Sources of

Metropolitan

Growth

Sources of
Metropolitan
Growth

edited by

Edwin S. Mills

and
John F. McDonald

Mary L. McLean
Associate Editor

CENTER
FOR URBAN
POLICY RESEARCH

Copyright © 1992 by Rutgers, the State University of New Jersey
All rights reserved

Published by the Center for Urban Policy Research
New Brunswick, New Jersey 08903

Printed in the United States of America

Library of Congress Cataloging-in-Publication Data

Sources of metropolitan growth / edited by Edwin S. Mills and
John F. McDonald.
      p. cm.
   Includes bibliographical references.
   ISBN 0-88285-135-7

   1. Metropolitan areas—United States—Congresses.   2. Cities and
towns—United States—Growth—Congresses.   3. United States—
Industries—Location—Congresses.   I. Mills, Edwin S.   II. McDonald,
John F., 1943–
HT334.U5S67   1992   91–8650
307.1'416'0973—dc20   CIP

FTW
AFL 0054

Contents

Foreword   ix

Acknowledgments   xi

Editors' Introduction   xiii

Contributors   xxvi

Part I. Theories of Metropolitan Growth and Development

1   EDWIN S. MILLS
Sectoral Clustering and Metropolitan Development   3

2   PATRICIA E. BEESON
Agglomeration Economies and Productivity Growth   19

Part II. Empirical Analysis of Metropolitan Growth

3   MARK A. SATTERTHWAITE
High-Growth Industries and Uneven Metropolitan Growth   39

4   BREANDÁN Ó HUALLACHÁIN
Economic Structure and Growth of Metropolitan Areas   51

5   JOHN F. MCDONALD
Assessing the Development Status of Metropolitan Areas   86

Part III. Empirical Analysis of Key Sectors

6 WILLIAM B. BEYERS
Producer Services and Metropolitan Growth and Development 125

7 TRUMAN A. HARTSHORN AND PETER O. MULLER
The Suburban Downtown and Urban Economic
Development Today 147

Part IV. Policy and Metropolitan Economic Development

8 RODNEY A. ERICKSON
Enterprise Zones: Lessons from the State Government
Experience 161

9 RICHARD FLORIDA AND DONALD F. SMITH, JR.
Venture Capital's Role in Economic Development:
An Empirical Analysis 183

10 CLAUDIA BIRD SCHOONHOVEN AND KATHLEEN M. EISENHARDT
Regions as Industrial Incubators of Technology-based
Ventures 210

Part V. Economic Change and Urban Social Problems

11 STEPHEN NORD AND ROBERT G. SHEETS
Service Industries and the Working Poor in
Major Metropolitan Areas in the United States 255

12 THOMAS R. HAMMER
Economic Determinants of Underclass Behavior 279

Reviewers 307

*This book was developed
as part of an ongoing
research program at
NCI Research in
Evanston, Illinois*

Foreword

This book is based on papers delivered at a symposium, "Sources of Metropolitan Growth and Development," held in Evanston, Illinois, on November 13 and 14, 1989.

The symposium was a collaborative effort by the Economic Development Administration (EDA) of the U.S. Department of Commerce and NCI Research in Evanston. Many of the symposium papers were based on research studies originally funded by EDA. As a collected body of work, the chapters of this volume evidence the commitment of the modest EDA research program to a better understanding of factors influencing the growth and development of local and regional economies. With more insight into why metropolitan areas develop as they do, policymakers will be in a stronger position to devise economic development strategies and programs in response to the needs of their communities.

Although the contributors to this volume represent a variety of disciplines, spatial orientation is the one characteristic their papers have in common. This being the case, geographers as well as regional economists are well represented.

The spatial framework in much of the research presented here gives rise to some intriguing insights, such as the notion of a region as an industrial incubator and the perception of a nationwide venture capital network, dispelling the myth of isolated local financial markets. The emergence of the suburban business center described here provides yet another observed phenomenon that needs to be formally explored as a new variation on agglomeration economies.

Overall, this book represents an opportunity for EDA to share some of the findings of its funded research with researchers and policymakers beyond the usual government channels.

I would like to express my thanks and appreciation to Jim Peterson and all of the staff at NCI Research for facilitating this symposium and the publication of this book. Economic development policy should be based on solid research such as the work presented in this collection. Today's accepted economic development tools, such as industrial incubators and venture capital networks, are the product of prior research illuminating the vital role of the small firm in new job creation. EDA is proud to have supported some of that research.

David H. Geddes
Director
Technical Assistance and Research Division
Economic Development Administration

Acknowledgments

In the field of economic development, it is a truism that experience is the best teacher. Yet as management philosopher W. E. Deming has observed, there can be no learning without theory. It is by organizing and interpreting facts—by developing theories about what we observe and experience—that we are able to learn. The more valid our theories, the more we are able to understand and apply our experiences.

Local economic policymakers and planners have a special need in this regard. Compared to macroeconomic theory, our understanding of the operation of local and regional economies is relatively undeveloped. Yet the effects of economic change are felt no less intensely locally than nationally, and willingly or unwillingly, local leaders are compelled to respond. The need to make intelligent use of development incentives is a powerful reason to seek a better understanding of local and regional economies.

This volume assembles some of the best recent research on patterns of economic growth in U.S. metropolitan areas. Clearly, the emergence of a post industrial global economy has called into question many aspects of economic development theory and practice. NCI Research was founded five years ago to focus critical research attention on this issue. In this book, we are pleased to have an opportunity to bring together our work and complementary research by others in this challenging field.

NCI's work is represented here in selections by Edwin S. Mills, John F. McDonald, Breandán Ó hUallacháin, and Mark A. Satterthwaite. As NCI Senior Fellows, they have been instrumental in defining and pursuing our initial research agenda. The editorial guidance of Mills and McDonald in shaping this volume and identifying contributors is especially appreciated. Also represented here is NCI Senior Economist Thomas R. Hammer, whose perceptive analyses help bridge the gap between theory and practice.

Special thanks are due to those who critiqued the papers in this volume when they were presented at an earlier symposium. Identified individually at the end of this book, these reviewers were most helpful in refining the papers for presentation to a broader audience.

Many others were involved in bringing this book to publication. Associate editor Mary McLean carefully edited each selection for substance and style, coordinating with multiple authors and the able publishing staff of the Center for Urban Policy Research (CUPR) at Rutgers University. It was the interest expressed by CUPR Director Norman J. Glickman that ultimately made publication possible. As ever, NCI administrator Catherine Frasunek handled manuscript production with deceptive ease.

Of course, this project would not have developed at all were it not for the funding that underwrites research in this critical but neglected area. NCI extends special thanks to the foundations that have supported our early research and to the respective program officers who have offered their encouragement and constructive suggestions, notably David Arnold of the Ford Foundation, Dan Martin of the John D. and Catherine T. MacArthur Foundation, and Jack Litzenberg of the Charles Stewart Mott Foundation.

In addition, much of the research reported here was made possible with funding support from the U.S. Economic Development Administration (EDA). The encouragement offered at the inception of this project by David H. Geddes, director of EDA's Technical Assistance and Research Division, assisted greatly in the book's realization.

James E. Peterson
President, NCI Research
Evanston, Illinois

EDWIN S. MILLS and JOHN F. MCDONALD

Editors' Introduction

Understanding Metropolitan Growth

This volume represents a coordinated examination of underlying influences on the economic growth and development of metropolitan areas. Why is it important to understand metropolitan growth? An obvious answer is that we have become an increasingly urbanized population: more than three-quarters of the U.S. population now resides in the country's 284 metropolitan areas. However, two additional observations provoke consideration.

First, metropolitan areas differ greatly in their rates of economic growth, with profound implications for the well-being of local residents. The wide variation in metropolitan growth is illustrated in Table I.1, showing changes from 1980 to 1986 in population, total employment, and manufacturing employment in the twenty largest metro areas. Population change ranged from a 4.5 percent loss in Pittsburgh to a gain of 22.8 percent in Dallas–Fort Worth. Changes in total employment varied from a 7.0 percent gain in Pittsburgh to a 42.7 percent gain in Atlanta. Most of the top twenty metropolitan areas (fifteen out of twenty) lost manufacturing jobs during this period, but in Atlanta, manufacturing employment was up more than 24 percent. One challenge is to understand better the reasons for these large variations among metropolitan areas.

A second point is that the composition of the national economy has shifted dramatically in terms of sectors and occupations. Manufacturing's share of employment dropped from 25.4 percent in 1969 to 18.7 percent in 1985 (Table I.2). This change was matched by the relative growth of the

TABLE I.1

Percentage Changes in Population and Employment
in the Twenty Largest Metropolitan Areas[1]
1980–1986

	Population	Private Employment	Manufacturing
New York	2.0%	7.9%	−17.8%
Los Angeles	10.3	9.2	−6.1
Chicago	2.8	1.9	−20.4
Philadelphia	2.2	11.8	−14.3
Boston	1.0	20.8	−3.2
Detroit	−3.2	7.7	−9.0
San Francisco/Oakland	7.9	15.4	−11.7
Dallas/Fort Worth	22.8	3.1	1.7
Houston	16.0	3.9	−22.9
Washington, D.C.	8.5	−1.3	−4.6
Minneapolis/St. Paul	7.0	11.8	−4.6
St. Louis	2.5	9.6	−10.31
Pittsburgh	−4.5	−7.0	−43.5
Atlanta	18.3	42.7	24.7
Newark	0.7	14.4	−15.6
Cleveland	−2.5	−.03	−20.6
Anaheim	11.0	27.2	9.5
Nassau/Suffolk	1.1	28.3	10.1
Baltimore	3.3	19.8	−13.2
Denver	13.0	18.4	2.7

Note: 1. Based on 1980 definitions of standard metropolitan statistical areas (SMSAs).

Source: Data diskette, U.S. Department of Commerce, Bureau of Economic Analysis, Regional Information System, Washington, D.C.

broad category of personal, professional, and business services, from 16.9 percent to 23.2 percent of total employment. The shares of employment in retail trade and in the finance, insurance, and real estate sector have also increased appreciably. The transformation of the U.S. economy has reverberated differently throughout U.S. metropolitan areas, and this also needs to be better understood. Associated causes and effects are explored in several of the chapters that follow.

TABLE I.2

Distribution of Employment, 1969–1985

| | *Percent of Jobs in Activity* | | |
	1969	*1979*	*1985*
Goods-producing sector	35.7	32.1	28.1
Agriculture	4.0	3.3	2.9
Mining	0.8	1.0	0.9
Construction	5.4	5.9	5.7
Manufacturing	25.4	21.98	18.7
Service-producing sector	64.3	67.9	71.9
Transportation	5.7	5.4	5.1
Wholesale trade	5.1	5.6	5.6
Retail trade	13.4	14.7	15.5
Finance, insurance, real estate	4.6	5.6	6.2
Services	16.9	19.7	23.2
Government	18.6	16.9	16.3
Total	100.0	100.0	100.0

Source: Reprinted from Garnick in *Urban Change and Poverty*, 1988, with permission from the National Academy Press.

Theories of Metropolitan Growth

Our focus on metropolitan economic growth contrasts with treatments that take the changing internal spatial patterns of metropolitan areas as their point of departure (Peterson, 1985; Solomon, 1980). Both are recognized aspects of the field of urban economics, as recently defined by Mieszkowski (1987):

> Urban economics addresses two central positive issues. First, it explains the internal form, or density gradient, of a city vis-à-vis a centralized place of employment, the central business district (CBD); and second, it analyzes the determinants of relative city size.[2]

Though we agree with this identification of key issues, we would reverse their order of relative importance. Studies of urban spatial organization are often motivated by concern for the plight of the central city, yet metropolitan economic growth is a primary determinant of the changes in spatial patterns within a metropolitan area. This point has been convincingly demonstrated by Norton (1979) in research linking the economic fortunes of a central city to the growth rate of its metropolitan area. Given that there is a strong underlying trend in all metropolitan areas for employment and population to move to the suburbs, the central city declines in absolute terms unless metropolitan economic growth is sufficient to offset suburbanization effects.

The agenda then is first to understand the causes of metropolitan economic growth and development. We begin by considering five leading theories: export base theory, neoclassical growth theory, the product cycle paradigm, cumulative causation, and disequilibrium dynamic adjustment.

EXPORT BASE THEORY

The traditional theory of metropolitan growth is the export base model: exports to purchasers outside the metropolitan area drive the local economy. This truism has been used many times in forms that range from very simple Keynesian multiplier models to very complex Leontief input-output models (Sullivan 1990). However, this approach leaves unasked and unanswered the fundamental question, "Why does a metropolitan area have demands for its export products and services and why do these demands change?" The other theories of metropolitan economic growth try to answer this question.

NEOCLASSICAL GROWTH THEORY

Neoclassical growth theory emphasizes the supply side of the economy. Economic growth depends upon the quantity and quality of labor, the quantity and quality of capital, and technical knowledge. This approach was first developed by Solow (1957) and then Denison (1985) to account for economic growth at the national level. Recently, neoclassical models have been applied to regional and metropolitan growth. These applications at the regional and metropolitan level represent an important addition to the basic neoclassical framework.

At the regional or metropolitan level, economic growth is also influenced by the economies generated by spatial proximity, so-called *agglomeration economies*. These include *localization economies*, which are industry-specific and result from the expansion of a particular industry in a certain place, as well as *urbanization economies* arising from the greater array of services and opportunities available in larger places. The first two chapters of this book elaborate these concepts within the context of the neoclassical growth model. In chapter 1, Edwin S. Mills considers the possible reasons for industry clustering in metropolitan areas, offering original insights on economies of information exchange. Patricia E. Beeson, in chapter 2, examines how agglomeration economies affect income and productivity, with consequences for the growth of metropolitan areas. In so doing, she points out that discussions of localization and urbanization economies need to distinguish between level and growth rate effects.

PRODUCT CYCLE THEORY

An important perspective on metropolitan growth has come from economic history. It is known variously as the product cycle model or the long-wave model or the product-profit cycle. Historical studies have established the existence of industrial life cycles. New industries experience a period of rapid growth after an initial phase of incubation, then eventually, as a consequence of competition from still newer industries, face a slowdown in growth or absolute decline. The existence of industrial cycles relates to the Schumpeterian concept of competition as a constant struggle in the marketplace among entrepreneurs to gain a monopoly position in a new commodity, a new technology, a new source of supply, or a new type of organization (Schumpeter 1942). Any competitive edge gained in this struggle is ultimately eliminated by competition from still newer marketplace innovations.

The private enterprise economy thus involves a constantly changing mix of products, technologies, sources of supply, and forms of business organization, with new technologies emerging to replace the older ones as growth leaders. The early stages of the industrial life cycle exhibit rapid technical change, requiring flexible, labor-intensive production processes. The later stages involve a stabilizing of technology, saturation of product markets, and increasing concern with cutting unit production costs through the attainment of scale economies.

There may be a connection between industrial life cycles and metropolitan growth and decline. The growth of a metropolitan area is stimulated by the presence of industries in the rapid growth phase of their life cycles and retarded by the presence of industries in the slow growth or decline phase. A metropolitan area with a good mix of growing and stable industries does not experience a period of decline in its growth rate. However, researchers such as Norton and Rees (1979), Markusen (1985), and Booth (1986) believe that a metropolitan area with aging industries suffers through relatively long periods of time without developing substantial economic activity in new growth industries.

If so, there must be barriers to the formation of new industries in metropolitan areas with a mature industrial base. Such barriers may arise because mature firms focus on management rather than entrepreneurship because their central problem is achieving scale economies and cutting costs. Such firms train managers, not entrepreneurs who would be capable of starting new firms in the metropolitan area. Once employment begins to decline in mature industries, the prospects for new business formation begin to improve. However, some suggest that the fundamental problem is the lengthy period often required for new businesses to grow to the point where they become major employers. In the meantime, metropolitan areas with mature industries experience slow or declining economic growth and social problems associated with inadequate employment opportunities.

The product cycle model is certainly plausible, but the evidence in support of the overall model is weak and subject to alternative interpretation. The evidence begins with the observations that (1) much of the growth in newer science-based industries has occurred in metropolitan areas in the South and West and not in the older industrial belt and (2) New England metropolitan areas seemed to enter a new long wave of development in the 1970s and 1980s. These developments might also be explained, however, by the presence of specific human and nonhuman capital, factor costs, threshold effects, and political influence over federal spending.

The basic notions of "mature" and "growth" industries are useful for understanding some aspects of metropolitan growth and development, but the product cycle theory needs more sharply focused empirical tests. An intriguing line of research is suggested by Ó hUallacháin and Satterthwaite's recent study of growth industries in metropolitan areas, reported in chapter 3.

CUMULATIVE CAUSATION THEORY

The first statement of a cumulative causation model was by Myrdal (1957) in the context of regional growth in less-developed countries. He argued that a few leading regions exploit initial advantages and that growth is self-sustaining if, for example, there are scale economies to be exploited. Linkages between growing regions and lagging regions are favorable (spread effects) as well as unfavorable (backwash effects), though the latter tends to dominate. It is not evident that this sort of mechanism is at work in regions of the United States, however.

In proposing cumulative causation models as the main rival to the neoclassical model, Richardson (1985) asserts that the basic difference between unelaborated versions of the neoclassical model and the cumulative causation model is that the latter allows for increasing returns to scale. Consequently, both capital and labor can flow in the same direction (rather than in opposite directions) and growth rate differentials may persist or even widen over time. Still, we contend that a neoclassical model does not have to become very complicated to permit increasing returns to scale. Moreover, an augmented neoclassical model offers a more complete and theoretically consistent approach, without necessarily ruling out the possibility that growth differentials may widen over some time period.

DISEQUILIBRIUM DYNAMIC ADJUSTMENT THEORY

One of the most sustained and technical attacks on neoclassical theory in recent years has been the work of Gordon Clark and his associates. They have compiled their views and empirical findings in Clark et al. (1986). Their basic point is simple enough: economies evolve historically and a theory of disequilibrium dynamics is needed to understand that history. One can agree with both the former and the latter propositions or with just the former. It may be that the neoclassical theory of equilibrium is sufficient to comprehend the process of metropolitan economic growth for some purposes. Their orientation, however, is somewhat different:

> Our goal is to show how the actual means and institutions of economic adjustment, the strategies and decisions concerning economic fluctuation and change are very important in determining the long-run economic fortunes of different regions.[3]

The Clark et al. (1986) characterization of the economic landscape assumes that corporations have the power to construct locational hierarchies that place the various types of production activities at different locations. This creates a spatial division of labor with several characteristics:

1. Variable demands are allocated to a periphery of small firms.
2. There is a separation of technical, control, and management functions.
3. There is an increasing specialization and division of labor.
4. A "dual" labor market with a spatial component emerges.

The authors emphasize that this spatial division of labor characterizes only certain sectors, such as electronics, plastics, and many "high-tech" industries, but that these sectors are important because they constitute the most recent round of capital investment. They also present a wide variety of empirical investigations that are loosely related to various versions of their dynamic adjustment framework, including studies of labor migration and capital growth. These two are important determinants of metropolitan and regional growth, of course.

Although the studies of labor migration are not very useful for those interested in metropolitan economic growth, their empirical analysis of capital growth at the state level is important and informative. They examined capital accumulation in manufacturing as a function of past profit levels, changes in profit, and the existing capital stock. This is a standard econometric formulation used to study investment at the national level in the 1950s. This emphasis on internal liquidity has a long history in investment modeling. Recently, Fazzari and coworkers (1988) have developed a more formal microeconomic model based on asymmetric information about investment prospects to justify this emphasis on internal liquidity.

In summary, Clark et al. (1986) have produced useful empirical evidence on capital growth at the state level that can be incorporated into an augmented neoclassical growth model. Their broader approach to disequilibrium dynamic adjustment is less helpful in the effort to understand the determinants of metropolitan growth.

TOWARD A SYNTHESIS

This survey of theories of metropolitan growth leads us to offer our own theory, summarized informally here. It is essentially an augmented neoclassical growth model that begins by recognizing that export demands are important determinants of metropolitan growth. Furthermore, modern metropolitan areas export a wide variety of goods and services to the region, the nation, and the world, and the exportation of services in various forms appears to be growing.

The capacity of a metropolitan area to respond to the demand for its exports depends on its supply characteristics, or "factors of production," broadly defined. All of the neoclassical supply variables are important—labor quantity and quality, capital quantity and quality, technical knowledge, and agglomeration economies. The area needs to develop, attract, and hold a high-quality labor force. This may not be easy. Education systems and the numerous factors that contribute to the quality of life are involved. Capital is needed in various forms. As the findings of Clark and colleagues (1986) suggest, metropolitan areas need methods to overcome the problem of asymmetric information that arises in the evaluation of potential capital investments. Lenders have difficulty figuring out how to evaluate loan applications for entrepreneurs in relatively untried lines of business. As suggested by the cumulative causation model, metropolitan areas also need to figure out how to enhance technical knowledge and agglomeration economies.

Finally, the factors that determine growth at the industry level are different for growing versus mature industries. Growth industries rely on high-quality workers, access to capital from outside the firm, technical change in the form of new products and processes, and numerous forms of agglomeration economies. Mature industries concentrate more on low-input costs and minimizing costs for wages, transportation, taxes, material, and so forth. This augmented neoclassical approach is adopted here as a particularly useful device for considering the growth and development of metropolitan economies.

Organization of the Book

EMPIRICAL ANALYSIS OF METROPOLITAN GROWTH

Following the introduction to theory provided in part 1, the second part of this book considers some results of recent investigations conducted at NCI Research. Chapters 3, 4, and 5 represent a coordinated empirical investigation consistent with the augmented neoclassical theory outlined above.

In chapter 3, Mark A. Satterthwaite explores the locational determinants of firms in high-growth industries, taking as his starting point the results of an analysis of employment growth patterns among metropolitan areas. His exposition of the types of localization economies that might be important for today's fast-growing service and high-technology industries extends the agglomeration theory developed in chapters 1 and 2 and provides a bridge to subsequent chapters.

In chapter 4, Breandán Ó hUallacháin examines spatial associations among industries as evidenced in modern metropolitan areas. This chapter provides the empirical counterpart to chapter 1's discussion of the economic forces that lead to industry clustering. Ó hUallacháin uses factor analysis to identify many recognized types of industry clusters, such as ports, petrochemical complexes, resort areas, and centers for traditional manufacturing and resource processing industries. He also finds some new types of clusters, including centers for fast-growing financial and legal services and business and professional services. His results should put to rest the notion that manufacturing is the basic sector of a local economy and everything else is in the local service sector.

In chapter 5, Ó hUallacháin's results are used by John F. McDonald to identify industry clusters common to most metropolitan areas for use in developing neoclassical models of growth. The purpose of the models is to provide benchmark estimates so that a local analyst can compare the actual growth performance of an industry cluster at the local level with an "expected" growth rate. The analyst can then identify and examine the particular industries that influenced the performance of these industry clusters and, in so doing, quickly arrive at the most relevant topics for further research.

CASE STUDIES OF IMPORTANT SECTORS

The two chapters of part 3 analyze two important sources of growth in contemporary metropolitan economies. In chapter 6, William B. Beyers presents a detailed look at the producer services sector. Beginning with a review of past and projected employment trends, he proceeds to examine the reasons for the recent rapid growth of the producer services. He also analyzes the location patterns of producer services firms, identifying variations in growth across metropolitan areas and regions.

In chapter 7, Truman A. Hartshorn and Peter O. Muller document the emergence of modern suburban business centers in large metropolitan areas. The authors offer an initial assessment of the function and impact of these suburban centers and outline the policy issues presaged by their recent history of rapid growth. This line of inquiry needs to be pursued; an improved understanding of how metropolitan areas grow must include a theory of how suburban business centers capture certain agglomeration economies.

POLICY AND METROPOLITAN GROWTH

In part 4, questions of policy receive more explicit attention than in the preceding theoretical and empirical investigations. Chapters 8, 9, and 10 provide perspective on three of the more popular economic development policy initiatives of the past decade: enterprise zones, venture capital programs, and efforts to "incubate" new businesses in an area.

In chapter 8, Rodney A. Erickson examines the structure and effectiveness of state enterprise zone programs. The state programs differ widely in terms of legislative intent, designation criteria, and the nature of the incentives offered. In addition to reporting the results of a comparative analysis of state program effects on job creation and investment, Erickson identifies factors that seem to be associated with the success of high-performing zones—those that generated much greater investment and employment than his analyses would have predicted.

Chapter 9, by Richard Florida and Donald F. Smith, Jr., is a detailed examination of location and investment patterns of the private venture capital industry, which substantiates the role of agglomeration economies in the growth of high-technology industry. The authors find that areas with an established high-technology infrastructure are able to attract venture capital irrespective of their distance from sources of supply. In areas without such a base, venture capital alone is not likely to generate innovation and high-technology development. The authors urge public policymakers to reconsider measures that simply attempt to redress perceived capital gaps, emphasizing that venture capital is only one element of a network of factors that support technology-based development.

This point is amplified in the following chapter by Claudia Bird Schoonhoven and Kathleen M. Eisenhardt, which reports the results of their comprehensive survey of new semiconductor firms. In examining the relationship between environmental factors and firm survival and growth, the authors focus particularly on the contribution of industry-specific regional resources. The concentration of the semiconductor industry in a few selected locations, notably Silicon Valley, offers an opportunity to test the concept of an "incubator region," defined as a confluence of industry-specific resources that may be mobilized to create and sustain new ventures. This detailed case study of a growth industry strongly confirms the importance of agglomeration economies, especially localization economies, and it suggests how metropolitan economic development policy might be aimed at improving the incubation effect.

ECONOMIC CHANGE AND URBAN SOCIAL PROBLEMS

The final section of the book examines the social problems that have emerged or that have been exacerbated by recent trends in metropolitan growth and development. As noted earlier, metropolitan economies have differed greatly in their overall growth rates as the economy has undergone a long-term transition away from employment in goods production to service sector jobs. Indeed, some metropolitan areas have lost a great deal of their older manufacturing base while experiencing lackluster overall growth, with negative repercussions for many workers.

In chapter 11, Stephen Nord and Robert G. Sheets report the results of research focusing on the impact of structural change on the lower tiers of the labor market, as measured by the earnings of the working poor. Their Poverty-level Earnings Index identifies the share of workers whose employment fails to generate earnings above poverty level. In examining the distribution of poverty-level earnings among service industries and metropolitan areas, they find that the transition to a service economy has been more problematic in some industries—often those with a disproportionate share of minorities and women. Their finding that almost a fifth of metropolitan-area workers failed to generate earnings above the poverty level at the time of the study sounds a warning note that bears further investigation once new census data become available.

The final chapter, by Thomas R. Hammer, summarizes a study of the differential effects of manufacturing job losses on blacks and nonblacks in urban areas. Focusing on youth and young adults in the 1970–80 period, the analysis traces the effects of job losses on labor force participation, house-hold income, and changes in family structure, such as numbers of female-headed households. Hammer finds strong statistical support for the assertion that the decline in blue-collar jobs has been a major contributor to the under-class syndrome—the intensification of joblessness, poverty, welfare depen-dency, and social disintegration among minorities in central city areas.

Although the book ends on a disturbing note, progress in solving the social problems discussed in the final two chapters requires further research of the types included in this volume. We need a deeper theoretical under-standing of the causes of metropolitan economic growth, such as the forces of agglomeration examined here by Mills and Beeson. Empirical studies along the lines of those by Satterthwaite, Ó hUallacháin, and McDonald are needed to establish basic facts and to test theories of metropolitan growth. Detailed case studies of particular industries and particular economic development policies are needed in abundance. The contributions of Beyers, Hartshorn and Muller, Erickson, Florida and Smith, and Schoonhoven and Eisenhardt provide some of this needed depth. Finally, we need the kinds of studies per-formed by Nord and Sheets and Hammer to gain a clearer understanding of the urban economic and social problems we seek to solve.

Notes

1. Based on 1980 definitions of standard metropolitan statistical areas (SMSAs).
2. P. Mieszkowski, 1987, p. 253.
3. G. Clark, M. Gertler, and J. Whiteman, 1986, p. 2.

References

Booth, D. "Long Waves and Uneven Regional Growth." *Southern Economic Journal* 52 (1986): 448–460.

Clark, G., M. Gertler, and J. Whiteman. *Regional Dynamics*. Boston: Allen & Unwin, 1986.

Denison, E. *Trends in American Economic Growth*. Washington, D.C.: The Brook-ings Institution, 1985.

Fazzari, S., G. Hubbard, and B. Petersen. "Investment, Financing Decisions and Tax Policy." *American Economic Review* 78 (May 1988): 200–205.

Garnick, D. "Local Area Economic Growth Patterns: A Comparison of the 1980s and Previous Decades." In *Urban Change and Poverty*. Eds. M. McGeary and L. Lynn, Jr. Washington, D.C.: National Academy Press, 1988.

Markusen, A. *Profit Cycles, Oligopoly and Regional Development*. Cambridge: Cam-bridge University Press, 1985.

Mieszkowski, P. "Urban Economics." In *The New Palgrave: A Dictionary of Economics*. Eds. J. Eatwell, M. Milgate, and P. Newman. New York: Macmillan, 1987.

Myrdal, G. *Economic Theory and Underdeveloped Regions*. London: Gerald Duckworth, 1957.

Norton, R. *City Life-Cycles and American Urban Policy*. New York: Academic Press, 1979.

Norton, R., and J. Rees. "The Product Cycle and the Spatial Deconcentration of American Manufacturing." *Regional Studies* 13 (1979): 141–151.

Peterson, P., ed. *The New Urban Reality*. Washington, D.C.: The Brookings Institution, 1985.

Richardson, H. "Regional Development Theories." In *Economic Prospects for the Northeast*. Eds. H. Richardson and J. Turek. Philadelphia: Temple University Press, 1985.

Schumpeter, J. A. *Capitalism, Socialism and Democracy*. New York: Harper, 1942.

Solomon, A. *The Prospective City*. Cambridge: MIT Press, 1980.

Solow, R. "Technical Change and the Aggregate Production Function." *Review of Economics and Statistics* 39 (1957): 312–320.

Sullivan, A. *Urban Economics*. Homewood, Ill.: Richard D. Irwin, 1990.

Contributors

Patricia E. Beeson, Department of Economics, University of Pittsburgh, Pittsburgh, Pennsylvania.

William B. Beyers, Department of Geography, University of Washington, Seattle, Washington.

Kathleen M. Eisenhardt, Department of Industrial Engineering and Engineering Management, Stanford University, Palo Alto, California.

Rodney A. Erickson, College of Business Administration, The Pennsylvania State University, University Park, Pennsylvania.

Richard Florida, School of Urban and Public Affairs, Carnegie-Mellon University, Pittsburgh, Pennsylvania.

Thomas R. Hammer, NCI Research, Evanston, Illinois.

Truman A. Hartshorn, Department of Geography, Georgia State University, Atlanta, Georgia.

John F. McDonald, Department of Economics, University of Illinois at Chicago, and former Research Director, NCI Research, Evanston, Illinois.

Edwin S. Mills, J. L. Kellogg Graduate School of Management, Northwestern University, Evanston, Illinois, and Chairman of the Senior Fellows of NCI Research.

Peter O. Muller, Department of Geography, University of Miami, Coral Gables, Florida.

Stephen Nord, Department of Economics, Northern Illinois University, De Kalb, Illinois.

Breandán Ó hUallacháin, Department of Geography, Arizona State University, Tempe, Arizona.

Mark A. Satterthwaite, J. L. Kellogg Graduate School of Management, Northwestern University, Evanston, Illinois.

Claudia Bird Schoonhoven, Department of Organization and Management, San Jose State University, San Jose, California.

Robert G. Sheets, Center for Governmental Studies, Northern Illinois University, De Kalb, Illinois.

Donald F. Smith, Jr., School of Urban and Public Affairs, Carnegie-Mellon University, Pittsburgh, Pennsylvania.

PART I

Theories of Metropolitan Growth and Development

EDWIN S. MILLS

1 *Sectoral Clustering and Metropolitan Development*

This paper presents thoughts about the relationship between sectoral clustering and metropolitan development. It can be viewed as a sequel to "What Makes Metropolitan Areas Grow?" (Mills, March 1988) and "A Transactions Cost Model of Metropolitan Size" (Mills, June 1988).

At one level, the issue can be stated simply. Many studies have found that similar sectors tend to cluster together in metropolitan areas. Among the most recent and elaborate studies are *Sectoral Growth Patterns at the Metropolitan Level* (Ó hUallacháin and Satterthwaite, 1988) and Henderson's *Urban Development* (1988). Although neither study formally examines clustering among two- or three-digit SIC[1] code sectors, both find that localization economies are more important than urbanization economies. That means that growth of employment within a sector tends to depend more on the size of the sector than on the size of the metropolitan area. Since sectors at the SIC code levels actually studied are collections of related subsectors, I interpret the strong findings about localization to be findings about the importance of clustering among related but not identical sectors.

In addition, work just completed at NCI Research does formally analyze the importance of clustering at the two- or three-digit level (see chapter 4 by Ó hUallacháin and chapter 5 by McDonald in this volume). There seems to be little doubt that narrowly defined sectoral groups tend to cluster and grow together. This paper addresses the possible explanations for such clustering.

First, a distinction is in order. Clusters can be intrametropolitan or intermetropolitan. The former refers to the fact that some sectors cluster together in certain parts of metropolitan areas. The latter refers to the fact that some

3

sectors cluster in one metropolitan area and some in another. The suburban shopping center is one example of intrametropolitan area clustering. The clustering of auto-related manufacturing sectors in Flint or of tourist service sectors in Miami illustrates the latter.

Intermetropolitan clustering is the subject of NCI's work. Nevertheless, I start with brief notes on intrametropolitan clustering. It has been studied extensively, and what is known about it may provide insight into intermetropolitan area clustering.

It is patent that there is something to explain. As just cited, the facts indicate considerable clustering. By contrast, classical location theory, fathered by Lösch (1954), indicates that dispersion of producers of identical or similar products should be the norm. Dispersion provides each producer limited monopoly power in its market area, which, in classical location theory equilibrium, is a hexagon or some closely related geographical shape. That the facts are frequently, perhaps typically, in contrast with the Lösch (1954) model indicates the need for explanation.

Intrametropolitan Area Clustering

An intrametropolitan cluster is a cluster of activities in a set of contiguous locations in a metropolitan area. An intermetropolitan cluster is a cluster of activities in a particular metropolitan area. The presumption is that intermetropolitan clusters are mainly of firms that sell goods and services outside the metropolitan area. Intrametropolitan clusters may be of firms that sell locally and/or outside the metropolitan area.

Consider the suburban shopping center, which has been extensively studied. Two factors account for these intrametropolitan clusters. The first is comparison shopping. Firms that sell closely related but not identical goods find it worthwhile to cluster because consumers like to compare goods for style differences. Thus, several firms can mutually benefit from proximate locations. The second factor is economies in shoppers' time and in transportation cost due to one-stop shopping by automobile. It is no accident that the shopping center became common when auto ownership became widespread.

I am inclined to think that the second reason is more important than the first because most shopping centers do not appear to offer many kinds of closely related goods. Indeed, having enough "space" between product lines seems to be a common goal in the leasing strategies of suburban shopping centers. However, the second reason—economies due to the availability of automobile transportation—presumably does not explain the retail area in the 600 to 900 blocks of North Michigan Avenue in Chicago, which is not advantageous for automobile-based shopping. There, comparison shopping and economizing on shoppers' travel time must be the purpose.

Downtown office activities and suburban office and industrial parks are the other prominent intrametropolitan clusters.[2] Clustering of office activities may relate to intrametropolitan or intermetropolitan considerations. Examples of the latter will be discussed in the next section. Here it suffices to mention one entirely intrametropolitan consideration. Suppose the only characteristics that large downtown office activities shared were that their employees and/or their customers were scattered around the entire metropolitan area; then a downtown location would minimize the total travel cost between the office cluster and such scattered points. If employees or customers are scattered, it leaves unanswered the question of why production must be concentrated in one lump instead of being similarly scattered. That could be because of traditional economies of scale or scope. Thus, it is at least possible that all downtown office activities are there because of scattered employees or customers and because of economies of scale or scope and not because they relate to each other in any way. How they might relate to each other is discussed in the next section.

Suburban industrial parks are a different matter. Manufacturing is in suburbs for well-understood reasons: the capital/land ratio is small and inputs and outputs are shipped into and out of the metropolitan area by truck. Therefore, manufacturing businesses locate in suburbs where land is cheap and where large trucks can undertake intermetropolitan area freight movement without having to cope with downtown congestion and lack of space to load and unload.

This explains suburban location but not clustering. One possibility is a common desire of many manufacturing activities to be near a transportation mode, such as an airport or expressway interchange. In fact, the industrial land near airports often has both advantages, as witnessed by many suburban industrial clusters around the country. In addition, local government land use controls may be important, in that they restrict manufacturing to a few segregated locations.

None of the above depends on manufacturing firms relating to each other in any way. Again, factors that depend on firms relating to each other will be discussed in the next section.

Clusters of research and development (R&D) activities are a relatively recent example of clustering. Route 128 in Boston, Research Triangle in North Carolina, and Silicon Valley in California are prime examples. (Although each of the three examples displays a substantial research component, none is an entirely research cluster.) Route 128 is a cluster by virtue of distance from the metropolitan center and location on the beltway rather than by contiguous location per se. For R&D clusters, local government policy is certainly involved. Research activities are very attractive (they are typically small and clean operations that attract mostly middle-class and upper-middle-class employees), and local governments have many programs to induce their location within their jurisdictions. Subsidized land, cheap loans, and other incentives may be offered for spatially contiguous locations. A second factor is that research is the most footloose of all activities, making the locational preferences of professional employees a prime consideration. Again, these factors may explain preferences for suburban locations but they do not explain clustering. Ways that research activities might relate to each other will be discussed in the next section.

The final illustrations in this section are of clusters that are both intrametropolitan and intermetropolitan areas. The wholesale fashion garment center in midtown Manhattan is a prime example. It is the only such center in the New York metropolitan area, and it is the largest among only a few such centers in the country. Comparison shopping and proximity to the garment manufacturing district a few blocks south in Manhattan are presumably the reasons for the cluster. Much, but not all, of the service production is exported to customers who come from outside the New York metropolitan area.

Likewise, the specialized financial markets in New York, Chicago, and, to a lesser extent, elsewhere are both intermetropolitan and intrametropolitan area clusters. The same is true of tourist hotels on the oceanfront in Atlantic City or of casinos in Las Vegas.

Perhaps the most important examples are state and national capitals, producing government services. They are both intermetropolitan and intrametropolitan clusters.

I now turn to the reasons for clusters that are, at least to some extent, intermetropolitan area in character.

Intermetropolitan Clusters

In this section, I discuss what I hope is an exhaustive set of plausible reasons for intermetropolitan area clustering. First, a few more words about the definition of intermetropolitan clustering. By such clustering, I mean a greater share of employment in one or a set of two- or three-digit SIC code sectors in one metropolitan area than in another.[3]

Even at the three-digit level, production is sufficiently diverse that any one of the causes of clustering to be discussed below could occur within one sector or among several sectors. Of course, production is even more diverse within a two-digit sector. At the four-digit level, some of the following phenomena might be implausible within a sector. However, disclosure rules prevent large samples of four-digit data from being analyzed at the metropolitan level. At the four-digit level, data are especially scarce for small metropolitan areas. Since small metropolitan areas tend to be more specialized than large metropolitan areas, use of four-digit data misses some of the most interesting and informative observations.

Both within and between SIC codes, we are at the mercy of government officials who design the codes. At any number of digits, an SIC code is intended to collect together similar products. "Transportation Equipment" is such a collection (two-digit). Automobiles and airplanes are three-digit codes within that two-digit code, but there is no guarantee that cross-elasticities of demand are greater within codes than between them. For example, small private airplanes may have a larger cross-elasticity with automobiles than with commercial jets, although private planes and commercial jets are in the same three-digit sector whereas autos are in a separate three-digit sector. Likewise, there is no assurance that technologies are more similar within than between codes, although there is a strong tendency for that to be true.

In addition, nothing about the definitions of sectors at any number of digits implies anything at all about input-output relationships. Firms A and B may or may not buy from or sell to each other if they are within a particular code, if they are in codes with adjacent numbers, if their code numbers are as far apart as possible, or if they are three-digit sectors within the same two-digit sector. Elaborate input-output tables, available at many levels of detail, do tell us about input-output relationships among SIC code sectors. However, most input-output tables are at the national level; intrametropolitan area tables may show quite different patterns of input-output relationships. (Although I have seen a few metropolitan area tables, I have never compared one with a national table.) A final comment is that although coefficient instability through time is a major and widely discussed defect of national input-output tables, especially at detailed levels, such instability is much worse at the metropolitan level. If a buyer were to switch from a vendor within the same metropolitan area to a vendor outside the metropolitan area, it would show up as a coefficient change in a metropolitan table although it might not in a national table.

INPUT-OUTPUT CLUSTERING

This discussion brings me to the first reason for clustering within and between SIC codes at the intermetropolitan area level: input-output relationships. Beyond doubt, this is an important reason for clustering. If A produces an input used by B in further production, and if A's product is expensive to ship between metropolitan areas (hereafter taken to include shipments from nonmetropolitan to metropolitan areas and vice versa), then A and B may be found in the same metropolitan area or areas. That is true regardless of the extent of scale economies in either A or B and regardless of why B is in the metropolitan area. If, for example, scale economies are important in A, then there may be lots of B producers in the same metropolitan area. Clustering of A and B firms is intersectoral, whereas clustering of B firms is intrasectoral. Thus, both intersectoral and intrasectoral clusters may result from input-output relationships.

A special kind of input-output relationship is often claimed to be important: the availability of a trained labor force. The allegation is that A-producing firms locate in a metropolitan area that contains other firms that produce A or similar products because the metropolitan area contains a labor force with skills needed by all such firms. On the face of it, the argument is not compelling. If the needed workers are all employed, there are literally no more workers of the needed types available in the metropolitan area than elsewhere. The scale economy in input suppliers that can explain product input-output clustering does not apply with respect to workers. Of course, if some of the needed workers are unemployed or underemployed, location of a potential employer in the metropolitan area where they live is more compelling. Otherwise, the claim must be that it is cheaper to induce needed workers to change jobs if they can remain in the same metropolitan area than if they must move to a new metropolitan area. It must also be cheaper to induce workers to make intrametropolitan area job changes than it is to train new workers in needed skills. The argument is plausible but not necessarily true and requires careful formulation and testing.[4]

Undoubtedly, a common kind of input-output clustering results from natural resource availability. Natural resources are unevenly distributed on and under the earth's surface. Metals and fossil fuels are in richer and more easily accessible concentrations in some places than others. Extraction occurs where concentrations are sufficiently rich and accessible to be economical to extract. Since much of what is mined is discarded at subsequent stages of processing, firms that use natural resources as inputs tend to be near mines, firms that use subsequent semifabricated products as inputs tend to be near the first processors, and so on. This is the simplest kind of input-output relationship and has been extensively studied in such sectors as steel and aluminum. Much of the resulting processing is in metropolitan areas.

Climate is a natural resource that can also affect input-output clustering. Jet aircraft production tends to be located in places with mild climates in order to avoid large heating and cooling bills because assembly requires large enclosed spaces. Input suppliers tend to locate in the same metropolitan areas and so on. Climate also affects nonmetropolitan production, notably agriculture, so food processing tends to cluster in metropolitan areas near rural areas that have a comparative advantage in agriculture. This could be intrasectoral clustering (flour production) or intersectoral clustering (for example, textiles and furniture manufacturing both use farming products produced in the Southeast).

To the extent that the natural resources are cheap to transport, clustering does not necessarily result near resource-rich places. Oil and natural gas are examples. Both are cheap to transport and their prices are nearly identical all over the country (indeed, all over the world except for tax effects), so the fact that most oil and gas are found in the southern part of the forty-eight contiguous states does not provide much incentive for oil- and gas-using firms to locate there. Southern California is a slight exception; not only is it oil rich but also oil exports from the region to other states are made expensive by the high cost of shipping oil across the Rocky Mountains or through the Panama Canal. Thus, energy prices are slightly lower in Southern California than in the rest of the country.

Similarly, climate and topography also generate nonproduced consumer amenities. Southern Florida has a comparative advantage in services for tourists and retired people. This generates both intersectoral and intrasectoral clustering in such areas.

COMPARISON SHOPPING CLUSTERS

I now return to comparison shopping. If it is advantageous to carry on comparison shopping on a large scale, it can lead to intermetropolitan clustering. The high-fashion wholesale garment market in midtown Manhattan is the classic example. Buyers go there from all over the country because visual inspection and face-to-face negotiation between buyer, wholesaler, and manufacturer are important. As was suggested above, there is also input-output clustering involving the manufacture and wholesaling of such garments in Manhattan. Neither activity can be subject to scale economies to an extent that justifies such incredible clustering. Presumably, this clustering results from the peculiarities of women's high-style clothing: the need for more or less simultaneous exchange of information among sellers, among sellers and buyers, and among sellers and producers about styles, quantities, modifications, delivery dates, and so forth. Although it is inappropriate to call this phenomenon an exchange of technology, it is a dramatic example of the importance of in-person contact in both institutionalized and informal exchanges of information. The institutionalized exchange (such as fashion shows, specifications, prices, or quantities) could be done easily on computer screens and closed-circuit TV, with brochures and flyers distributed by mail or by other means and computerized ordering. For that purpose, no one would need to travel to or be in New York. Presumably, it is the informal exchanges of trends and hints and the negotiations that demand face-to-face contacts. The suggestion is intriguing and will be elaborated below.

INFORMATION CLUSTERS

The argument here is that firms that deal with similar kinds of information find it advantageous to cluster in particular metropolitan areas for the purpose of information exchange.

The first observation is that information exchange could lead to any one of several kinds of clustering. Suppose that A and B need the same information. If they cluster in the same metropolitan area, they might get the needed information from each other. That is tricky because information that is valuable to B is not likely to be given up willingly by A if A and B compete. However, it is possible that sets of information are at issue and that there are economies of specialization in the production of subsets of the needed information, then A could produce one subset and B another, and both A and B might benefit from exchange of the two subsets. In the best of circumstances, relying on a competitor for information is of limited value; it is a bit like the United States and Russia agreeing that spying on each other is mutually beneficial. It may be, but the agreement is difficult to work out and enforce.

Perhaps, more likely, there may be simple scale economies in producing related information sets and A and B might benefit from locating in the metropolitan area where C, who produces the information, is located. In fact, this case is stronger. Even if there are no scale economies in information production, information is a pure public good: There is no additional input cost if a second consumer makes use of the information. Thus, A and B can get the needed information at roughly half the cost if they buy it from the same producer, compared with each generating the information itself or having a supplier who agrees not to provide the information to the other firm. That is precisely the reason why there is typically only one newspaper in a community.

Information may be, and frequently is, provided as a joint product with inputs. When a manufacturer of electronic equipment wants to design a new product, he is likely to go to his component suppliers and talk to them about designing new components for the new product. It should be noted that such discussions may be very complex, involving relationships between product and component designs and the many variables that characterize a satisfactory component. In such a case, input-output and information exchanges may reinforce each other as inducements to locate in the same metropolitan area.

Another question is what kinds of information exchange motivate proximate locations. These days, information can be transmitted electronically at costs that are almost independent of distance. Some recent research papers make the distinction between quantitative and qualitative information. The assumption is that quantitative information can be transmitted electronically and inexpensively. Qualitative information, by contrast, is assumed not to be possible to transmit efficiently by electronic means; it is further assumed that qualitative information is used by decision makers who must have face-to-face contact to transmit information efficiently. The distinction is misconceived. Any information that can be transmitted verbally can be transmitted electronically; it makes no difference whether it is quantitative or qualitative.

I believe that a more relevant distinction is between ambiguous and unambiguous information. Ambiguous information is information that requires an interactive and convergent set of exchanges before the final exchange can be consummated. A good example is that given above between buyer and seller of a new component of electronic equipment. A series of discussions among buyers' and sellers' design, production, marketing, accounting, and legal specialists may be required before information about the final product is known. Once things are at that stage, an agreement with detailed product specifications can be written down and conveyed electronically or otherwise.

A second example is information exchanged between a corporation's research and production activities. If a research team comes up with a bright new product idea, elaborate and sequential discussions may be required between research, production, product design, marketing, accounting, and legal specialists. Furthermore, continuing discussions may be advantageous as the R&D activity proceeds. It is easy to believe that face-to-face communication may be advantageous in such circumstances.

An example close to home is a research seminar. The function of a research seminar is for a speaker to convey an idea and for similar but not identical specialists to suggest lines of further research and to criticize ideas presented. Sometimes the most productive seminars involve an exchange that approximates free association. In any case, it is the back-and-forth exchange that generates valuable ideas, corrections, and ways of thinking about problems.

Protection of proprietary information is an issue in all exchanges of ambiguous information. Economists, for example, are much more willing to present unambiguous information at conferences if paper publication is far along before the conference (for instance, by inclusion in a conference volume or by prior submission to a scholarly journal).

In some cases, an important component of ambiguity is exploration by each side of what exchange the other side is willing and able to make. "What will he tell me about his fall fashion styles in exchange for various things I might tell him about mine?" might be asked by a fashion designer prior to a meeting. A real estate syndicator might wonder what he can extract from a real estate lawyer about new ideas to avoid taxes under the 1986 tax reform law. The lawyer, in turn, might try to find out what knowledge of tax gimmicks the syndicator has and attempt to convey—without giving his ideas away—that he has ideas that will reduce the syndicator's taxes.

Quite generally, it is easy to imagine mutually profitable exchanges of ambiguous information among people with common problems. The problems might be technical production issues, finance issues, product design, marketing matters, tax issues, legal issues, research issues, and many others, or the problems might involve several such issues.

Does the exchange of ambiguous information require face-to-face contact? Clearly, it does not. Much ambiguous information is conveyed and exchanged over telephones, in TV advertising, in newspaper stories and advertising, and in trade journals. Many articles in trade journals have the following format: the author gives a few examples of wonderful things he has accomplished in the past (to establish credibility), then a few hints about what he can do for readers if paid his fee, and then finally how he can be contacted if the reader wants to pursue the matter.

Nevertheless, it seems clear that face-to-face exchanges may be efficient for the exchange of ambiguous information. The interactive convergence to a solution may be difficult or impossible without such interactions. Likewise, electronic transmission may be inefficient if more than two or three parties are involved and must interact several times in order to converge to a solution. Finally, in-person exchanges may build trust and help clarify what information other parties have or can obtain, what kinds of expertise and judgment they have, and so on.

An exchange of ambiguous information is closely related to technical change, broadly construed. The case for this hypothesis is strengthened if it is appreciated that much technical change comes not from new ideas but from new combinations of existing ideas. An idea may be well known in one field but important technical change can result from applying it in another field, where no one previously thought of applying it.

A persuasive analogy can be made to genetics. Ultimately, all evolution depends on genetic mutations. However, geneticists inform us that evolution would continue for many generations if mutations suddenly ceased because much of evolution results from new combinations of existing gene sets made possible by bisexuality. Also, all technical progress would eventually cease if new ideas ceased to appear, but much technical progress results from new "mixtures" of ideas, just as much evolution results from new mixtures of genes.

The informational interpretation is even stronger than the genetic interpretation. Mutations do not result from bisexual reproduction, but new ideas can and do result from ambiguous information exchange. Frequently, research topics or ideas are stimulated by discussion between researchers and people with practical problems. This is analogous to a world in which sexual activity caused genetic mutations! Of course, some research and other activities that generate new ideas are stimulated by formal communication (for example, by reading published research papers). I would guess that research that is toward the basic end of the basic-applied spectrum is most likely to be stimulated by formal communication (and training), whereas research that is toward the applied end of the spectrum is more commonly stimulated by ambiguous informational exchanges. My reason for this guess is the notion that applied research is frequently stimulated by practical problems and therefore by ambiguous exchanges between production, marketing, and other people, on the one hand, and research people on the other hand. Empirical support is provided by the fact that most applied research is financed by profit-making firms, whereas most basic research is financed outside the profit-making sector.

What kinds of clusters might be stimulated by the need for the exchange of ambiguous information? Some exchanges are intrafirm, between a firm's research and production people, for example. That is not the subject of primary interest here. Some exchanges of ambiguous information are horizontal and intrasectoral, as when high-fashion garment dealers cluster in one building in Manhattan. Another example is when electronic engineers in some metropolitan area meet once a month for dinner to exchange ideas informally. In addition, mercantile traders might meet for lunch at a club and exchange information about likely trends and other ideas. Many more examples could be imagined.

Exchanges might be among firms that relate in an input-output sense, as was suggested earlier. Indeed, some of the electronic engineers mentioned in the previous paragraph might be employed in firms with input-output relationships. Exchanges might be among professionals with common technical interests but who work in different and unrelated sectors. Again, some of the electronic engineers might illustrate that possibility, or a set of accountants employed in unrelated sectors might meet occasionally to discuss the latest rulings of the accounting standards board or of the IRS or tax laws passed by Congress or by state legislatures. My conclusion is that it is difficult to speculate a priori about what kinds of clusters might result from the desire for the exchange of ambiguous information.

It is clear that locations within a single metropolitan area are not necessary for the exchange of ambiguous information. People from all over the country come several times a year to an O'Hare Airport motel to exchange ambiguous information at meetings on trends in the cosmetics industry. The same is true in many other business sectors. Also, scholars meet to exchange ideas in conferences. The point is that the exchange of ambiguous information is most likely to justify location in a single metropolitan area if such exchanges are needed frequently.

A final question concerns firm size. It is frequently contended that information exchange is an aspect of the "incubator" effect that is important for new and small firms and a reason that they benefit from central locations in metropolitan areas. There is no reason to think that the exchange of ambiguous information is less important for large than for small firms. Insofar as proximate locations are important for such exchanges, it is as important for large as for small firms. More such exchanges can be intrafirm in large firms;

most such exchanges must be interfirm in small firms. All electronic engineers in GTE meet once a year for a three-day "retreat" whereas those in smaller firms must have interfirm meetings for the same purposes. Thus, interfirm clustering must be more important among workers in small firms, although clustering of workers with common problems may be independent of firm size.

Is clustering for the exchange of ambiguous information peculiarly important in service sectors? If so, in which service sectors? My guess is that the answer is "yes." I am thinking of office-type service sector firms that are typically located downtown. For one thing, such firms usually have relatively few employees compared with manufacturing firms. That means that much of the information exchange must be interfirm. That, in turn, may increase the need for the exchange of ambiguous information. To some extent, employees within a firm are united in pursuit of the same goal; there may be relatively little need for ambiguity in the form of jockeying, partial concealment, and secrecy. However, anyone familiar with large firms knows that such strategies are by no means absent within large firms.

Among the sectors that are prominently clustered in downtown offices are manufacturing company headquarters, accounting firms, legal firms, business consultants, advertising concerns, financial institutions, insurance companies, an enormous variety of small-scale business services, and firms that provide real estate services. There is obviously an enormous amount of interacting among these firms and much of it is presumably the exchange of ambiguous information.

My conclusion is that the exchange of ambiguous information is almost certainly a substantial reason for intermetropolitan clustering. Whether it is a major or minor factor in location decisions remains to be explored. In principle, the importance of the exchange of ambiguous information for intermetropolitan clustering depends on the state of communications technologies. Inexpensive electronic transmission of data may have reduced the need for some kinds of clustering. Nevertheless, the communications revolution in recent years probably has had only a slight effect in reducing the incentive to cluster. Theoretically, one can engage in arbitrage anywhere there are long-distance phones and good personal computers, yet most such workers are still in the small set of metropolitan areas in which such activities are common. The exchange of ambiguous information may be an important reason.

Government Policy

Do markets provide adequate incentives to cluster? If not, what government policies should strengthen market incentives?

First, it is clear that market incentives to cluster are weaker than they previously were. Most of the growth of both goods- and service-producing firms has been in suburbs during the last quarter century or so and, to a remarkable extent, outside metropolitan areas altogether since about 1970. Undoubtedly, the incentive to cluster has been weakened because electronic devices have reduced the cost of transmitting information over long distances. In addition, the growth of metropolitan areas and incomes, as well as household suburbanization, has generated large enough markets that clusters of sufficient size have been replicated in suburbs. Whereas previously only downtown could generate clusters of sufficient size to be efficient, suburban clusters can now also be efficient. Beyond doubt, that trend will continue, regardless of government policies to further it or to inhibit it. The point is that a variety of changes during the postwar period has reduced the need for downtown clusters, but that does not imply that market incentives for clustering have become increasingly inadequate.

Most of the reasons for clustering discussed above provide no presumption of market inefficiency. For example, input-output clustering presumably leads to the right amount of clustering, taking account of social benefits and costs.

The basic argument in support of the contention that markets insufficiently motivate clustering is the public good character of information. Once information is produced, little or no additional inputs are needed if a second firm uses it instead of just one. TV is a classic example; once resources have been devoted to produce and transmit a program, no additional resources are needed if an extra viewer is added. Likewise, there is no additional cost of producing a newspaper of given content if the number of readers is doubled. There are relatively small extra manufacturing and distribution costs but no extra costs for information assembly, writing, and so forth.

To some extent, the same is true of all information, ambiguous or otherwise. The basic cost is in generating information; only distribution costs depend on how many recipients there are. However, most information that is germane to the discussion here is valuable to only a small group of users, even if clustering is optimally great. Much information is valuable only to small groups of people with highly specialized training, experience, and business interests. If the group to whom information is potentially useful is sufficiently small, private agreements can optimize distribution of the information without justification for government intervention.

A couple of examples will fix the ideas. Suppose a mathematician invents linear programming. That new information has enormous and diverse applications. Many applications become known only gradually as some are tried and found to work, as new computer hardware and software are developed, as additional research is done on solving particular problems with the new mathematical techniques, and as people gradually learn about the technique and think about applications. This in fact has been the history of linear programming during the last forty years or so. Linear programming undoubtedly developed with the aid of an enormous number of informal exchanges of ambiguous information. However, it was socially important that the basic mathematical techniques be in the public domain from the beginning, and they were. The cost of doing the basic research was not dependent on the number of subsequent uses to be made of the new technique. It was a pure public good.

By contrast, suppose a real estate tax lawyer has an idea about a form of organization for a real estate venture that has the advantages of a limited partnership but avoids the double taxation that Congress recently imposed on some limited partnerships. The idea, which may require technical notification for each user, is of value to only a few dozen people or organizations who are positioned to benefit from it. Almost all those people can be cheaply contacted through publications in trade journals. Once it has worked for a few people, word quickly gets around the relevant group that it is valuable. The attorney can "sell" his idea to the first few users. Gradually, it becomes well known and other attorneys can work out the details for their clients. This idea is a public good in only a limited sense, and private agreements probably adequately motivate both the generation and the distribution of such ideas.

The point of these examples is that information, and exchanges of ambiguous information, can have highly varying degrees of publicness. The more limited the public good aspect of an exchange, the weaker the presumption of market failure. I suspect that many examples of ambiguous information exchange in which physical clustering is important involve publicness to only a limited extent and that market failure may be minimal or nonexistent. That is only a presumption, not a substitute for evidence.

In a way, a more serious issue is a practical one. Suppose we all agreed that clustering for information exchange was important and that market incentives provided too little clustering. What would we advise local governments to do? Undoubtedly, local governments (or economists, for that matter) have only limited ability to identify clusters that are socially beneficial but for which market incentives are inadequate. Government policies to facilitate locations of private research firms or high-tech manufacturing firms near universities appear to be almost obviously desirable, and hundreds of state and local governments have pursued the strategy. But what sectors lack market incentives to undertake such clustering even though it is socially desirable? How frequent, extensive, and ambiguous must needed contacts be to justify government encouragement?

If we think governments cannot answer these questions, we are restricted to recommending general policies that can facilitate clustering but do not require local governments to identify sectors that should cluster. Examples might include making sure that public schools produce people who can qualify for emerging jobs; making sure that the transportation system provides easy access to downtown jobs both from within the city and from the suburbs (not all the workers in such jobs will want to live in the city); reducing crime rates because high crime rates are bad for downtown job creation; making sure that land use controls do not unduly restrict commercial development; and keeping tax rates at reasonable levels in the city so as not to deter downtown business growth. Most of these suggestions are aimed at central city governments because that is where the inadequacy of traditional local government services is worst, but to the extent that they are applicable, the suggestions apply to suburban governments as well.

My final point is that recent research findings at NCI and elsewhere that certain clusters tend to locate or grow in some metropolitan areas, although an important first step in understanding the dynamics of metropolitan growth, have no implications for government policy. In addition, the finding that a cluster of sectors tends to grow in a metropolitan area in which it was strong in an initial year has no implications for government policy. Both findings are perfectly consistent both with the hypothesis that markets provide optimum incentive for clustering and with the hypothesis that government intervention is justified.

A finding that particular clusters of activities tend to locate or grow in metropolitan areas in a particular region may provide hints as to causes, but it has no government policy implications per se. A finding that some clusters are found in large, but not small, metropolitan areas would suggest that metropolitan size or a correlate of size is a factor, but that finding also has no implications for government policy. It merely indicates that large metropolitan areas provide a comparative advantage for the clusters in question. There is no presumption that markets generate insufficient numbers of large metropolitan areas. A finding that certain clusters are found where educational attainment is especially great suggests that a high-quality school system may have large social return but no more. (High educational attainment is strongly correlated with high income. High income creates strong local demand for the products of certain clusters of activities. Thus, it would be necessary to establish that the correlation between educational attainment and the strength of activity clusters was not spurious.) Even finding that the size or growth of an industry cluster is correlated with a set of government policies only hints about desirable government policies. It suggests places to look in further investigation.

As most of the papers in this volume illustrate, we are making rapid progress in understanding the dynamics of clustering and metropolitan development, but government policy issues are yet to be addressed.

Notes

1. The Census Bureau's Standard Industrial Classification (SIC) system exhaustively categorizes industries by primary product. Data for metropolitan areas

are generally available at four levels of industry detail, ranging from the "one-digit" level of broad industry divisions to the "four–digit" level of industry subsectors.

2.   Other common examples of intrametropolitan area clusters are antique furniture stores and art galleries. Both are presumably explained by comparison shopping.

3.   A formal definition of a cluster might go as follows. Let

$$X_i = \{x_{i1}, \cdots x_{iN}\} \; i = 1, \ldots, I$$

be the amounts of N commodities or services produced in the ith of I metropolitan areas. Alternatively, x_{ij} could refer to employment in sector j in metropolitan area i or to the growth of production or employment in sector j in metropolitan area i.

Suppose there exists a subset J' of the set J of product subscripts such that

$$X_i' = \{x_{ij}/j\epsilon J'\}$$

and

$$\frac{x_{ij}}{Y_i} > Mj$$

If $J \epsilon J'$, then we say that the activity set J' is a cluster in i. Here $Y_i = \Sigma_j w_j x_{ij}$ is a weighted average of i's activities. Weights might be wage rates or product prices. If the x's are total employment, then $w_j = 1$ for all j,

$$Mj = \underset{i}{\Sigma} xij/Y$$

is the average importance of sector j in all I metropolitan areas. Here, $Y = \underset{i}{\Sigma} Y_i$

The definition simply defines a cluster to be a set of activities that are more important in i than in an average metropolitan area.

An easy generalization would make the right side of the inequality ϕM_j. $\phi = 2$, for example, would define a cluster in i as a set of activities that were at least twice as large a share of metropolitan area i as of the average metropolitan area.

4.   On the subject of this paragraph, see the paper by Satterthwaite, chapter 3, in this volume.

References

Henderson, J. V. *Urban Development: Theory, Fact and Illusion.* New York: Oxford University Press, 1988.

Lösch, A. *The Economies of Location.* New Haven, Conn.: Yale University Press, 1954.

Mills, E. "A Transactions Cost Model of Metropolitan Size." Mimeo. June 1988.

_____ . "What Makes Metropolitan Areas Grow?" Mimeo. March 1988.

Ó hUallacháin, B., and M. Satterthwaite. *Sectoral Growth Patterns at the Metropolitan Level: An Evaluation of Economic Development Incentives.* Report to the U.S. Department of Commerce, Economic Development Administration. Evanston, Ill.: NCI Research, 1988.

PATRICIA E. BEESON

2 Agglomeration Economies and Productivity Growth

The question of why some areas grow while others stagnate and decline is of perennial interest to economists and policymakers. In the short run, exogenous changes in the demand for goods produced in a region or in the technology used to produce these goods may cause growth rates to differ. However, growth rates differ not just in the short run in response to exogenous changes. There are also persistent differences in growth rates across regions. Between 1950 and 1980, for example, family incomes in Jackson, Mississippi, increased by 2.7 percent annually, more than twice the annual increase in South Bend, Indiana (1.05 percent), El Paso, Texas (1.14 percent), Binghamton, New York (1.2 percent), and Spokane, Washington (1.35 percent).

Over time, these differences in growth rates have tended to reduce interarea income differences as low-income areas have experienced more rapid income growth on average than high-income areas. Despite this tendency toward convergence, however, considerable differences remain—even across Standard Metropolitan Statistical Areas (SMSAs), centers of production that are relatively well developed. In 1980, family incomes in the richest SMSAs were nearly twice those in the poorest. In San Jose, California, Washington, D.C., and Stamford, Connecticut, for example, family incomes

The author would like to thank Cynthia Rogers and John McDonald, among others, for their comments on an earlier draft, as well as Neil Bania for providing the data on patent rates by SMSA and Stanko Racic for his research assistance.

19

ranged from $30,000 to $36,000 in 1980. Meanwhile, family incomes in Columbus, Georgia, El Paso, Texas, and Ashville, North Carolina, were considerably lower, ranging from $17,000 to $19,000. Family incomes outside these SMSAs were lower still.

In addition, despite the general tendency for low-income areas to experience relatively rapid growth, a large number of low-income areas have not benefited from this trend. This raises the question of why? Why do some areas, such as Jackson, grow while others, such as El Paso, continue to stagnate? Is there anything governments can and should do to change the fate of areas such as El Paso?

Agglomeration Economies and Metropolitan Growth

One of the primary sources of income growth is growth in the productivity of inputs used in production. In the study of urban economies, productivity tends to be linked to city size. The higher wages and rents paid in large cities suggest that productivity is higher in these areas. If this were not the case, why would firms locate in the large cities and pay the high wages and rents rather than locate in smaller cities where wages and rents are lower?

This ability to pay higher wages and rents may be related to the existence of some natural site advantage, such as a natural port, that reduces other costs of production and thus allows firms located in these areas to compete in a national market despite the higher wages and land rents. Alternatively, there may be externalities associated with the agglomeration of activity, independent of where that agglomeration may be, that increase productivity, allowing firms in large cities to pay higher factor costs.

These agglomeration economies may contribute to observed differences in both levels and growth rates of income and productivity across cities. In this paper, I discuss the nature of the externalities associated with the agglomeration of economic activity in cities and the relationship between these agglomeration economies and productivity growth. Following Kaldor (1970), I consider agglomeration economies to be:

> ... nothing else but the existence of increasing returns to scale—using that term in the broadest sense—in processing activities. These are not just the economies of large-scale production, commonly considered, but the cumulative advantages accruing from the growth of industry itself—the development of skill and know-how; the opportunities for easy communication of ideas and experience; the opportunity of ever-increasing differentiation of processes and of specialization in human activities.[1]

It is the "cumulative advantages accruing from the growth of industry itself" that I consider as a source of productivity growth. The process is one where increases in the scale of economic activity generate externalities that increase productivity, thereby generating additional growth.[2] If individuals do not take into account the effect their actions have on the productivity of others (if there is no way to internalize these external effects), there may be policies that the government can pursue that will increase productivity and welfare.

The idea that productivity and growth are related to the scale of production is not new—it has been part of economics at least since the time of economist Adam Smith—nor is it specific to the study of urban economies; it is also part of the discussion of why nations grow at different rates.[3] However, it seems that in many cases these economies are most naturally thought of as occurring within cities because they depend not just on scale of production but also proximity.

Here I focus my attention on externalities associated with increases in the scale of activity in cities, but there may be implications for the growth of nations as well. As Jacobs (1984) stresses in *Cities and the Wealth of Nations*, productivity increases associated with the agglomeration of economic activity in cities may be an engine of growth for nations as well as regions. After all, what are nations but systems of cities and their hinterlands?

There are three related issues concerning the relationship between agglomeration and productivity: Does agglomeration affect *levels* of income and productivity? Does the agglomeration of economic activity in cities affect the *growth* of income and productivity, perhaps affecting nations as well as cities, as Jacobs (1984) suggests? Do agglomeration economies affect the relative growth rates of income and productivity across cities? While this paper focuses on the second and third issues regarding growth, some attempt is made to distinguish between factors that affect levels of income and productivity and those that affect growth.

Empirical Evidence and Underlying Issues

There is considerable evidence that productivity levels increase with city size (Henderson, 1986; Moomaw, 1981; Segal, 1976; Sveikauskas, 1975). It is unclear from these studies the extent to which the higher productivity is related to city size per se or to other site characteristics. Locational characteristics, such as a natural port, could be the source of both higher productivity and city size. However, the simple fact that cities exist suggests that agglomeration has some effect on the productivity of firms. There is also some evidence concerning the relationship between agglomeration and productivity *growth*. Several recent studies employ methods similar to those used to analyze national and international productivity growth to examine regional productivity growth. In these studies, productivity growth is measured as a residual—the difference between the growth rate of value added and the portion of that growth that can be attributed to increased input usage. Productivity growth, so measured, is then compared across regions to determine the extent to which agglomeration and productivity growth are related.

In the first of these regional studies, state-level manufacturing data were used to examine the relationship between agglomeration and productivity growth (Beeson, 1987). The overall measure of productivity growth was decomposed to identify the contribution of scale economies and residual growth, attributed to technical change. The relationship between each of these two components and various measures of agglomeration, as well as the relationship between agglomeration and the composite measure of productivity growth, were then examined. Productivity growth due to scale economies was found to be positively related to the share of the state's population living in SMSAs and negatively related to the presence of one of the nation's twenty largest SMSAs. The opposite was true for technical change and overall productivity growth. Both technical change and the composite measure of productivity growth were found to be higher in states with a large SMSA and lower in states with more metropolitan populations, though in the case of the composite measure neither relationship was statistically significant.

Moomaw and Williamson (1988) also found that productivity growth is higher in states with one of the country's twenty largest SMSAs and lower in states with a higher percent metropolitan population; in this study, both relationships were statistically significant. This study used an approach similar to Beeson (1987) but did not separately identify the two sources of productivity growth. In addition, in the statistical analysis of the relationship between productivity growth and agglomeration, they controlled for a larger number of state characteristics and used a more efficient three-stage least-squares estimator, both of which may have contributed to their finding a statistically significant relationship where the earlier study did not.

Studies using metropolitan-level data have also found productivity growth to be highest in the largest SMSAs. Fogarty and Garofalo (1988) used metropolitan area data to examine productivity growth for a sample of large SMSAs. Within this group of large SMSAs, they found evidence of increasing returns to city size and a small positive relationship between city size and the rate of technical change.

Fogarty and Garofalo (1988) focused on differences in productivity growth among the largest SMSAs. In a subsequent study (Beeson, mimeo, 1988 and update, *Journal of Urban Economics* 28, 1990), Fogarty and Garofalo's SMSA data were combined with state data to compare productivity growth inside and outside large SMSAs over the 1959–78 period. Large SMSAs were defined as those for which value added in manufacturing exceeded $2 million in 1978.[4] This study found that the productivity rate was 15 percent higher inside than outside these large SMSAs (2.26 percent annually compared with 1.96 percent). However, while productivity growth was higher on average in large SMSAs over the full time period, this was not true in all regions nor for all shorter time periods examined. In particular, we found productivity growth was consistently lower inside than outside the large SMSAs in the South and that the productivity growth advantage of large SMSAs has tended to decline over time.

To summarize, the empirical evidence to date indicates that productivity growth tends to be highest in the largest metropolitan areas, though it does not appear to be uniformly higher for large SMSAs in all regions or for all time periods. In addition, Beeson's (1987) and Moomaw and Williamson's (1988) findings of lower productivity growth in the more metropolitan states, after accounting for the productivity advantage of the largest SMSAs, suggest that the relationship between city size and productivity growth may be nonlinear, with the growth rate of productivity higher for very large and small cities and lower for those in between.

PRODUCTIVITY GROWTH AND EMPLOYMENT GROWTH

A natural question that arises given this evidence is that if the largest SMSAs have the highest productivity growth rates, shouldn't they also have the highest employment growth rates? Shouldn't employment be increasingly concentrated in a relatively few large cities over time rather than becoming less concentrated, as we observe?

There are at least two reasons why higher productivity growth rates in large SMSAs may not translate into higher employment growth rates in these areas. First, even if productivity growth is higher, wage growth may be lower in large cities if other costs of production, such as land costs, are increasing more rapidly in large than small cities. Second, the growth rate of wages required to sustain a given growth rate of employment may be higher in large than small cities if the compensation workers require for the increases in housing costs, crime rates, pollution, and so on, associated with increased city size is higher in large than small cities.

GEOGRAPHIC AND INTERINDUSTRY SPILLOVERS

Before turning to the discussion of how agglomeration might affect productivity growth, I would like to raise two general issues concerning spillovers associated with agglomeration. The first concerns the extent to which the benefits associated with agglomeration extend beyond the geographic boundaries of a city (von Boventer, 1970). There is sound evidence that such spillovers occur (Beeson, 1987). The extent of these spillover effects has implications for which level of government should be responsible for policy.

If they are limited, local policies may be most appropriate; if they are extensive, it may be desirable for a government representing a larger geographic area to assume responsibility.

The second issue concerns whether the advantages of scale and proximity relate primarily to increases in the scale of activity in a particular industry, with all benefits accruing primarily to that industry (localization economies), or whether they relate more generally to the overall scale of activity in an area, thereby affecting the productivity of all firms (urbanization economies). A number of studies examining the relationship between levels of productivity and the scale of production in cities conclude that localization economies tend to dominate. This conclusion is supported by the tendency for cities to specialize in the production of specific goods (Henderson, 1986) and by evidence from studies of the relationship between industrial clustering and employment growth (see Satterthwaite, chapter 3, Ó hUallacháin, chapter 4, and McDonald, chapter 5). To the extent that localization economies tend to dominate, industry-specific as opposed to general economic policies may be in order.

Sources of Agglomeration Economies

INCREASING RETURNS TO SCALE FROM SPECIALIZATION

Adam Smith proposed that productivity will increase with the scale of production because increased scale allows firms and workers to specialize in specific tasks and this specialization and division of labor increases productivity. The ability to exploit these economies of scale, in turn, depends on the size of the market. To the extent that the size of the market depends on population density and is limited by transport costs, the ability to exploit economies of scale depends on city size.

One can think of a number of examples where city size allows for greater specialization. The large labor force allows individual workers to specialize in specific tasks where their productivity will be higher. In addition, when a person leaves a job, firms may spend less time and effort searching for replacements because the pool of labor from which to hire is large.

Specialization may also occur in the production of intermediate goods, including those produced by private firms, such as business services, steel, and machine tools, as well as those that are publicly provided, such as education and transportation. The large demand for these intermediate inputs in cities supports the presence of firms that specialize in providing these goods. Similarly, in the production of final goods, the density of demand in large cities allows firms to specialize in the production of local goods that require a minimum density of demand to support production—goods such as restaurants and theaters, which by their nature are too expensive to transport.[5]

All of these can be viewed as instances in which the scale of economic activity in cities enables greater specialization and division of labor. In this way, agglomeration can generate productivity growth leading to higher per capita income in large cities.[6] The remaining question is whether this can explain differences in productivity growth across cities. The answer depends on the strength of the economies of scale associated with agglomeration. If they are strong enough, the growth as well as the levels of income and productivity will be higher in large cities. If not, growth rates (but not levels) of income and productivity will be higher in the smaller cities.

This relationship between the scale of production and productivity suggests a role for government if individual firms do not consider the effect of their production decisions on the productivity of other firms in the area. In this case, government policies designed to increase the level of production in an area, such as subsidies to new or existing firms, may be desirable—especially if some minimum level of production is required before increases in production generate productivity growth. This is the basis for "big push" strategies of economic development where local governments initially subsidize production in the hope of achieving the threshold size. The question of whether or not a specific industry should be targeted depends on whether agglomeration benefits depend primarily on the scale of a single industry (localization economies) or on the general level of activity (urbanization economies).

This discussion has focused on positive externalities associated with agglomeration. However, beyond some point, agglomeration may also generate negative externalities, such as congestion, that reduce productivity. If this is the case, there may be a role for government in limiting the extent of these negative spillovers by limiting urban growth.

THE RATE OF TECHNICAL CHANGE

Specialization of the sort discussed above increases productivity by allowing workers and firms to engage in more refined tasks. Productivity will also increase if the productivity of workers at a given task increases. Agglomeration, in turn, may affect this type of productivity growth through its effects on the rate at which new technologies are developed and incorporated into the production processes and through its effect on the rate at which workers learn and human capital accumulates.

If patent applications are any indication, rates of innovation are higher in large SMSAs than in small.[7] If we again define large SMSAs as those for which value added in manufacturing exceeded \$2 million in 1978, large SMSAs averaged more than four thousand patent applications in 1980 compared with less than five hundred for small SMSAs. The patent rate was 60 percent higher in large SMSAs (2.15 patent applications per one thousand people in large SMSAs versus 1.32 per one thousand in small).[8]

A number of factors may explain this higher rate of innovation. On the supply side, if there are scale economies associated with the development of new technologies, a more-than-proportionate number of innovations may be developed in urban areas. For a variety of reasons, a disproportionate number of researchers, skilled technicians, and entrepreneurs willing to invest in the development of new technologies may be found in urban areas. Furthermore, the interaction of these groups is facilitated by the proximity afforded by cities and by formal institutions such as university and corporate research centers that tend to be concentrated in these areas (Jacobs, 1969; Pred, 1966; Richardson, 1978).

To the extent that proximity increases the rate at which new technologies are developed, the agglomeration of economic activity in cities may generate productivity growth through its effect on the rate of technical change. It is in this way that Jacobs (1969) suggests that cities may serve as the engines of growth—the endogenous source of productivity growth—for nations. Clearly, if this is the case and if these externalities in the development of new technologies only occur when cities have reached a minimum size, then there may be some benefit to the nation, as well as to cities, of helping some cities reach this minimum threshold size.

On the demand side, it has been argued that new innovations in products and processes are more likely to appear first in large economies because the demand for new products is highest in these areas (Vernon, 1966). According to these product life cycle models, during the early stages of production when rates of innovation are highest, production tends to take place close to the market so that firms can adapt the product and process in response to consumer demand. As the product and processes become more standardized in later stages, production moves away from the centers of demand to areas where other production costs are lower.

If innovations are generated at a constant rate in large cities and then appear in smaller cities with a constant lag, then the growth rates of per capita income and productivity will be the same in both areas. Income and productivity levels, however, will be higher in large cities because they are the first to benefit from the new technologies. Income and productivity growth rates will be different only if the rate at which new technologies appear in large cities is different from the rate at which they appear in small cities. This depends on the rate at which new technologies are developed in large cities, the rate at which this technical knowledge is transmitted from large to small cities, and the rate at which this knowledge is incorporated into production processes in small and large cities.

Changes in the rate of innovation in large cities over time can lead to differences in growth rates between large and small cities. If new technologies appear in the production processes of firms in small cities with a constant lag, then productivity growth rates will be higher in large cities than in small if the rate at which new technologies are being developed in large cities is increasing over time. Similarly, if the rate at which new technologies are being developed is decreasing over time, productivity growth rates will be higher in the small cities.

On the other hand, if new technologies are being generated at a constant rate but the rate at which this information is spreading to other areas is increasing over time, due to improvements in communication, then the growth rate of productivity will be higher in the smaller cities as long as there is a backlog of innovations available.[9]

Productivity growth depends not only on the availability of technical knowledge but also on the ability of firms in an area to incorporate this knowledge into the production process. Differences in the ability of firms in large and small cities to implement technology may cause growth rates to differ. Several recent studies provide evidence that the ability to incorporate new technologies depends on the availability of skilled labor (Bartel and Lichtenberg, 1987; Wozniak, 1984, 1987). This suggests that areas with skilled labor will have the advantage in implementing new technologies.

This skilled labor, in turn, tends to be concentrated in large cities. Individuals in large SMSAs, on average, have completed more years of schooling than individuals in smaller SMSAs (10.3 years compared with 9.9 years in small SMSAs). They are also more likely to be employed in what might be considered high-skill occupations (the share of workers who are scientists and engineers is 17 percent higher in large than in small SMSAs).[10]

While this concentration of skilled labor may cause levels of income and productivity to be higher in large cities, simply having a more skilled labor force will not lead to higher income and productivity growth rates in large cities as long as the difference in skills is constant over time. For example, assume that there is no lag between the rate at which new technology is developed and the rate at which this information reaches smaller cities and that the skilled labor available in large cities is always sufficient to implement the new technologies. Then if small cities always have half the skilled labor of large cities, they can always implement half of the new technologies generated, and while the levels of technology may be different, the growth rates will not.

Productivity and income growth rates may differ, however, if the gap between skilled labor in large and small cities is changing over time. This raises the question of what determines the growth of skills and how agglomeration might affect this growth of human capital.

THE RATE OF HUMAN CAPITAL ACCUMULATION

Human capital accumulation can be thought of as an improvement in technology in that it increases the productivity of individual workers at a given task. To the extent that agglomeration aids in the process of human capital accumulation, it will then contribute to productivity growth. Here I address two questions regarding the effects of agglomeration on human capital accumulation and productivity growth: Does the agglomeration of economic activity in cities increase the stock of human capital in the national economy, thereby serving as a source of growth for the nation as well as for individual cities? Does agglomeration affect the relative distribution of human capital among cities, thereby affecting relative growth rates of income and productivity across cities?

It has been argued that an individual's ability to learn depends on the average knowledge of those around him. If so, then once human capital increases for any reason, it will continue to increase forever because the initial increase will raise the average level, which in turn will increase learning—and the process goes on.[11] If the ability to learn from each other is enhanced by proximity, then cities will contribute to this process of human capital accumulation by affording people the opportunity to learn from each other. In this way, agglomeration can be a source of productivity and income growth for the nation as well as cities.

Whether this can also explain differences in growth rates across cities depends on the exact nature of the relationship between average human capital and learning. Skills will increase most rapidly in areas that have the highest initial stock of human capital only if the rate of learning increases with increases in the average human capital of those around us.

Another method of acquiring knowledge and skills is through learning on the job. In learning-by-doing models, learning depends on the level of output per capita. Once output per capita increases for any reason, it will continue to increase forever as today's higher output increases learning, which increases tomorrow's productivity, increasing output tomorrow, and so it continues.[12]

Earlier it was noted that productivity levels and city size are correlated. This correlation may be due to the presence of a locational advantage, such as a natural port, or it may reflect agglomeration economies of the sort discussed in this paper. Learning-by-doing models suggest that independent of the source, the higher productivity associated with agglomeration will lead to further productivity growth because the higher output per worker gives rise to more opportunity for learning by doing.

Whether this can also explain why the rate of increase in productivity is higher in large cities depends on the exact relationship between learning and output per worker. If learning accelerates as output per worker increases, then the growth rate of productivity will be higher in large cities. On the other hand, if there are diminishing returns to learning on the job, the growth rate of productivity will be higher in small cities.

In addition to the level of output, the technology used to produce goods may influence learning on the job. The production of high-technology goods, for example, may provide many opportunities for learning while the production of other goods may provide few. Learning by doing will then be highest in the high-technology industries. This suggests that the same factors that determine comparative advantage, or industry mix, also determine the rate of growth of human capital if the production of different goods has different potentials for human capital growth. To the extent that large cities have a comparative advantage in the production of high-technology goods, they will also have the highest rate of increase in productivity through learning by doing. If we consider the percent of the work force employed in high-tech industries as an indication, large SMSAs with their high concentration of these industries have an industry mix that is more conducive to acquiring skills through learning by doing.

A final way in which agglomeration may affect the rate of human capital accumulation and hence productivity growth is through migration. If skilled and educated workers are drawn disproportionately to large cities, the rate of human capital accumulation will be higher in large cities than in small. This could account for differences in the levels and growth rates of productivity and income across cities. By itself, however, it cannot affect productivity growth for the nation as a whole because it does not represent an addition to the nation's stock of human capital.

Skilled workers may be drawn to large cities because the demand for their services is higher in these cities, perhaps because production in the early stages of the product cycle requires skilled labor. On the other hand, skilled labor may be concentrated in large cities because these workers place a higher value on the amenities relative to the costs of big-city life than do less skilled workers.

These relationships between agglomeration and human capital accumulation suggest a number of policies that may be successful in encouraging local economic growth. To the extent that there are externalities associated with learning, subsidies to improve the average level of education and training may be successful in promoting economic growth. On the other hand, if there are learning externalities associated with the production of advanced technology goods, an industrial policy that subsidizes high-tech industries may be appropriate.

It is important to remember, though, that the success of any policy designed to improve skills and education of the local labor force depends on the ability of the local area to retain these workers once they are trained. Once educated and trained, people may leave the small cities for large cities, further increasing the human capital of large cities relative to small cities. Direct evidence on the ability of local areas to retain skilled labor is limited. However, there is evidence that local investments in education are associated with higher growth rates of per capita income, employment, and net investment—at least suggesting that such a strategy may be successful (Helms, 1985; Mofidi, 1988).

COLLEGES AND UNIVERSITIES

Finally, there is a set of institutions that tends to be concentrated in large cities that may contribute to productivity growth, namely, colleges and universities. Table 2.1 shows mean values for various measures of the quality and size of local colleges and universities in large and small SMSAs. These measures indicate that the number of degrees awarded, the amount of research and development (R&D) funding, the number of top-rated science and engineering programs, and the share of graduates who are scientists and engineers are all higher on average in large SMSAs.

One obvious way in which these colleges and universities may contribute to the higher productivity growth in large cities is through their effect on the skill composition of the local labor force. As noted earlier, a highly educated and trained labor force may generate productivity growth by (1) increasing the ability of firms to implement new technologies and (2) increasing the average level of education, thereby increasing the rate of learning in an area. Consistent with this idea that colleges and universities may increase the skills of workers in an area, Beeson and Montgomery (1989) found that the portion of the labor force employed as scientists and engineers tends to be higher in areas with colleges and universities engaged in large amounts of R&D.

Colleges and universities may also affect productivity by increasing the rate of innovation in the local area. It was suggested earlier that large cities provide a natural environment for the development of technology and in this way affect productivity growth. Colleges and universities may also serve as incubators for new technology. A number of recent studies provide evidence of links between basic research facilities, such as universities, and technological innovation in private industry (Nelson, 1986). This may be related to direct university-industry cooperation, as suggested by Cox (1985), the

TABLE 2.1

Quality and Size of
Colleges and Universities
in Large and Small SMSAs

	Average in Large SMSAs[a]	Average in Small SMSAs
University R&D funding	$61 million	$9.9 million
Number of science and engineering programs rated among the top twenty in the country[b]	6.7	1.3
Number of bachelor's degrees awarded	697	1,729
Portion of bachelor's degrees awarded in science and engineering	27%	21%

[a]Includes the fifty large SMSAs used in Beeson (1988) for which value added in manufacturing exceeded $2 million in 1978.

[b]Science and engineering programs include math, biological and physical sciences, computer science, and engineering programs.

Source: Based on data from 1980 NSF survey of academic institutions and reported in Beeson and Montgomery (1989). Figures refer to totals for all four-year colleges and universities in the SMSA.

National Science Foundation (1983), and the Office of Technology Assessment (1984), or it may be related to benefits to private industry from technology spillovers of the type discussed by Bernstein and Nadiri (1988), Jaffe (1986), and Kennedy (1986).

To the extent that these spillovers depend on proximity, the presence of research universities may contribute to productivity and income growth in a local area. Empirical research by Jaffe (1989) using state data and Bania (1989) using SMSA level data found that technological spillovers from universities to firms depend to some extent on proximity.

If there are externalities associated with education and training that individuals do not take into account when deciding on their schooling, or if there are technology spillovers from universities to industry, a reasonable policy might be to subsidize universities. Whether this should be done by the local, state, or national government depends on the extent to which these benefits spill over to larger geographic areas through migration and technology transfers.

Conclusion

One intriguing aspect of metropolitan growth is the extent to which growth feeds upon itself. A number of researchers have speculated that the agglomeration of activity in cities generates positive externalities that increase the productivity of firms in such a way that growth itself becomes endogenous. In this paper, I have discussed one aspect of this process, the relationship between agglomeration and productivity growth.

Agglomeration may affect productivity growth in a number of ways. The scale of activity in an area may allow for greater specialization in production on the part of workers and firms, it may increase the rate at which new technologies are developed and implemented in a firm's production process, or, more generally, it may increase the rate of human capital accumulation. Agglomeration may also foster the development of institutions, such as colleges and universities, that facilitate the development of new technology and human capital.

To the extent that these sorts of externalities exist, productivity may increase even in the absence of external changes in the demand for goods produced in the city or in the technology used to produce these goods. The scale of activity in the city itself may be the source of productivity growth. The arguments suggest that, at least over some range, the agglomeration of activity in cities may generate productivity growth. The relationship between the rate of productivity growth and the degree of agglomeration, however, is unclear. Whether the rate of productivity growth is higher in the early or later stages of development depends on the exact nature of the externalities and the interaction between different sources of agglomeration economies. Moreover, the benefits of agglomeration may exist only for a range of city sizes. A minimum scale may be needed before any benefits of agglomeration accrue, and beyond some size there may be no additional benefits from further agglomeration or these benefits may be offset by negative externalities, such as congestion.

A final issue concerns the extent to which agglomeration economies of the sort discussed in this paper translate into employment growth. Although productivity and employment growth are related, a number of other factors, including the effects of agglomeration on factor costs, such as land rents and wages, are also important. In order to understand the relationship between agglomeration and metropolitan growth and to develop informed policy, these countervailing negative effects of agglomeration on employment growth, as well as the positive effects of agglomeration on productivity growth discussed here, need to be considered.

Notes

1. Kaldor, 1970, p. 340.
2. Cumulative causation models of regional growth based on this positive relationship between productivity and city or region size predict that regional incomes will diverge over time. See Malecki and Varaiya (1986) or Richardson (1978) for a discussion of these models and comparison with models that predict income convergence.
3. Recent papers in this area include Ekstein and Kollintzas (1988), Lucas (1988), Romer (1986), Stokey (1986), and Vassilakis (1989). While the size of the economy being considered is not always made explicit in these papers, implicit in most is a concern with national growth.
4. While defined in terms of value added at the end of the period, 1978, these SMSAs would also be considered large at the beginning of the period, 1959.
5. To the extent that individuals value diversity, the variety of products offered in large cities will increase individuals' utility, attracting them to large cities. The effects of this migration on productivity growth are discussed later.
6. A number of recent theoretical models show how these economies of scale can serve as an "engine of growth" causing productivity growth in the absence of exogenous shocks, such as changes in technology (Romer, 1986; Vassilakis, 1989).
7. See Bania (1989) for a discussion of problems associated with using patent rates as an indication of rates of innovation for SMSAs.
8. Patent applications by SMSA were calculated using data from the patent office.
9. A number of researchers have examined the spatial diffusion of technology. These studies suggest that there may be spatial barriers to the transmission of technology that may be especially important in countries with less-developed communication systems (Brown, 1981; Clapp and Richardson, 1984; Morril, 1968; Pederson, 1970).
10. Education and occupation figures are based on 1980 census data using the same definition of large SMSAs as Beeson (mimeo, 1988). Scientists and engineers are defined to be individuals with occupation codes 44–83.
11. See Azariadis and Drazen (1988) and Lucas (1988) for theoretical models in which the technology of human capital accumulation leads to endogenous growth differentials.
12. See Krugman (1979), Lucas (1988), and Stokey (1986) for a more complete discussion of learning-by-doing models.

References

Azariadis, C., and A. Drazen. "Threshold Externalities in Economic Development." Mimeo. University of Pennsylvania and Tel-Aviv University, 1988.

Bania, N. "Technological Spillovers and Innovation in Research and Development Laboratories." REI Working Paper. Cleveland: Case Western Reserve University, 1989.

Bartel, A., and F. Lichtenberg. "The Comparative Advantage of Educated Workers in Implementing New Technology." *Review of Economics and Statistics* 69 (1987): 1–11.

Beeson, P. "Sources of the Decline of Manufacturing in Large Metropolitan Areas." Mimeo, 1988 and update. *Journal of Urban Economics* 28 (1990): 71–86.

———. "Total Factor Productivity and Agglomeration Economies in Manufacturing, 1959–73." *Journal of Regional Science* 27 (1987): 183–200.

Beeson, P., and E. Montgomery. "The Effects of Colleges and Universities on Local Labor Markets." Mimeo. University of Pittsburgh, 1989.

Bernstein, J., and M. Nadiri. "Interindustry R&D Spillovers, Rates of Return and Production in High-Tech Industries." *American Economic Review* 78 (1988): 429–434.

Brown, L. *Innovation Diffusion: A New Perspective*. London: Methuen, 1981.

Clapp, J., and H. Richardson. "Technical Change in Information-Processing Industries and Regional Income Differentials in Developing Countries." *International Regional Science Review* 9 (1984): 241–256.

Cox, R. "Lessons from 30 Years of Science Parks in the USA." In *Science Parks and Innovation Centers: Their Economic and Social Impact*. Ed. J. M. Gibb. New York: Elsevier, 1985.

Ekstein, Z., and T. Kollintzas. "An Exact Log-Linear Endogenous Economic Growth Model." Working Paper No. 242. University of Pittsburgh, 1988.

Fogarty, M., and G. Garofalo. "Urban Spatial Structure and Productivity Growth in the Manufacturing Sector of Cities." *Journal of Urban Economics* 23 (1988): 60–70.

Helms, L. "The Effects of State and Local Taxes on Economic Growth: A Time Series-Cross Section Approach." *Review of Economics and Statistics* 67 (1985): 574–582.

Henderson, J. V. "Efficiency of Resource Usage and City Size." *Journal of Urban Economics* 19 (1986): 47–70.

Jacobs, J. *Cities and the Wealth of Nations: Principles of Economic Life*. New York: Random House, 1984.

———. *The Economy of Cities*. New York: Random House, 1969.

Jaffe, A. "Real Effects of Academic Research." *American Economic Review* 79 (1989): 957–970.

———. "Technological Opportunity and Spillovers of R&D: Evidence from Firms' Patents, Profits and Market Value." *American Economic Review* 76 (1986): 984–1001.

Kaldor, N. "The Case for Regional Policies." *Scottish Journal of Political Economy* 17 (1970): 337–347.

Kennedy, D. "Basic Research in the Universities: How Much Utility?" In *The Positive Sum Strategy: Harnessing Technology for Economic Growth*. Eds. R. Landau and N. Rosenberg. Washington, D.C.: National Academy Press, 1986.

Krugman, P. "A Model of Innovation, Technology Transfer, and the World Distribution of Income." *Journal of Political Economy* 87 (1979): 253–266.

Lucas, R. "On the Mechanics of Economic Development." *Journal of Monetary Theory* 22 (1988): 3–39.

Malecki, E., and P. Varaiya. "Innovation and Changes in Regional Structure." Ed. P. Nijkamp. *Handbook of Regional and Urban Economics* 1 (1986): 629–642.

Mofidi, A. "Taxes, Expenditures, and State Economic Performance." Ph.D. dissertation. Department of Economics, University of Oregon, 1988.

Moomaw, R. "Productivity and City Size: A Critique of the Evidence." *Quarterly Journal of Economics* 94 (1981): 675–688.

Moomaw, R., and M. Williamson. "Total Factor Productivity Growth in Manufacturing: Evidence from the States." Mimeo. Oklahoma State University, 1988.

Morril, R. "Waves of Spatial Diffusion." *Journal of Regional Science* 8 (1968): 1–18.

National Science Foundation. *University-Industry Research Relationships: Dead Ends and New Departures*. Washington, D.C.: U.S. Government Printing Office, 1983.

Nelson, R. "Institutions That Support Technical Advance in Industry." *American Economic Review* 76 (1986): 186–189.

Office of Technology Assessment. *Technology, Innovation, and Regional Economic Development*. Washington, D.C.: U.S. Government Printing Office, 1984.

Pederson, P. "Innovation Diffusion Within and Between National Urban Systems." *Geographic Analysis* 2 (1970): 203–254.

Pred, A. "The Spatial Dynamics of U.S. Urban-Industrial Growth, 1800–1914." Cambridge: MIT Press, 1966.

Richardson, H. W. "Regional and Urban Economics." Harmondsworth: Penguin, 1978.

Romer, P. "Increasing Returns and Long-Run Growth." *Journal of Political Economy* 94 (1986): 1002–1038.

Segal, D. "Are There Returns to City Size?" *Review of Economics and Statistics* 58 (1976): 339–350.

Stokey, N. "The Dynamics of Industry-Wide Learning." In *Equilibrium Analysis: Essays in Honor of K. J. Arrow*. Vol. II. Ed. W. P. Heller. Cambridge: Cambridge University Press, 1986.

Sveikauskas, L. "The Productivity of Cities." *Quarterly Journal of Economics* 89 (1975): 393–413.

Vassilakis, S. "Increasing Returns and Strategic Behavior: The Worker-Firm Ratio." *The Rand Journal of Economics* 20 (Winter 1989): 622–636.

Vernon, R. "International Investment and International Trade in the Product Cycle." *Quarterly Journal of Economics* 80 (1966): 190–207.

von Boventer, E. "Optimal Spatial Structure and Regional Development." *Kyklos* 23 (1970): 903–924.

Wozniak, G. "The Adoption of Interrelated Innovations: A Human Capital Approach." *Review of Economics and Statistics* 66 (1984): 70–79.

_____. "Human Capital, Information, and Early Adoption of New Technology." *Journal of Human Resources* 22 (1987): 101–112.

PART II

Empirical Analysis of Metropolitan Growth

MARK A. SATTERTHWAITE

3 High-growth Industries and Uneven Metropolitan Growth

Metropolitan areas do not grow evenly. At different times, different cities have boomed while others have lagged. For example, in the late 1800s and continuing into the twentieth century, Chicago's growth far outstripped Philadelphia's. The reasons for this, presumably, were classical locational factors: Chicago was a natural transportation hub for opening up the agricultural richness of the Midwest and it was fortuitously located relative to mineral deposits for the development of a large steel industry. More recent history, however, is not so transparent. Boston and the San Francisco Bay area have no obvious locational advantage over Cleveland for the development of industries based on microelectronics, yet most definitely the microelectronic revolution has transformed the former two cities while the latter has lagged seriously.

This unevenness of urban growth is this paper's focus. Consider an industry that, for whatever reason, is exhibiting rapid employment growth nationally. Why does this growth tend to occur in some metropolitan areas and not in others, particularly when geography per se is not the dominant determinant of either demand or costs? In the next section, I propose a theory

Substantial parts of this paper are taken from the author's article, "Location Patterns of High-Growth Firms," which appeared in the Spring 1988 issue of *Economic Development Commentary*, published by the National Council for Urban Economic Development, Washington, D.C.

of localization economies as an explanation of lopsided growth across metropolitan areas. The idea is that the presence within a metropolitan area of existing firms in the industry reduces costs both for new firms that locate nearby and for existing firms that decide to expand their operations. Therefore, growth in employment within a fast-growing industry tends to occur where the industry already has a lot of employment. The third section of this paper summarizes some of the empirical evidence in favor of this theory. The paper concludes by considering the implications these results have for economic development practice.

Reinterpreting Location Theory

In this section, I offer a reinterpretation of classical location theory that is consistent with the strong tendency of growth industries to grow primarily in those metropolitan areas where they already have a strong presence.[1] The central theme of this reinterpretation is that within many rapidly growing industries, strong localization economies exist that reduce the costs of firms in the industry if they locate in proximity to other firms in the industry.

LOCATION THEORY

Location theory as applied to firms' choices of geographical location states that a firm chooses its location to maximize its expected profits. Location decisions thus involve a balancing of demand and cost considerations. The location of steel mills in the United States is a classic example of this behavior. Steel making (crudely construed) involves bringing together large quantities of iron ore, limestone, and coal in the form of coke. Since these materials are not found together in nature, the siting of a steel mill is important to minimize transportation costs. This led to a great deal of U.S. steel-making capacity being located on the shores of the Great Lakes because the iron ore could be shipped by water from the Mesabi Range. The cost considerations that influenced the siting of steel mills and other great industrial enterprises, such as refineries, are obvious, they are easily separated out into components, and they appear as identifiable items in accounting reports.

Explaining concentrations of high-tech manufacturing in areas such as the San Francisco Bay and Boston on the basis of cost and demand considerations is not as easy. Accounting reports do not have identifiable items that show a cost advantage for these areas. High-tech products tend to have a high value-to-weight ratio and therefore transportation costs are unlikely to be decisive in obtaining access to either materials or markets. Should location theory be abandoned for high-growth and high-tech services and manufacturing because of its failure to explain the agglomeration that is the outstanding feature of the geography of most of these industries? I think not for two main reasons.

First, when it comes to straight manufacturing of already designed products, high-tech firms do act like traditional manufacturers in making their location decisions. Immigration restrictions prevent firms from importing inexpensive labor from Taiwan and Hong Kong directly into the United States for use in manufacturing, but the relative insignificance of transport costs for moving high-tech products great distances has allowed American firms to take the product to the labor. That the placing of manufacturing facilities offshore has occurred to a substantial degree in high-tech industries demonstrates that the firms involved have the same sensitivity to location-specific costs that traditional manufacturers have long demonstrated.

Second, for high-tech firms, the design of new products and services and the improvement of existing offerings are as necessary for continued success as is the low-cost manufacturing or production of an existing service or product. This involves professionals—scientists, engineers, designers, analysts, managers, entrepreneurs—whose varied functions are difficult for an accounting report to capture adequately. For example, in any dynamic and growing professional group, a substantial proportion of the professionals' time is spent on recruitment of new professionals and evaluation of already present professionals. These personnel functions cannot be delegated to a personnel department that is separate from the group. If the costs of recruitment, for whatever reason, are different in two metropolitan areas, then the area with the lower costs will give the firm located in it a cost advantage that may be quite important if the professionals in question are critical for the firm's success. Yet accounting reports are unlikely to reveal the difference in the two areas' costs because of the difficulty of accurately allocating professionals' time among activities.[2]

Considerations of feasibility and verifiability cause accounting reports, particularly financial accounting reports that are accessible to outside observers, to be based on identifiable transactions between the firm, its employees, its suppliers, and its customers. This results in a good picture of the firm's costs and efficiency whenever (1) output is easily measurable in well-defined physical units and (2) individual functions, such as purchasing, personnel, transportation, and so forth, are performed by identifiable individuals whose time in different functions is easily tracked. Both conditions are largely met in traditional manufacturing, but both are violated to a substantial degree in high-tech services and manufacturing. In other words, the reason location theory may not appear to explain the location decisions of high-tech firms may be due to poor data rather than to a failure of the theory.

LOCALIZATION ECONOMIES

If one takes seriously this argument that location theory may be an important determinant of the location of high-tech firms, then the next step is to try to identify phenomena that might have strong enough effects on an industry's costs across metropolitan areas to explain the agglomeration of individual industries in particular areas. To my mind, the best candidate is localization economies. This concept is a refinement of the idea that an important reason cities form and grow is urbanization economies. For example, to repeat two classic cases, a firm that locates in a city (1) shares the use of roads and other transportation facilities that already exist to serve other unrelated businesses and (2) participates in an existing labor market that offers workers a wide variety of general purpose and specialized skills. If the firm is located in a small town, good transportation might be available if the town is carefully chosen and the firm's needs for a variety of modes are quite limited, but in such a town, the labor market is inevitably restricted in the variety of skills that are available. Therefore, a firm that has unpredictable needs for a variety of transportation services and human skills is likely to obtain a significant cost advantage if it selects an urban location.

Generalized urbanization economies are undoubtedly important to high-growth service industries and high-tech manufacturing. My conjecture, however, is that industry-specific localization economies are more important than the generalized economies. These localization economies are not fundamentally different than urbanization economies generally; they are just more specialized and confer benefits primarily on firms within a single industry. At least three distinct ways exist by which firms in an industry generate positive externalities for other firms in that industry:

1. High-tech firms that are growing quickly need to be able to recruit specialized, experienced, and skilled professionals who can meet specific requirements. Being part of a large, local, intraindustry labor market makes this far easier. Identifying, evaluating, and hiring candidates can be done quicker and less expensively locally than nationally. From the viewpoint of the candidate, changing employers locally is easier than changing to a new employer in a new city.
2. A firm located within a city that has many other firms in the same industry automatically has easy access to a wide spectrum of suppliers, distributors, and specialized business services. As a result, the growing firm does not have to do everything itself. It can contract with other firms to provide those services that it is not ready to produce in-house.

3. Within a city that has a concentration of rapidly growing firms in an emerging dynamic industry, there is almost inevitably an atmosphere of excitement that envelops all firms. This ferment of ideas and possibilities makes all participants more effective and innovative. Smart people are smarter when surrounded and interacting with other smart people. Constructive criticism, divergent viewpoints, and competition all play a role.

The effect is that firms that locate within a city with a high concentration of firms in the same industry have higher productivity from critical professionals and lower costs overall than they would otherwise.

A second way to understand localization economies is in terms of the theory of optimal search. When a firm is surrounded by other firms, suppliers, and distributors all working in the same industry, its costs of searching for supplies, services, and personnel is reduced. This cost reduction has a direct effect on profits. A second, perhaps more important, effect also exists. With search being easier, the searching firm can raise its standards and look for a supplier or engineer that fits its needs more perfectly. Firms are less likely to have to settle for second best.

JOBS FOLLOW PEOPLE AND PEOPLE FOLLOW JOBS

A continuing controversy in regional economic development is whether jobs follow people or people follow jobs.[3] If localization economies are important in determining where an industry grows and where it does not grow, then the controversy may be unresolvable because both are true in important ways. Bright, ambitious, young professionals do follow jobs. This process begins with their graduation from high school, when a substantial fraction of the United States's most promising young people travel long distances to obtain top-quality college educations that match their particular interests and ambitions. Upon graduation, many choose to enter an industry that is currently "hot" because that is where excitement and opportunity lie. This often requires another move, sometimes across the country. It is exactly these people—the bright, ambitious, highly educated—who are critical to the success of high-tech manufacturing and service industries. Thus, a small but important segment of the labor market apparently is quite willing to follow jobs.[4]

Once an industry becomes concentrated in a few cities, then the jobs-follow-people phenomenon becomes important in two different ways. First, a firm making a deliberate geographical choice for a new facility is likely to recognize the benefits of the localization economies that exist in a few cities and make one of those cities its choice. Second, even if a firm does not make a deliberate choice but happens to choose a city with substantial localization economies, the firm is likely to benefit from the externalities and to be more successful, grow faster, and generate more jobs than it would otherwise.

AN EXAMPLE: GREAT UNIVERSITY DEPARTMENTS

The academic labor market illustrates these ideas. Pick a discipline, such as economics, think of it as an industry, and think of each scholar who is or aspires to be a professor as an individual firm. The goal of almost every aspiring scholar of outstanding talent is to receive an appointment within a department that is composed of outstanding, productive, and creative scholars. The reason for this strong preference is not that young scholars are prestige hounds but rather their sense that they can do better work if they are surrounded by other, equally talented colleagues in their own field. In other words, participants in the economics industry believe that localization economies are very important.

The jobs-follow-people versus people-follow-jobs distinction is tangled within a great department of a university. People do follow jobs in the sense that appointments into the faculty ranks are almost always made after a national search. On the other hand, great departments tend to attract graduate students. The presence of the students, who would like to be supported as research assistants, makes possible large-scale research projects that the faculty could not even consider if this pool of skilled labor did not exist. Faculty seek funding for these projects and, in those cases where they are successful, create new jobs. Thus, jobs for research assistants have followed graduate students.

Localization economies are of great advantage to those departments within a university that have them, but they do not necessarily spill over to the university as a whole. For example, a university's great economics department does not create many externalities for its indifferent physics department. Therefore, to understand the strengths and weaknesses of a university, it is necessary to examine it department by department as well as from an overall perspective. This implies that a plan to improve a university's academic quality cannot be general; it must be specific and explicitly recognize that improvement in some areas will be easier than others because of the presence or absence of localization economies.

DYNAMICS OF METROPOLITAN GROWTH

To the extent that localization economies are important for a particular, growing industry, agglomeration tends to occur as the industry grows. Those firms that are located in close proximity to other firms in the industry tend to produce higher quality output in a more timely fashion at lower cost. The advantage this gives these firms tends to cause them to grow faster than firms that are less favorably located. This creates further localization economies and causes the advantageously located firms to grow even faster relative to other firms.

This self-reinforcing cycle continues with the industry agglomerating into a small number of metropolitan areas, even though initially those areas had an imperceptible advantage over other metropolitan areas that did not share in the industry's growth. Ultimately, this dynamic tends to limit itself because, after some point, further agglomeration produces no further economies but instead merely produces increasing congestion costs. For this reason, the process of agglomeration stops short of its logical conclusion of all firms within an industry locating in a single metropolitan area. Instead, several metropolitan areas may coexist as centers for that industry.[5]

An implication of this argument is that the root cause for one city becoming a center for an industry while a second city languishes may be impossible to determine. The reason is that small, unmeasured differences between the cities when the industry was in its infancy may have provided the successful city with its initial, and ultimately decisive, productivity advantage. Years later, after the growth has occurred in one city and not the other, the subtle differences that existed initially between the two cities may be impossible to reconstruct with any reliability.

Evidence on the Existence of Localization Economies

The literatures of both urban and industrial economics suggest that localization economies are important. I wish to briefly mention work from both literatures here and then describe at more length a recent study (Ó hUallacháin and Satterthwaite, 1990). First, Henderson's comprehensive book (1988) on urban development contains a critical survey of the urban economics literature that bears on the existence of localization economies. He also reports the results of a cross-sectional study of his own that measures the strength of localization economies directly. The study involves sixteen different industries and finds localization economies to be statistically significant in eight of them.

Second, in the industrial economics literature, a large body of work documents the learning (or experience) curve. This literature has recently been reviewed by Argote and Epple (1990). The learning curve is the tendency for the unit costs of producing a given product to decline as a function of the firm's cumulative output of the product. The reason for this decline of costs is, presumably, that with practice a firm becomes more efficient at making a product. For example, Lieberman (1984) showed that in the chemical industry (1) learning economies have generally been far more important than scale economies and (2) learning has not been kept proprietary within any particular company but has diffused throughout the industry. Whenever learning does diffuse among all firms within an industry, it becomes a localization economy. The reasoning is simple. As any competitor in the industry grows and produces more, its costs fall from learning economies. If these learning economies spill over to other nearby firms, causing their costs to fall, then learning economies are a special form of localization economies.

The only difference between the learning curve concept and the localization economies concept developed here is that the learning concept normally does not explicitly consider the effect of geography on the rate of diffusion of learning within an industry. Lieberman (1988), however, in his comparative discussion of rates of learning with U.S. and Japanese industry, suggests that geography does make a difference: Learning within Japanese firms tends to diffuse more rapidly to other Japanese firms than is the case for U.S. firms. Interestingly, he suggests that Japanese firms for many years have made a deliberate and reasonably successful effort to overcome geographical barriers and share in the learning of U.S. firms. Harder evidence on the importance of geography on diffusion of learning is provided by Jaffe (1989). Using U.S. data on patents and research and development (R&D) expenditures, he shows that university research has a positive effect on innovation within corporations that are geographically nearby.

Complementing this evidence is a cross-sectional study of the rate of employment growth for thirty-seven rapidly growing industries in 265 U.S. metropolitan areas between 1977 and 1984 (Ó hUallacháin and Satterthwaite, 1988). Out of the thirty-seven industries, nine are manufacturing industries and twenty-eight are service industries. Examples of industries included in the sample are computer and data processing services (Standard Industrial Classification [SIC] 737), hospitals (SIC 806), and communication equipment (SIC 366). For each industry, the specific equation estimated was:

$$E_{1i} - E_{0i} = aE_{0i}^{\alpha} U_i^{\beta} \, \text{Exp}\{bX_i + cZ_i + \epsilon_i\}$$

where E_{1i} is Standard Metropolitan Statistical Area (SMSA) i's 1984 employment for the industry, E_{0i} is SMSA i's 1977 employment in the industry, U_i is SMSA i's 1977 civilian labor force, X_i is a vector of variables describing some of SMSA i's economic development programs, Z_i is a vector of other variables describing SMSA i (such as the average wage rate), ϵ_i is a stochastic error term, and (a, b, c, α, β) is the vector of estimated coefficients.

Two points are particularly important regarding this research design. First, the study is at a disaggregated level. This is important because localization economies are an industry phenomenon, not a macro phenomenon. Moreover, working at a disaggregated level alleviates problems of simultaneity bias in the estimation. Second, in estimating the equation for each industry, only those SMSAs for which the industry's employment grew ($E_{1i} - E_{0i}$ positive) were included. The reason for excluding SMSAs for which the industry's growth was negative is that the process governing the decline of an industry within a community is likely to be different than the process governing growth.

A dominant explanation emerges from the regression analysis: that an industry grew between 1977–84 in a metropolitan area if it was already large in that metropolitan area in 1977. That is, in thirty-two of the thirty-seven industry regressions, the coefficient α on E_{0i} is positive and significant at the .01 level. We interpret this as evidence of localization economies.[6] In only fourteen of the thirty-seven industry regressions is the coefficient β on U_i positive and significant at the .01 level. Thus, in most of the industries we examined, it was the industry's base year size that drove growth of the industry, not the overall size of the community in which the industry was located.

The other interesting result is that economic development incentives entered the regressions surprisingly often, though usually only at a .10 level of significance instead of a .01 level. Specifically, the presence within a SMSA of a university research park or an enterprise zone was positively associated with employment growth while—surprisingly—heavy use of industrial revenue bonds was negatively associated with employment growth. These effects are weak but suggestive of the following tentative explanation. A community that in the 1977–84 period had either a university research park or an enterprise zone was a community whose governmental and private leadership was alert and responsive to development needs. Our hypothesis is that it is this alertness and responsiveness that is responsible for the positive effect of research parks and enterprise zones in the regression, that is, the presence of a research park or enterprise zone is a signal of the underlying character of a community's leadership.

The unexpected negative effect of industrial revenue bonds also fits this signaling explanation. Industrial revenue bonds are, in a sense, an attempt by a community to "buy" development, but if one community can buy development, so can any other competing community because offering a company a cash inducement takes no special leadership or skill on the part of a community. Such competition for economic development may easily escalate to the point that the winning community may have bid so much to attract a company that its success is at best no more than a break-even proposition socially. At worst, the community may have overbid. To the extent a community does overbid, then the overall effect is to transfer wealth from it to the firm that receives the financing help. Ultimately, this impoverishes the community's local government and makes the community as a whole an undesirable place to locate. Thus, heavy use of industrial revenue bonds may signal that a community is a poor place for a firm to locate.

Implications for Economic Development

If one accepts the idea that localization economies are important in determining where employment growth occurs, then the primary implication is that economic development efforts should be micro oriented. Metropolitan areas must have a data system with the ability to spot a nascent concentration of an emerging industry. Once an industry is identified that is believed to have the potential to become a significant growth industry in terms of generating exports from the metropolitan area, then economic development efforts should be focused on heightening the growth of localization economies among the existing firms in the industry.

How this can be done effectively is not clear, but some suggestions can be offered here:

1. Aid may be provided to the industry in setting up networks of information exchange, both at the executive level and at the professional level. For example, is there a local trade organization? Do local professional societies exist where the technical professionals in these companies can meet to share ideas? The economic development agency might provide staff assistance in establishing such organizations.

2. An emerging concentration of firms needs to be publicized. If no one outside of the city realizes the amount of industry activity that is going on in the community, then other firms will not think to locate there and individuals will be hesitant to accept positions there because it will lack the image of excitement and movement that attracts ambitious and talented individuals. An economic development agency may be able to provide public relations support that leads to articles in trade publications and helps create the image that the industry is growing dynamically in the community. Another possibility is to aggressively seek to have industry meetings and trade shows in the city.

3. A university, college, or research institute can have important benefits for an identified industry. For example, if a research group within a university develops special expertise and interest in an area of knowledge that is fundamental to the industry, then that group can become a nucleus around which ideas are exchanged and developed. Moreover, the group may train a small but significant number of students who, if opportunities are available, are likely to stay in the community. An economic development agency may help this process by introducing practitioners and academics to develop-

ing forums where they can meet and exchange ideas. More broadly, the agency can push for the upgrading and development of those academic programs that most closely interface with the industry.

These suggestions are micro in their focus. The reason is that localization economies are a micro phenomenon. Thus, for example, general publicity about a city will not influence a scientist who is trying to decide whether to accept a job there nearly as effectively as an article that describes all the activity occurring in that city in his particular field.

The fact that these approaches are micro oriented makes them hard to implement. One person at the top of a city or county government cannot effectively implement them because such a person does not have the time necessary to get involved at the level of detail required. Instead, implementation can only be accomplished by an economic development team that is flexible, responsive, and oriented to the long run. Moreover, even if these approaches are successful overall, documentation of their success is difficult because only a few of the several industries that receive help will grow as hoped, and, even in those cases, it will be difficult to establish unambiguously the causal relationship between the development activities and the increased employment in the industries.

Notes

1. My analysis has been greatly influenced by Jane Jacobs (1969).
2. This, of course, is not uniformly true. Law firms and consulting firms keep accurate records of how their professionals allocate their time.
3. See the discussion on this issue in Carlino and Mills (1987).
4. Kim (1989) has developed a clever model that captures important aspects of this phenomenon. He shows that as the size of the labor market that a student plans to enter increases, the student tends to specialize more narrowly, but at greater depth, in a particular area. The reason is that as the labor market increases in size, the probability of the student finding a job that matches his or her specialized skills increases. Thus, as firms within an industry agglomerate in a few cities, students who wish to work for that industry find it optimal, first, to get deeper, more specific training and then to migrate to one of the cities where a concentration of the industry exists and good matches are likely to be available. The resulting, more highly qualified labor force in those cities where agglomeration is occurring leads to further productivity gains (that is, localization economies) for the firms that have located in those cities.
5. For detailed analyses of the dynamics of metropolitan growth that localization economies imply, see Arthur (1990) and David and Rosenbloom (1990).
6. Some caveats exist regarding this interpretation. See Ó hUallacháin and Satterthwaite (1990) for a full discussion.

References

Argote, L., and D. Epple. "Learning Curves in Manufacturing." *Science* 247 (February 23, 1990): 920–924.

Arthur, W. B. " 'Silicon Valley' Locational Clusters: When Do Increasing Returns Imply Monopoly?" *Mathematic Social Sciences* 19 (1990): 235–251.

Carlino, G., and E. Mills. "The Determinants of County Growth." *Journal of Regional Science* 27 (1987): 39–54.

David, P., and J. Rosenbloom. "Marshallian Factor Market Externalities and the Dynamics of Industrial Localization." *Journal of Urban Economics* 28 (November 1990): 349–370.

Henderson, V. J. *Urban Development: Theory, Fact, and Illusion.* New York: Oxford University Press, 1988.

Jacobs, J. *The Economy of Cities.* New York: Random House, 1969.

Jaffe, A. "Real Effects of Academic Research." *American Economic Review* 79 (1989): 57–70.

Kim, S. "Labor Specialization and the Extent of the Market." *Journal of Political Economy* 97 (1989): 692–705.

Lieberman, M. "The Learning Curve and Pricing in the Chemical Processing Industries." *Rand Journal of Economics* 15 (1984): 213–228.

———. "Learning, Productivity, and U.S.-Japan Industrial 'Competitiveness.' " Duplicated. February 1988.

Ó hUalláchain, B., and M. Satterthwaite. "Sectoral Growth Patterns at the Metropolitan Level." Duplicated. April 1990. *Journal of Urban Economics,* forthcoming 1991.

———. *Sectoral Growth Patterns at the Metropolitan Level: An Evaluation of Economic Development Incentives.* Report to the U.S. Department of Commerce, Economic Development Administration. Evanston, Ill.: NCI Research, 1988.

Satterthwaite, M. A. "Location Patterns of High-Growth Firms." *Economic Development Commentary* 12 (Spring 1988): 7–11.

BREANDÁN Ó HUALLACHÁIN

4 Economic Structure and Growth of Metropolitan Areas

The economic structure of U.S. metropolitan areas has changed dramatically in the past few decades. The geography and regional science literature documents Sunbelt/Frostbelt shifts in manufacturing (Schmenner, 1982; Wheat, 1986), the emergence of high-technology centers in California and New England (Barff and Knight, 1988; Saxenian, 1983, 1985; Scott, 1986), and the increasing role of financial and business services in the economies of many national and regional centers (Noyelle and Stanback, 1984). These changes are reflected in new spatial associations between services, high-technology manufacturing, and corporate administration. Such associations are the cornerstones of metropolitan economies, as important to today's cities as those based on metals, chemicals, and automobiles were in the past.

The objectives of this paper are to identify similarities in sectoral location patterns across metropolitan areas and to ascertain the relationship between metropolitan economic structure and employment and income growth. Also examined are temporal shifts as revealed by changes in spatial associations among sectors. Emphasis is placed on spatial associations between fast-growing services and other sectors of larger metropolitan economies.

51

Agglomeration and the Development of Sectoral Clusters

Aside from spatial associations that reflect a unique local combination, such as the juxtaposition of unrelated natural or agricultural resources, spatial association among sectors can stem from a variety of agglomeration forces. At the intermetropolitan scale, industry clustering occurs for several important reasons. First, locating successive vertical stages of production adjacently reduces the transportation costs to each participating firm. Second, as a sector expands in a given location, firms can realize savings by using jointly supplied products or by specializing in the production of complementary products. Spatial association can also arise from common attraction to particular kinds of places, such as low labor cost locations, large cities with the threshold populations that can support unusual products, and specialized centers where firms can more easily access important information flows.

Access to information is particularly important for innovating service and high-tech goods-producing sectors. Research and development (R&D) information can spill over from one innovating firm to another as skilled professionals switch jobs within a metropolitan area. Informal information exchanges can also develop as skilled professionals exchange ideas through private information networks.

For innovating business and professional services firms, an additional factor may be the location of corporate headquarters and regional offices, which some argue consume a larger proportion of business services than do production facilities (Marshall et al., 1987; Noyelle and Stanback, 1984). In addition, Browne (1983) has noted the strong links between high-tech manufacturing and several business services. Recent empirical evidence suggests that locational patterns are further complicated by the increasingly multidivisional nature of service firms, which allows back-office functions to locate some distance from the source of demand (Nelson, 1986), and by growing intermetropolitan trading in services (Beyers et al., 1985).

Investigating Spatial Associations Among Industries

There has been little attempt to determine the role spatial associations among sectors play in explaining metropolitan growth. The results presented here are based on an extensive enumeration of metropolitan employment structure using factor analysis, a technique for identifying the basic patterns of variance in a body of data.

The data analyzed include employment in all two-digit Standard Industrial Classification (SIC) sectors, as well as government and corporate auxiliary and administrative (A&A) activities.[1] A comprehensive approach permits evaluation of some of the more recent statements about the changing organization of the U.S. urban system. Of particular interest is the growing emphasis on the spatial association between high-order financial, business, and professional services and high-technology manufacturing and corporate administrative and control activities (Noyelle and Stanback, 1984; Pred, 1977; Simmie, 1983; Stanback et al., 1981; Wheeler, 1986).

In addition to analyzing metropolitan employment structure in 1977 and 1986, I used the clusters of sectors identified by the factor analysis as independent variables in two regression models of growth. The dependent variables were the rate of growth of total employment and the rate of growth of personal per capita income in the 1977–86 time period. This nine-year period is long enough to capture real structural change. It also minimizes cyclical effects since both 1977 and 1986 had identical national unemployment rates of 7 percent (U.S. Department of Commerce, 1979, 1989).

The results presented below support four main conclusions. First, spatial associations among sectors are identifiable and provide useful information on metropolitan economic character. Second, these spatial associations are good predictors, having predicted more than 50 percent of metropolitan economic growth. Their relationship to growth varied according to whether growth is measured in terms of per capita income or total employment. Third, spatial associations change over time. One noteworthy shift was the division of a miscellaneous collection of high-order services identified in 1977 into two distinct clusters by 1986. Finally, the results fail to support the hypothesis that the location of high-order financial and business services is strongly tied to the location of corporate headquarters activities. An important characteristic of the location of high-order services is their common attraction to national and selected regional centers.

METHODOLOGY

In examining spatial association among industries, I extracted the common factors from matrices of employment in seventy-eight sectors in the 150 largest metropolitan areas in 1977 and 1986. Counties were assigned to metropolitan areas based on the 1979 Standard Metropolitan Statistical Area (SMSA) definitions. The 150 largest metropolitan areas were determined by 1979 population.

Several decisions were required prior to extracting the common factors from the employment matrices. These related to the level of sectoral aggregation, the geographical scale of the observations, and the measurement of employment concentration.

Sectoral Aggregation. Any level of sectoral aggregation generates trade-offs. Very disaggregated schemes are often favored in locational analysis because they minimize heterogeneity in products and processes. However, a high level of disaggregation produces a very skewed size distribution of sectors (that is, employment in some three-digit sectors is very small whereas in others it is very large). The variance in a data matrix may be strongly influenced by the geographical distribution of the smaller specialized sectors, usually found only in the larger SMSAs. Disaggregated schemes also favor manufacturing sectors because there are far more three- and four-digit manufacturing sectors than services. The degree of disaggregation is also limited by the number of observations. Since the analysis is based on the 150 largest metropolitan areas, only a limited number of three- or four-digit sectors could be used. This would require an arbitrary selection. Finally, operating at the three- or four-digit level may identify many spatial associations that have no meaningful interpretation in terms of agglomeration theory.

In view of these considerations, most of the sectors are observed at the two-digit level. Also included are A&A employment at the nine one-digit division levels, military employment, federal government civilian employment, and state and local government employment. Data for private industries were obtained from *County Business Patterns* computer tapes (U.S. Department of Commerce, 1977, 1986). Disclosure problems are seldom a major problem at the two-digit level of sectoral aggregation. In those cases where the data were suppressed, a proportional adjustment procedure was used to obtain employment estimates (Gardocki and Baj, 1985). Data for the three government sectors were obtained from the *Regional Economic Information System* (Bureau of Economic Analysis, 1988).

Geographical Scale of Observations.   I chose to operate at the metropolitan level for the following reasons. First, metropolitan areas closely approximate labor markets and are the most relevant units for expressing human resources. Second, the economies of individual cities and counties within a metropolitan area interact and are difficult to understand without simultaneously studying the metropolitan area as a whole. Third, the alternative of using states would have obscured the considerable variability within state boundaries and would have provided only fifty observations.

Measurement of Employment Concentration.   Metropolitan employment structure derives from both the absolute employment of each local industry and its relative local importance. This analysis is based on a relative measure of sector size rather than absolute employment. I did not use absolute employment because the large metropolitan areas would dominate the results for two reasons. First, even at the two-digit level, certain sectors exist in meaningful numbers only in the large SMSAs. Second, large SMSAs have large employment levels in many sectors due to a common attraction to larger cities (urbanization effects) rather than to any mutual attraction. Factors extracted from a matrix of absolute employment levels would provide information on spatial associations only in the largest SMSAs. A relative measure of employment structure eliminates much of this bias, and so I converted the data to employment shares in each sector. Unfortunately, by giving equal weight to all SMSAs, this raises the opposite problem: Because there are many more small SMSAs than large ones, the factor analysis would tend to describe the structure of the lower end of the urban hierarchy. The solution here is to focus on results for the 150 largest SMSAs.

Factor Analysis Procedure. Unlike regression analysis, where the objective is to identify and measure the degree to which the variance in a set of independent variables explains the variance in a single dependent variable, the objective of factor analysis is to identify the basic variance "pattern" in a set of variables. No distinction is made between dependent and independent variables, so no cause-and-effect conclusions are possible. The method compresses a body of data in such a way as to eliminate the duplicative and less important information and express the great bulk of the total variation through a small number of secondary derived variables, called factors. The factors are simplifying abstractions that describe the underlying structure of the data around which the variables are arranged.

In this analysis of metropolitan employment structure, each industry sector is a variable and the observations are the 150 largest SMSAs. The strength of the association between the sectors and each factor is indicated by a set of weights called factor loadings. The bigger the loading, the stronger the relationship between a sector and a factor. Interpreting the factors requires judgment. Some factors group sectors that intuitively go together, especially in terms of input-output relationships. In other cases, interpretation is problematic and speculative. Factor analysis identifies rather than explains patterns in data.

A second set of weights called factor scores indicates the strength of the relationship between the SMSAs and the factors. Since each SMSA has a score on each factor, the factors can be used in a regression analysis of metropolitan growth. My objective was to determine the degree to which the clusters of industries identified by the factors could explain total employment and per capita income growth in metropolitan areas.

Metropolitan Employment Structure in 1977

I extracted and rotated eighteen common factors that explained more than 1 percent of the variation in sectoral employment shares in the largest SMSAs in 1977. These eighteen factors accounted for 47.35 percent of the total variance among all the sectors.

FACTOR ANALYSIS RESULTS

Retail and Federal Military/Government Complexes.   The first factor, as shown in Table 4.1, grouped numerous retail trade sectors and consumer services with federal military and civilian employment. The factor is bipolar, having several high negative loadings associated with manufacturing A&A and heavy manufacturing activity. The twenty SMSAs with the highest factor scores were mainly located in the Southeast and California. A concentration of government and military employment seems to support a strong retail base. The demography of military base areas often includes disproportionate numbers of young transitory people with discretionary income to spend on apparel, entertainment, and cars. The spatial association between credit agencies, eating and drinking places, car dealerships, retail activities, and military and government employment reflects the unique economic and demographic structure of military base areas.

High-Order Service Centers.   The second factor identified an assortment of high-order services, including real estate, security brokers, legal services, business services, and transportation services. In addition to strong interindustry linkages that bind them together, these sectors are drawn to the large populations of large SMSAs. The factor scores revealed concentrations of these activities in large national and regional centers, including New York, Miami, San Francisco, Los Angeles, and Chicago. However, several medium-size SMSAs were also strongly tied to this group. Albuquerque, Eugene, and Melbourne (Cape Kennedy, Florida) are regional centers for high-order services. These areas are important innovation centers with large proportions of skilled professionals. The location of manufacturing seemed to have little effect on the location of high-order services. The only spatial association between high-order services and manufacturing were the negative loadings on this factor for Stone, Clay, and Glass Products and Fabricated Metal Products. Factor 2 also showed little association between the location of high-order services and A&A employment—a finding at odds with Noyelle and Stanback's (1984) emphasis on the close functional and spatial links between corporate headquarters and high-order services. This discrepancy is discussed further below (see "Temporal Changes").

Insurance, Wholesale, and Administrative Services.   The third factor grouped insurance sectors, wholesale trade, communications, and A&A employment of the finance, insurance, and real estate (FIRE) sector. Unlike the previous high-order services group, few large national and regional centers are among the SMSAs having the top twenty factor scores. The association between insurance carriers and brokers is based on interindustry linkages. The inclusion of the other sectors in the cluster is unclear. Attraction to the same intermediate-size SMSAs probably reflects the common need to locate in low-cost regional distribution centers rather than in high-cost large SMSAs.

Petrochemical Complexes. The fourth factor identified petrochemical complexes. Chemicals and petroleum products, two sectors with strong inter-industry linkages, had high loadings on this factor. Heavy construction was also associated with this group, as was port activity. Most of the SMSAs that scored high on this factor are located on the Gulf and Atlantic coasts.

Resort Areas. The fifth factor identified a clustering of hotels and recreation services. SMSAs with high factor scores were predominantly resort areas in Florida and the Southwest.

Textiles and Construction. The sixth factor grouped textile sectors and construction and was associated with medium-size SMSAs in the Southeast. This grouping is difficult to interpret. It may have occurred because of the generally fast growth of medium-size southeastern SMSAs that have had a strong tradition of textile manufacturing.

Food Production and Distribution Centers. The seventh factor combined sectors engaged in the production, processing, and distribution of food. The factor is based on agricultural production that requires speedy processing following harvesting. High-scoring areas are in agricultural regions in California, Florida, and Texas.

Routinized Production Centers. The eighth factor grouped apparel, leather, and miscellaneous manufacturing. Locations in the Northeast had the highest factor scores, especially New York and surrounding SMSAs. A long tradition of diversified manufacturing in these SMSAs, rather than interindustry linkages among the sectors, probably accounts for the common location patterns.

Mining and Oil Complexes. The ninth factor is a natural resources group that exhibited strong interindustry linkages, combining mining activities and pipelines. Locations scoring high on this cluster are in Texas, Oklahoma, California, the Gulf Coast, and Pennsylvania.

State and Local Government and Social Services. The tenth factor combined an assemblage of social and professional services and state and local government. State capitals are strongly represented among high-ranking factor scores. State capitals function as regional centers for a variety of educational, social, and governmental services.

TABLE 4.1

Factor Analysis of Employment Shares
in the Largest 150 MSAs in 1977

	SIC	Industry	Factor Loading
Factor 1: *Retail Trade and Government/*			
Military Sectors			
Variance Explained: 8.66 Percent	55	Automotive Dealers & Service Stations	.8636
	72	Personal Services	.8094
	57	Furniture & Home Furnishing Stores	.7892
		Government: Military	.6703
		Government: Federal Civilian	.6484
	52	Building Materials & Garden Supplies	.6419
	53	General Merchandise Stores	.6354
	59	Miscellaneous Retail	.6314
	75	Auto Repair, Services, & Garages	.6306
	58	Eating & Drinking Places	.6250
	54	Food Stores	.6081
	61	Credit Agencies, Other than Banks	.5701
	76	Miscellaneous Repair Services	.5377
	17	Special Trade Contractors	.5049
	56	Apparel & Accessory Stores	.4709
		Government: State & Local	.4394
	48	Communications	.4106
	65	Real Estate	.3835
		Agriculture, Forestry, & Fisheries	.3556
	35	Machinery Except Electrical	-.3670
	34	Fabricated Metal Products	-.4034
		Auxiliary & Administrative: Manufacturing	-.4922

Top Twenty MSAs: Fayetteville (NC), Colorado Springs, Vallejo (CA), Charleston (SC), Salinas, Columbus (GA), Norfolk, Macon, Sacramento, Tucson, Fort Lauderdale, Pensacola, Washington, D.C., San Antonio, Melbourne (FL), Daytona Beach, Bakersfield, Long Branch (NJ), Austin, Tacoma.

Factor 2: **High-order Financial, Legal, and Business Services**

Variance Explained: 5.24 Percent

65	Real Estate	.7251
62	Security, Commodity Brokers, & Services	.6517
81	Legal Services	.6259
73	Business Services	.6124
45	Transportation by Air	.6088
47	Transportation Services	.6010
89	Miscellaneous Services	.5672
78	Motion Pictures	.4159
60	Banking	.3996
61	Credit Agencies Other than Banks	.4509
67	Holding & Other Investment Offices	.4579
75	Auto Repair, Services, & Garages	.3551
	Auxiliary & Administrative: Retail Trade	.3507
32	Stone, Clay, & Glass Products	-.3105
34	Fabricated Metal Products	-.3414

Top Twenty MSAs: New York, Miami, Honolulu, San Francisco, Washington, D.C., Santa Barbara, Fort Lauderdale, Los Angeles, West Palm Beach, San Diego, Denver, Seattle, Albuquerque, Atlanta, Houston, Phoenix, Chicago, Anaheim, Melbourne (FL), Eugene (OR).

TABLE 4.1 (Continued)

Factor Analysis of Employment Shares
in the Largest 150 MSAs in 1977

	SIC	Industry	Factor Loading
Factor 3: *Insurance, Wholesale,*	64	Insurance Agents, Brokers, & Services	.7487
and Administrative Industries	63	Insurance Carriers	.6254
Variance Explained: 2.80 Percent	50	Wholesale Trade: Durable Goods	.6038
	48	Communications	.4618
		Auxiliary & Administrative: FIRE	.4186
	60	Banking	.3645

Top Twenty MSAs: Columbia (SC), Des Moines, Jackson (MS), Little Rock, Jacksonville (FL), Omaha, Erie, Richmond (VA), Lansing, Baton Rouge, Austin, Newburgh (NY), San Francisco, Atlanta, Shreveport, Spokane, Madison, Nassau, Charleston (WV), New York.

	SIC	Industry	Factor Loading
Factor 4: *Petroleum and Chemicals*	28	Chemicals & Allied Products	.6788
Variance Explained: 2.50 Percent	16	Heavy Construction Contractors	.6502
	29	Petroleum & Coal Products	.6214
	76	Miscellaneous Repair Services	.4573
	44	Water Transportation	.4254
	35	Machinery Except Electrical	–.3201

Top Twenty MSAs: Beaumont, Baton Rouge, Charleston (WV), Wilmington, Corpus Christi, Pensacola, Johnson City, Houston, Mobile, Richmond, New Brunswick, Ann Arbor, Lakeland, New Orleans, Huntington (WV), Newark, Long Branch, Roanoke, San Antonio, Melbourne (FL).

Factor 5:   *Recreation Services*

       Variance Explained: 2.49 Percent

70	Hotels & Other Lodging Places	.9179
79	Amusements & Recreation Services	.9150
41	Local & Interurban Passenger Transit	.4099

Top Twenty MSAs: Las Vegas, Orlando, Daytona Beach, Honolulu, Lakeland (FL), Salinas, West Palm Beach, Fort Lauderdale, Miami, Madison, Tampa, Newport News, Harrisburg, New Brunswick, Anaheim, Jacksonville (FL), Des Moines, Binghamton, Atlanta, Riverside.

Factor 6:   *Textiles and Construction*

       Variance Explained: 2.49 Percent

22	Textile Mill Products	.8046
15	General Contractors & Operative Builders	.4861
23	Apparel & Other Textile Products	.3821
32	Stone, Clay, & Glass Products	.3600
80	Health Services	–.7132

Top Twenty MSAs: Greenville, Columbus (GA), Augusta (GA), Charlotte, Chattanooga, Columbia, Greensboro, Huntsville, Allentown, Montgomery, McAllen, Albuquerque, Baton Rouge, Macon, Johnson City (TN), Atlanta, Reading, Fayetteville, Raleigh-Durham, Paterson (NJ).

TABLE 4.1 (Continued)

Factor Analysis of Employment Shares
in the Largest 150 MSAs in 1977

	SIC	Industry	Factor Loading
Factor 7:		*Food Products and Wholesale Trade*	
		Variance Explained: 2.37 Percent	
	51	Wholesale Trade: Nondurable Goods	.7990
		Agriculture, Forestry, & Fisheries	.5827
	20	Food & Kindred Products	.5624
	56	Apparel & Accessory Stores	.4389

Top Twenty MSAs: McAllen, Visalia, Modesto, Lakeland, Stockton, Salinas, Fresno, Jersey City, Santa Rosa, Bakersfield, New York, Oxnard, Paterson (NJ), Lancaster, Johnson City, Shreveport, Orlando, West Palm Beach, New Brunswick, Lexington.

	SIC	Industry	Factor Loading
Factor 8:		*Apparel and Leather Products*	
	23	Apparel & Other Textile Products	.6609
	31	Leather & Leather Products	.5620
	60	Banking	.4631
	41	Local & Interurban Passenger Transit	.4474
	39	Miscellaneous Manufacturing	.4224
	61	Credit Agencies, Other than Banks	-.3052

Top Twenty MSAs: Newburgh, New York, Jersey City, NE Pennsylvania, Columbus (GA), Utica, Allentown, El Paso, Boston, Lancaster, Johnstown, Binghamton, Knoxville, Long Branch, Nassau, Reading, Miami, Johnson City, York, Vallejo.

Factor 9: *Mining and Oil*

Variance Explained: 2.22 Percent

Auxiliary & Administrative:	Mining	.7254
Pipelines, Except Gas		.6862
Auxiliary & Administrative:	Transportation	
Communications & Public Utilities		.6408
Mining		.5674

Top Twenty MSAs: Tulsa, Houston, Bakersfield, Duluth, Colorado Springs, New Orleans, Corpus Christi, Allentown, Johnstown, Shreveport, Wichita, Oxnard, Tucson, Visalia, Oklahoma City, Denver, Charlestown (WV), Charlotte, Lexington, Gary.

Factor 10: *Government and Related Services*

Variance Explained: 2.21 Percent

Government:	State & Local	.5601
Social Services		.5375
Miscellaneous Services		.3888
Membership Organizations		.3471
Auxiliary & Administrative:	Agriculture,	
Forestry, & Fisheries		.3395
Fabricated Metal Products		−.3855

Top Twenty MSAs: Madison, Trenton, Albany, Washington, D.C., Duluth, Harrisburg, Austin, Ann Arbor, Salem (OR), Raleigh-Durham, Wilmington, Santa Barbara, Boston, Long Branch, Sacramento, Lakeland, Newburgh, Lansing, Tucson, Reading.

63

TABLE 4.1 (continued)

Factor Analysis of Employment Shares
in the Largest 150 MSAs in 1977

SIC	Industry	Factor Loading
Factor 11:	*Distribution Industries*	
	Variance Explained: 2.15 Percent	
42	Trucking & Warehousing	.6950
50	Auxiliary & Administrative: Retail Trade	.6495
20	Wholesale Trade: Durable Goods	.4924
54	Food & Kindred Products	.3213
	Food Stores	–.3046

Top Twenty MSAs: Jersey City, Omaha, Harrisburg, Atlanta, Charlotte, Nashville, Memphis, Indianapolis, Lakeland, Roanoke, Salt Lake City, Akron, Modesto, New Brunswick, Jackson (MS), Washington, D.C., Dallas, Eugene, Birmingham, San Antonio.

SIC	Industry	Factor Loading
Factor 12:	*High-technology Manufacturing*	
	Variance Explained: 2.10 Percent	
36	Electric & Electronic Equipment	.7651
38	Instruments & Related Products	.4724
35	Machinery Except Electrical	.3524
27	Printing & Publishing	.3518
31	Leather & Leather Products	.3444
33	Primary Metal Products	–.4137

Top Twenty MSAs: Binghamton, Poughkeepsie, San Jose, Rochester (NY), Melbourne, Huntsville, Ann Arbor, Boston, Colorado Springs, Anaheim, Phoenix, York (PA), Lexington, Milwaukee, Lancaster, Austin, Albuquerque, Dayton, Visalia, Shreveport.

Factor 13: *Headquarters and Cultural Activities*
Variance Explained: 1.82 Percent

84	Auxiliary & Administrative: Services	.5889
	Museums, Zoos, & Botanical Gardens	.5516
46	Pipelines, Except Gas	.3680
	Auxiliary & Administrative: Manufacturing	.3489

Top Twenty MSAs: Colorado Springs, Wilmington, New York, Rochester (NY), Newport News, Santa Barbara, Chicago, Memphis, Augusta, Tulsa, Nashville, Johnson City (TN), Kalamazoo, Trenton, Chattanooga, Macon, New Brunswick, Cincinnati, Corpus Christi, Columbus (OH).

Factor 14: *Miscellaneous Industries*
Variance Explained: 1.72 percent

30	Rubber & Miscellaneous Products	.6884
	Auxiliary & Administrative: Wholesale Trade	.4678
	Auxiliary & Administrative: Manufacturing	.4116
15	General Contractors & Operative Builders	-.3661

Top Twenty MSAs: Akron, Fayetteville, Wilmington, New Brunswick, Trenton, Salinas, Dayton, Fort Wayne, Detroit, Newark, Jersey City, Richmond, Oxnard, Long Branch (NJ), Bakersfield, Newburgh, Columbus (GA), Melbourne (FL), Paterson, Tulsa.

TABLE 4.1 (Continued)
Factor Analysis of Employment Shares
in the Largest 150 MSAs in 1977

	SIC	Industry	Factor Loading
Factor 15: *Ports and Related Activities*			
	44	Water Transportation	.5824
	47	Transportation Services	.4647
		Auxiliary & Administrative: Contract Construction	.3633
	82	Educational Services	.3212
	49	Electric, Gas, & Sanitary Services	–.3535

Variance Explained: 1.62 Percent

Top Twenty MSAs: New Orleans, Charleston (SC), Honolulu, Mobile, Norfolk, Jersey City, Newport News, Newark, Houston, Trenton, Jacksonville, Macon, Beaumont, Boston, Columbus (GA), Philadelphia, Appleton, Nassau, Omaha, Baltimore.

	SIC	Industry	Factor Loading
Factor 16: *Wood Products*			
	24	Lumber & Wood Products	.6870
	26	Paper & Allied Products	.3219
	49	Electric, Gas, & Sanitary Services	–.3269
	56	Apparel & Accessory Stores	–.3477

Variance Explained: 1.57 Percent

Top Twenty MSAs: Eugene, Salem, Columbus (GA), Appleton, Santa Rosa, Tacoma, Hamilton (OH), Beaumont, Kalamazoo, Los Angeles, Portland (OR), Greenville, Modesto, Seattle, Bakersfield, Vallejo, Visalia, Lakeland, Johnson City, Lancaster.

Factor 17: *Transportation Equipment*

	Transportation Equipment	37	.8159
	Paper & Allied Products	26	-.3491

Variance Explained: 1.51 Percent

Top Twenty MSAs: Flint, Newport News, Saginaw, Lansing, Ann Arbor, Binghamton, Wichita, Lorain (OH), Seattle, Los Angeles, Youngstown, Erie, Detroit, Kansas City, Buffalo, Lakeland, Albuquerque, Johnstown (PA), South Bend, Johnson City (TN).

Factor 18: *Furniture and Tobacco*

Furniture & Fixtures	25	.7322
Tobacco Manufacturers	21	.6837

Variance Explained: 1.47 Percent

Top Twenty MSAs: Greensboro, Grand Rapids, Richmond (VA), Roanoke, Raleigh-Durham, Louisville, Nashville, York (PA), Lexington, Madison, Santa Barbara, Austin, Fayetteville, Tacoma, Evansville, Hamilton, Vallejo, Paterson, Chattanooga, Daytona Beach.

Distribution Centers. The eleventh factor combined distribution sectors exhibiting interindustry linkages. It is dominated by trucking and warehousing, wholesale trade, and retail trade A&A. Favored locations included Jersey City and New Brunswick, both close to New York City, and regional distribution centers, such as Omaha, Atlanta, Memphis, and Dallas.

High-technology Manufacturing. The twelfth factor is a manufacturing grouping dominated by electric and electronic equipment and scientific instruments. These sectors are linked by interindustry flows and are also attracted to centers of scientific innovation. Well-known high-technology metropolitan areas in California and the Northeast were associated with this grouping. These metropolitan areas have an abundance of skilled labor with talents specific to high-tech manufacturing.

Other Factor Groupings. Each remaining factor accounted for less than 2 percent of the variance among all the variables. Most of the industrial associations made intuitive sense. Factor 13 identified a spatial association between various corporate office functions and cultural activities. Though New York and Chicago scored high on this factor, no other large national or regional centers were among the twenty SMSAs scoring highest on this factor. Corporate A&A functions and cultural facilities are important in Colorado Springs, Wilmington, and Rochester (New York). Corporate support for cultural facilities and the recreational demands of corporate office staff may account for the similarities in locational patterns.

Factor 14 is difficult to interpret. Two A&A sectors and rubber and miscellaneous manufacturing are associated with this factor. Most of the SMSAs scoring high on the factor are medium-size metropolitan areas in the Northeast and the Midwest. The highly diversified nature of the miscellaneous manufacturing sector may help explain the cluster. The sector is composed of many multisite firms whose corporate offices are geographically separate from their production plants but still in the same metropolitan area.

Factor 15 grouped water transportation and transportation services. These are complementary port activities that are important employment sources in New Orleans, Charleston, Honolulu, and Mobile. Factor 16 is a wood products grouping based on strong interindustry linkages between lumber and paper products sectors. This cluster is located mainly in SMSAs in the Pacific Northwest, California, and the Southeast. Factor 17 combined transportation equipment and paper products manufacturing. Both sectors are very large. Spatial association may occur because both sectors are important in many SMSAs rather than as a result of any mutual attraction.

Factor 18 combined tobacco and furniture manufacturing, which are frequently located in the same SMSAs in the Southeast. This particular grouping of sectors is a good example of a spatial association that is an outcome of juxtaposed raw materials rather than mutual attraction. Both sectors use outputs of local primary industries for which the Southeast has an environmental comparative advantage and an historical legacy. Also, they are both labor-intensive and the Southeast has low wage rates.

Metropolitan Economic Structure and Employment and Income Growth

In addition to describing the economic structure of metropolitan areas, these sectoral groupings are likely determinants of metropolitan growth and decline. Using the eighteen factors extracted in 1977 as independent variables, I tested two regression models of growth. The dependent variables were the rate of growth of per capita personal income and the rate of growth of total employment in the 1977–86 time period (Bureau of Economic Analysis, 1988). My purpose was to determine the usefulness of industrial clusters in explaining metropolitan growth. I also wanted to identify those particular groupings that had the strongest effects on total employment and income growth. This was not a formal model of growth nor did I generate formal employment and income multipliers. I was simply seeking to determine the degree to which metropolitan employment structure in a given period of time influences subsequent growth.

Table 4.2 shows the regression results. The R^2 values were .58 and .57 for the models of per capita income growth and total employment growth, respectively.

Only five sectoral groupings were positively related to growth of both per capita income and total employment: high-order services, high-technology manufacturing, state and local government and social services, textiles and construction, and the insurance cluster. These sectors are themselves fast growing and serve as propulsive segments of metropolitan economies, speeding up the growth of income and employment. The strong positive relationship of the textiles and construction cluster with per capita income and employment growth may be a regional effect. As noted above, this cluster is strongly associated with medium-size metropolitan areas in the Southeast. In the 1977–86 time period, these SMSAs experienced a large influx of diverse manufacturing firms. Low wages and a nonunion tradition are frequently cited as an explanation for this growth (Norton, 1986).

The federal government and retail trade cluster and the recreation services cluster had positive effects on employment growth yet were not related to income growth. Sectors in these clusters generate large numbers of relatively low-paying jobs. The distribution cluster likewise had no effect on income growth, though it was negatively related to employment growth. The slow growth of jobs in high-scoring SMSAs may be due to the introduction of computer-based information technology in trucking, warehousing, and

TABLE 4.2

Regression Results of Models of Total Employment and Per Capita
Personal Income Growth Using Common Factors of Matrix of
Employment Shares in 1977 as Independent Variables

	Dependent Variable			
	Total Employment Growth Rate 1977–1986		Per Capita Income Growth Rate 1977–1986	
Independent Variable	Coefficient	T-ratio	Coefficient	T-ratio
Intercept	34.148	321.591	10.0045	18.239
Factor 1	14.8746[a]	9.280	0.6487	1.167
Factor 2	6.3921[a]	3.926	2.8386[a]	5.027
Factor 3	2.8605[c]	1.721	1.0186[c]	1.767
Factor 4	−1.6537	−1.020	−0.2999	−0.533
Factor 5	6.5984[a]	4.089	0.5368	0.959
Factor 6	6.7109[a]	4.137	1.4587[b]	2.593
Factor 7	1.5326	0.933	−1.6540[a]	−2.904
Factor 8	0.1978	0.121	2.2334[a]	3.950
Factor 9	−1.1689	−0.701	−2.2408[a]	−3.872
Factor 10	3.2839[c]	1.971	1.6372[a]	2.833
Factor 11	−5.0392[a]	−3.042	−0.5026	−0.875
Factor 12	6.1201[a]	3.773	3.7115[a]	6.598
Factor 13	1.0772	0.640	2.3197[a]	3.977
Factor 14	0.6147	0.370	1.6268[a]	2.825
Factor 15	0.8594	0.540	1.4134[b]	2.390
Factor 16	3.0643[c]	1.842	−1.3653[b]	−2.367
Factor 17	−0.7755	−0.506	−0.5840	−1.098
Factor 18	1.0375	0.621	1.2711[b]	2.194

$R^2 = .57$, Adj $R^2 = .52$ $\qquad\qquad$ $R^2 = .58$, Adj $R^2 = .52$

$F = 9.8^a$ $\qquad\qquad\qquad$ $F = 10.1^a$

[a]Significant at .01 level.
[b]Significant at .05 level.
[c]Significant at .10 level.

wholesaling; the substitution of capital for labor may have led to relatively
slow employment growth.

Some groupings were positively related to income growth but had no
relationship to employment growth: corporate A&A and cultural activities,
apparel and leather products, port activities, and the furniture-tobacco cluster. The food products and mining and oil clusters were also unrelated to

employment growth but evidenced a negative relationship to income growth. Finally, the wood products cluster was negatively related to income growth and positively related to employment growth. The strong negative relationship between the natural resources clusters and income growth is probably due to declines in natural resources prices over the time period and outflows of unearned income from natural resources regions.

Temporal Changes in Metropolitan Economic Structure

To investigate changes in spatial associations over time, the factor analysis of employment shares was repeated using 1986 data for the group of 150 large SMSAs. Table 4.3 shows that many of the factors extracted from the 1986 data were quite similar to those for 1977. However, several important differences exist. The most important change is the separation of the high-order financial, legal, and business services grouping associated with factor 2 in 1977 into two distinct clusters in 1986.

EVOLUTION OF BUSINESS AND PROFESSIONAL SERVICES

As shown in Table 4.3, in 1986, factor 2 merged financial, legal, real estate, communications, and transportation services. Most of the top twenty ranking SMSAs are large national and regional centers. Absent from this factor are business services (SIC 73) and miscellaneous professional services (SIC 89). By 1986, these last sectors had evolved into a second high-order service grouping, as indicated by factor 3 in Table 4.3. Other sectors associated with this 1986 grouping include real estate, electric and electronic equipment, and special trade construction. Locations favored by this high-order complex include Washington, D.C., Melbourne (Cape Kennedy), San Jose, Trenton, Huntsville, and Boston. Interestingly, the two distinct high-order service groupings failed to emerge when the factor analysis was conducted on matrices of employment shares in all SMSAs. Adding the small SMSAs to the matrix produced a single high-order service cluster in both 1977 and 1986 that combined financial, legal, communications, business, and professional services.

Key characteristics of the distinct business services grouping that emerged in 1986 include the following:

- Strong links between the location of business services and miscellaneous professional services.
- Spatial association between the location of business and professional services and electric and electronic equipment manufacturing, real estate, and special trade construction.

TABLE 4.3

Factor Analysis of Employment Shares
in the Largest 150 MSAs in 1986

SIC	Industry	Factor Loading
Factor 1:	**Retail Trade and Government**	
	Variance Explained: 5.63 Percent	
72	Personal Services	.8238
	Government: Military	.7686
57	Furniture & Home Furnishing Stores	.7091
	Government: Federal Civilian	.6682
55	Automobile Dealers & Service Stations	.6570
58	Eating & Drinking Places	.5851
53	General Merchandise Stores	.5237
59	Miscellaneous Retail	.5228
52	Building Materials & Garden Supplies	.4873
79	Auto Repair, Services, & Garages	.4797
54	Food Stores	.4189
17	Special Trade Contractors	.3165
56	Apparel & Accessory Stores	.3139
61	Credit Agencies, Other than Banks	.3067

Top Twenty MSAs: Fayetteville (NC), Charleston (SC), Vallejo (CA), Norfolk, Macon, Columbus (GA), Salinas, Washington, D.C., Newburgh (NY), Colorado Springs, El Paso, Sacramento, Tacoma, Long Branch (NJ), South Bend, Santa Rosa, San Antonio, Newport News, Pensacola, Riverside.

Factor 2: *High-order Legal and Financial Services*
      Variance Explained: 4.87 Percent

81	Legal Services	.7785
62	Security, Commodity Brokers, & Services	.6695
64	Insurance Agents, Brokers, & Services	.6240
65	Real Estate	.6145
67	Holding & Other Investment Offices	.5944
60	Banking	.5556
48	Communications	.5255
61	Credit Agencies, Other than Banks	.4762
45	Transportation by Air	.4444
47	Transportation Services	.3337
	Auxiliary & Administrative: FIRE	.3066
50	Wholesale Trade: Durable Goods	.3051
35	Machinery Except Electrical	-.3083
30	Rubber & Miscellaneous Plastics	-.3031

Top Twenty MSAs: New York, San Francisco, Miami, Seattle, Austin, Dallas, Spokane, Honolulu, Los Angeles, West Palm Beach, Chicago, Jackson (MS), Albuquerque, Portland (OR), Salt Lake City, San Diego, Santa Barbara, Atlanta, Birmingham, Kansas City.

Factor 3: *Producer Services and an*
      Absence of Heavy Manufacturing
      Variance Explained: 3.99 Percent

73	Business Services	.7879
89	Miscellaneous Services	.7562
65	Real Estate	.4512
36	Electric & Electronic Equipment	.3465
17	Special Trade Construction	.3428
34	Fabricated Metal Products	-.4044
86	Membership Organizations	-.4393
33	Primary Metal Products	-.4563
80	Health Services	-.5386

TABLE 4.3 (continued)

Factor Analysis of Employment Shares
in the Largest 150 MSAs in 1986

SIC	Industry	Factor Loading

Top Twenty MSAs: Washington, D.C., Melbourne (FL), San Jose, Trenton (NJ), Huntsville (AL), Boston, Newport News (VA), Albuquerque, Raleigh, San Diego, Phoenix, Santa Barbara, Baltimore, Los Angeles, Anaheim, Colorado Springs, Oxnard, Ann Arbor, Bakersfield, Austin.

Bottom Twenty MSAs: Erie, Gary, Lorain (OH), Canton (OH), Youngstown, Huntington (WV), Kalamazoo, Hamilton (OH), Salem (OR), Peoria, Eugene, McAllen, Appleton, Duluth, Spokane, Saginaw, Utica, Rockford, Columbus (GA), Grand Rapids.

	SIC	Industry	Factor Loading
Factor 4:	*Distribution Industries*		
		Variance Explained: 3.35 Percent	
	42	Trucking & Warehousing	.8110
		Auxiliary & Administrative: Retail Trade	.7119
	50	Wholesale Trade: Durable Goods	.6830
		Auxiliary & Administrative: Wholesale Trade	.4383
	51	Wholesale Trade: Nondurable Goods	.4363
	58	Eating & Drinking Places	–.3260
	36	Electric & Electronic Equipment	–.3136

Top Twenty MSAs: Jersey City, New Brunswick, Charlotte, Memphis, Atlanta, Richmond, Harrisburg, Little Rock, Newburgh, Lakeland (FL), Portland (OR), South Bend, Orlando, Dallas, Des Moines, Omaha, Eugene, Akron, Columbus (OH), Indianapolis.

Factor 5:   *Specialized Wood Products*
      Variance Explained: 3.09 Percent

52	Agriculture, Forestry, & Fisheries	.7884
24	Building Materials & Garden Supplies	.5617
55	Lumber & Wood Products	.4999
59	Automotive Dealers & Service Stations	.4309
17	Miscellaneous Retail	.3906
57	Special Trade Contractors	.3385
51	Furniture & Home Furnishings Stores	.3335
58	Wholesale Trade: Nondurable Goods	.3301
54	Eating & Drinking Places	.3286
	Food Stores	.3117

Top Twenty MSAs: Visalia (CA), Eugene, Bakersfield, Salem (OR), Santa Rosa, Lakeland (FL), Fresno, Salinas, Riverside, Vallejo, McAllen, Duluth, Oxnard, Modesto, Stockton, Daytona Beach, Lancaster, West Palm Beach, Sacramento, Santa Barbara.

Factor 6:   *Mining and Oil*
      Variance Explained: 2.66 Percent

	Mining	.8412
	Auxiliary & Administrative: Mining	.7911
46	Pipelines, Except Gas	.6743
	Auxiliary & Administrative: Transportation	
	Communications & Public Utilities	.5742

Top Twenty MSAs: Tulsa, Bakersfield, Corpus Christi, Duluth, Houston, New Orleans, Oklahoma City, Oxnard, Shreveport, Dallas, Allentown (PA), Johnstown (PA), Lexington, Wichita, Huntington, Lakeland, Denver, Charleston (WV), Birmingham, Salt Lake City.

TABLE 4.3 (continued)

Factor Analysis of Employment Shares
in the Largest 150 MSAs in 1986

	SIC	Industry	Factor Loading
Factor 7:		*Recreation Services*	
	70	Hotels & Other Lodging Places	.9457
	79	Amusement & Recreation Services	.8970
	41	Local & Interurban Passenger Transit	.4339
		Variance Explained: 2.57 Percent	

Top Twenty MSAs: Las Vegas, Honolulu, Orlando, Daytona Beach, Salinas, West Palm Beach, Lakeland, Miami, Fort Lauderdale, New Orleans, NE Pennsylvania, Riverside, Tucson, Newport News, Johnstown, Harrisburg, Nashville, Jersey City, Charleston, Syracuse.

	SIC	Industry	Factor Loading
Factor 8:		*Leather, Apparel, and*	
		Miscellaneous Manufacturing	
	39	Miscellaneous Manufacturing Industries	.7601
	31	Leather & Leather Products	.7054
	23	Apparel & Other Textile Products	.6383
	41	Local & Interurban Passenger Transit	.4400
		Variance Explained: 2.56 Percent	

Top Twenty MSAs: El Paso, Utica, Newburgh, Jersey City, NE Pennsylvania, New York, Lancaster, Allentown, York, Johnstown, Reading, Binghamton, Vallejo, Paterson (NJ), Nashville, Los Angeles, San Antonio, Santa Rosa, Nassau, Des Moines.

	SIC	Industry	Factor Loading
Factor 9:		*Ports and Related Industries*	
	44	Water Transportation	.7527
	76	Miscellaneous Repair Services	.6953
	29	Petroleum & Coal Products	.4958
	47	Transportation Services	.4149
	27	Printing & Publishing	–.4469
		Variance Explained: 2.55 Percent	

Top Twenty MSAs: Beaumont, New Orleans, Mobile, Charleston (SC), Jersey City, Baton Rouge, Jacksonville (FL), Honolulu, Norfolk, Hamilton (OH), Wilmington, Pensacola, Gary, Corpus Christi, Houston, El Paso, Miami, Baltimore, Fort Lauderdale, Tacoma.

Factor 10: Social and Educational Services
Variance Explained: 2.18 Percent

83	Social Services	.7295
82	Educational Services	.7051
80	Government: State & Local	.3721
24	Health Services	.3356
41	Lumber & Wood Products	.3124
	Local & Interurban Passenger Transit	.3025

Top Twenty MSAs: Trenton, Salem (OR), Eugene (OR), Poughkeepsie (NY), Albany, Tacoma, Johnstown, Boston, Syracuse, Rochester (NY), Duluth, New Orleans, Philadelphia, Harrisburg, Newburgh (NY), Pittsburgh, NE Pennsylvania, South Bend, Raleigh, Spokane.

Factor 11: Apparel and Distribution Industries
Variance Explained: 2.10 Percent

56	Apparel & Accessory Stores	.7368
51	Wholesale Trade: Nondurable Goods	.5856
23	Apparel & Other Textile Products	.3573
34	Fabricated Metals Products	.3492

Top Twenty MSAs: McAllen (TX), Jersey City, Salinas (CA), Visalia (CA), Poughkeepsie, Huntsville (AL), Miami, Honolulu, New Orleans, Paterson (NJ), Huntington (WV), Binghamton, Reading (PA), Saginaw, Columbus (GA), Modesto (CA), Davenport, Nassau, Ann Arbor, Lansing.

Factor 12: Heavy Construction and Textiles
Variance Explained: 2.10 Percent

16	Heavy Construction Contractors	.8274
22	Textile Mill Products	.7342
80	Health Services	-.3901

TABLE 4.3 (continued)

Factor Analysis of Employment Shares
in the Largest 150 MSAs in 1986

SIC	Industry	Factor Loading

Top Twenty MSAs: Greenville (SC), Columbus (GA), Baton Rouge, Charlotte (NC), Chattanooga, Houston, Montgomery (AL), Fayetteville (AL), Greensboro, Akron, Columbia (SC), Lakeland, Jackson (MS), Augusta (GA), West Palm Beach, York (PA), Salem, Austin, New York, Daytona Beach.

Factor 13: *Manufacturing Administration and Cultural Activities*
Variance Explained: 1.99 Percent

	Auxiliary & Administrative: Manufacturing	.7437
84	Museums, Zoos, & Botanical Gardens	.4526

Top Twenty MSAs: Wilmington (DE), Akron, New York, Long Branch (NJ), Kalamazoo, Peoria, Paterson (NJ), Allentown, Dayton, Trenton, Charleston (SC), Minneapolis, Richmond (VA), Salinas (CA), Detroit, Chicago, Greensboro, Newark, Fayetteville, New Brunswick.

Factor 14: *Insurance and Administration of Agriculture, Forestry, & Mining*
Variance Explained: 1.93 Percent

63	Insurance Carriers	.7817
	Auxiliary & Administrative: Agriculture, Forestry, & Mining	.6238
86	Membership Organizations	.3299

Top Twenty MSAs: Madison, Des Moines, Omaha, Harrisburg, Columbus (OH), Hamilton (OH), Modesto, Fort Wayne, Jacksonville, Columbia, Appleton, Jackson (MS), Lansing, Indianapolis, Austin, Sacramento, Chattanooga, Salinas, Salem, Fresno.

Factor 15: *Miscellaneous Industries*
  Variance Explained: 1.68 Percent

30	Rubber & Miscellaneous Products	.5301
78	Motion Pictures	.3707
25	Furniture & Fixtures	.3215
17	Special Trade Contractors	-.3194
54	Food Stores	-.4068

Top Twenty MSAs: Los Angeles, Fayetteville, Eugene, Grand Rapids, South Bend, Fort Wayne, Greensboro, Evansville, Miami, Paterson, Canton, Akron, Dayton, Huntsville, Jersey City, Trenton, Erie, Charlotte, Newark, Allentown.

Factor 16: *Petroleum and Chemicals*
  Variance Explained: 1.67 Percent

| 28 | Chemicals & Allied Products | .8064 |
| 29 | Petroleum & Coal Products | .4153 |

Top Twenty MSAs: Beaumont, Johnson City, Augusta (GA), Charleston (WV), New Brunswick, Baton Rouge, Knoxville, Columbia, Eugene, Newburgh, Newark, Huntington, Paterson, Corpus Christi, Las Vegas, Duluth, Pensacola, Madison, Cincinnati, Kalamazoo (MI).

Factor 17: *Paper and Related Activities*
  Variance Explained: 1.67 Percent

49	Electric, Gas, & Sanitary Services	.7551
26	Paper & Allied Products	-.4962
27	Printing & Publishing	-.3321

Bottom Twenty MSAs: Appleton, Eugene, Memphis, Hamilton, New Orleans, Honolulu, Modesto, Augusta, Miami, Johnson City (TN), Kalamazoo, Ann Arbor, Mobile, York, Macon, Lancaster, Kansas City, Denver, Huntsville, Chattanooga.

Factor 18: *Food Processing*
  Variance Explained: 1.66 Percent

| 32 | Stone, Clay, & Glass Products | .7108 |
| 20 | Food & Kindred Products | .5285 |

TABLE 4.3 (continued)

Factor Analysis of Employment Shares
in the Largest 150 MSAs in 1986

	SIC	Industry	Factor Loading
	66	Combined Real Estate, Insurance, Etc.	.4255
		Auxiliary & Administrative: Contract Construction	.3631
	15	General Contractors & Operative Builders	.3148
	38	Instruments & Related Products	-.3233
	33	Primary Metal Products	.3482

Factor 19: *Construction and Primary Metals*
  Variance Explained: 1.47 Percent

Top Twenty MSAs: Gary, Birmingham, Montgomery, Colorado Springs, Duluth, Memphis, Davenport, Washington, D.C., Charlotte, Nashville, Pittsburgh, Greensboro, Peoria, Tucson, Honolulu, Orlando, Allentown, Appleton (WI), Newport News, Little Rock.

	SIC	Industry	Factor Loading
	21	Tobacco Manufacturers	.7520
	25	Furniture & Fixtures	.6308

Factor 20: *Tobacco and Furniture*
  Variance Explained: 1.46 Percent

Top Twenty MSAs: Greensboro, Richmond, Macon, Grand Rapids, Louisville, Raleigh-Durham, Roanoke, Hamilton, Eugene, Appleton, Lexington (KY), York, Salt Lake City, Wilmington, Nashville, Shreveport, Birmingham, Paterson, Columbia, Tacoma.

Top Twenty MSAs: Modesto, Augusta (GA), Stockton, Trenton, Montgomery, Toledo, Vallejo, McAllen, Pensacola, Johnson City, Rochester, Riverside, Tulsa, Fresno, Allentown, Birmingham, Macon, Chattanooga, Lakeland, Bakersfield.

Factor 21: *Transportation Equipment and*
Vehicle Manufacturing

Transportation Equipment	37	.7260
Instruments & Related Products	38	–.4794
Electric & Electronic Equipment	36	–.3282

Variance Explained: 1.42 Percent

Top Twenty MSAs: Flint, Newport News, Lansing, Ann Arbor, Wichita, Saginaw, Youngstown, Los Angeles, Detroit, Johnstown, Wilmington, Huntsville, Harrisburg, Salem, Lorain, New York, Richmond, Seatle, Toledo, Jersey City.

Bottom Twenty MSAs: Rochester (NY), Poughkeepsie, Binghamton, Santa Rosa, San Jose, Canton, Davenport, Anaheim, Portland, Peoria, Fayetteville, Fort Wayne, New Brunswick, Johnson City, Paterson (NJ), Erie, Newark, Milwaukee, Grand Rapids, Appleton.

Industries with Strong Links to More than One Industrial Complex

Furniture & Home Furnishing Stores, Automotive Dealers & Service Stations, Eating & Drinking Places, General Merchandise Stores, Miscellaneous Retail, Food Stores, Credit Agencies Other than Banks, Special Trade Contractors, Wholesale Trade: Durable Goods, Building Materials & Garden Supplies, Local & Interurban Passenger Transit, Apparel & Accessory Stores, Wholesale Trade: Nondurable Goods, Health Services, Lumber & Wood Products, Apparel & Other Textile Products, Petroleum & Coal Products, Furniture & Fixtures, Membership Organizations, Primary Metal Products, Fabricated Metal Products, Electric & Electronic Equipment.

81

- An absence of metal processing sectors.
- No evidence of spatial association between the location of business and professional services and corporate office functions.
- Favored locations that are medium-size regional centers rather than national centers (except for Los Angeles).

It would appear that the location of the business and professional services complexes is driven more by interindustry linkages (localization economies) than by generalized urbanization forces. Although the financial and legal high-order complexes favor large SMSA locations, business and professional services complexes are frequently located in smaller SMSAs.

The factor analysis using employment shares in 1986 did not show a spatial association between business and professional services and corporate A&A functions. Moreover, the results of the analysis of metropolitan growth showed that the corporate A&A factor was not significantly related to employment growth, though it was positively related to per capita personal income growth. The results fail to support the findings of other studies that the location of business services is closely linked to the location of headquarters activities and other high-order services.

There may be several reasons for the contradiction between the results presented here and the prevailing view in the literature. First, Noyelle and Stanback's (1984) analysis terminated in 1977, before the emergence of the distinct business and professional services complexes. Business and professional services grew very fast in the period 1977 to 1986. This growth was fastest in several major regional centers included among the top twenty SMSAs associated with factor 3 in Table 4.3. Second, by using employment shares rather than absolute employment, we avoided spurious correlations caused by the common attraction of almost all industries to large SMSAs. The large national centers of New York, Los Angeles, Chicago, and San Francisco accounted for 19.51 percent of U.S. employment in business and professional services in 1986 (U.S. Department of Commerce, 1986). However, when measured in terms of employment shares, the economies of Washington, D.C., Melbourne, Huntsville, San Jose, Boston, and Trenton functioned to a greater extent as business and professional service centers. Finally, employment data may fail to fully document the role of corporate headquarters and regional offices in an SMSA. Increasingly, corporations are run by small A&A staffs (Tomasko, 1987). Back-office functions are being decentralized to low labor cost locations (Nelson, 1986). Crucial information flows between offices engaged in corporate control and high-order services may be based on interactions among a small number of individuals. Analysis of employment shares may underestimate the importance of these vital personnel.

OTHER TEMPORAL SHIFTS

Another change that occurred in the factor structure over the period 1977 to 1986 is the separation of the wood products complex identified by factor 16 in 1977 into two distinct complexes in 1986. In 1986, factor 5 grouped lumber processing and construction-related activities and factor 17 identified a paper and printing complex. SMSAs scoring high on factor 5 in 1986 are mainly located in the Pacific Northwest and California. The SMSAs associated with the paper and printing complex are more widely distributed and include Memphis, Honolulu, and Denver. Other developments over the time period included (1) the growing importance of educational services in the social services and state and local government complex (factor 10 in 1986), (2) the elimination of A&A functions in services from the corporate office and cultural activities complex (factor 13), and (3) the divergence of the high-technology manufacturing sectors and other types of manufacturing, including certain heavy manufacturing sectors (see factors 12 and 17 in 1977 and factors 3 and 21 in 1986).

These shifts in spatial associations indicate that metropolitan functions, though in general rather stable, do change over time. As particular sectors grow and others decline, the fortunes of metropolitan areas vary. Some metropolitan areas have a comparative advantage in the production of growing products or services. Comparative advantage is not solely a function of conditions that favor any one particular sector. Sectors grow and decline in groups as they mutually reinforce each other. The new business and professional services complexes are growing rapidly in areas where these services are in demand by linked industries.[2] In addition, linked industries are growing in the same areas due to the supply of these services.

Conclusion

Factor analysis of employment shares identified spatial industrial clusters in the larger U.S. metropolitan areas. These clusters are good predictors of total employment and per capita income growth and provide insights into structural change in metropolitan economies. Approximately half the variances in employment structure and employment and income growth are explained by the factor and regression analyses. SMSAs with a concentration of high-order services, government activity, and high-technology manufacturing experienced the fastest growth in total employment and per capita income. In contrast, a concentration of natural resources activities depressed income growth.

An important shift that occurred in the 1977–86 time period relates to the growth and location of business services. By 1986, the location of business services appeared more tied to the location of professional services, high-tech manufacturing, real estate, and specialized trade construction than to corporate administrative locations.

The results presented here substantiate the continued role of metropolitan specialization by groups of sectors. Metropolitan areas function as resorts, military and retail centers, natural resource processing centers, state capitals, high-technology manufacturing centers, ports, wholesale distribution points, and high-order service centers. These functions influence income and total employment growth. Though the results explain only about half the variance in metropolitan character and growth, they may help provide a context for evaluating government incentives to industry. Government incentive programs can become more effective by taking account of the nature and strength of spatial associations among sectors.

Notes

1.   Corporate auxiliary and administrative (A&A) establishments are primarily engaged in providing management and support services for other establishments of the same enterprise. A&A jobs located in establishments whose primary function is to produce goods and services sold to markets outside the enterprise are included in the sector associated with the primary function.

2.   For an expanded discussion of these linkages, see Ó hUallacháin, "The Location and Growth of Business Services in U.S. Metropolitan Areas," Appendix B, in McDonald et al., 1989.

References

Barff, R. A., and P. L. Knight. "The Role of Federal Military Spending in the Timing of the New England Employment Turnaround." *Papers of the Regional Science Association* 65 (1988): 151–166.

Beyers, W. B., M. J. Alvine, and R. Johnson. "The Service Sector: A Growing Force in the Regional Export Base." *Economic Development Commentary* 9 (1985): 3–7.

Browne, L. E. "High Technology and Business Services." *New England Economic Review* (July/August 1983): 5–17.

Bureau of Economic Analysis. *Regional Economic Information System.* Computer tapes. Washington, D.C.: U.S. Department of Commerce, 1988.

Gardocki, B. C., and J. Baj. *Methodology for Estimating Nondisclosure in County Business Patterns.* De Kalb, Ill.: Center for Governmental Studies, Northern Illinois University, 1985.

McDonald, J. F., B. Ó hUallacháin, and T. M. Beam. *Assessing the Development Status of Metropolitan Areas.* Final Report to the U.S. Department of Commerce, Economic Development Administration, Project #99–07–13719. Evanston, Ill.: NCI Research, 1989.

Marshall, J. N., P. Damesick, and P. Wood. "Understanding the Location and Role of Producer Services in the United Kingdom." *Environment and Planning A* 19 (1987): 575–595.

Nelson, K. "Labor Demand, Labor Supply and the Suburbanization of Low Wage Office Jobs." In *Production, Work, Territory: The Geographical Anatomy of Industrial Capitalism*. Eds. A. J. Scott and M. Storper. Boston: Allen & Unwin, 1986.

Norton, R. D. "Industrial Policy and American Renewal." *Journal of Economic Literature* 24 (1986): 1–40.

Noyelle, T. J., and T. M. Stanback. *The Economic Transformation of American Cities*. Totowa, N.J.: Rowman & Allanheld, 1984.

Pred, A. *City-Systems in Advanced Economies*. New York: John Wiley, 1977.

Saxenian, A. "The Genesis of Silicon Valley." *Built Environment* 9 (1983): 7–17.

_____. "Silicon Valley and Route 128: Regional Prototypes or Historic Exceptions?" In *High Technology, Space, and Society*. Ed. M. Castells. Beverly Hills: Sage, 1985.

Schmenner, R. W. *Making Business Location Decisions*. Englewood Cliffs, N.J.: Prentice-Hall, 1982.

Scott, A. J. "High Technology and Territorial Development: The Rise of the Orange County Complex, 1955–84." *Urban Geography* 7 (1986): 3–45.

Simmie, J. M. "Beyond the Industrial City?" *Journal of the American Planning Association* 49 (1983): 59–76.

Stanback, T. M., P. Bearse, T. J. Noyelle, and R. Karasek. *Services: The New Economy*. Totowa, N. J.: Allanheld, Osmun & Co., 1981.

Tomasko, R. M. *Downsizing: Reshaping the Corporation For the Future*. New York: American Management Association, 1987.

U.S. Department of Commerce. *County Business Patterns*. Computer tapes. Washington, D.C.: U.S. Government Printing Office, 1977, 1986.

_____. *Statistical Abstract of the United States*. Washington, D.C.: U.S. Government Printing Office, 1979, 1989.

Wheat, L. F. "The Determinants of 1963–77 Regional Manufacturing Growth: Why the South and the West Grow." *Journal of Regional Science* 26 (1986): 635–659.

Wheeler, J. O. "Corporate Spatial Links with Financial Institutions: The Role of the Metropolitan Hierarchy." *Annals of the Association of American Geographers* 76 (1986): 262–274.

JOHN F. MCDONALD

5 Assessing the Development Status of Metropolitan Areas

Industry clustering patterns provide the starting point for the research described in this paper. The research had two main objectives: to estimate a basic economic model of the factors that contribute to the growth of industry clusters and then to demonstrate the use of these results in assessing the economic development status of a given metropolitan area.

The industry clusters used in this analysis are based on the results obtained by Ó hUallacháin for the 150 largest metropolitan areas in the United States in 1986 (see chapter 4 and McDonald et al., 1989). Ó hUallacháin identified and measured spatial associations among U.S. industries on the basis of common location patterns. As he pointed out in chapter 4, and as Mills elaborated in chapter 1, geographical associations can stem from a variety of forces. These include strong interindustry linkages between industries; locational attractions among industries that make complementary products or use jointly supplied materials; common attraction to particular kinds of places, such as low labor cost locations or large cities that provide the threshold populations that can support specialized production; and information clusters. Ó hUallacháin identified spatial associations by extracting statistically the common factors from a matrix of employment in seventy-eight industries.

Underlying the analysis of clusters is the notion that urban areas with a relatively large proportion of employment in one industry in a cluster will tend to have relatively large employment proportions for the other industries in that cluster. Thus, it can be inferred that the industries in that cluster will

86

tend to grow or decline together in any metropolitan area in which the industries exist.

Once clusters had been identified, the next step in the research was to develop a basic model of the growth of a local industry cluster. The model that was developed is a basic economic model of labor demand that focuses on the fundamental determinants of employment change in a cluster of industries in a metropolitan area. The model assumes that changes in local employment are the result of changes in underlying demand and supply. This model of employment change was estimated for the period 1983 to 1986 for the six most common local industry clusters. These empirical estimates provide a benchmark for comparing the performance of an industry cluster in any particular subject metropolitan area.

The final step in the project involved using the model results to examine the economic strengths and weaknesses of a subject metropolitan area. The essence of this procedure is to:

1. Examine the performance of each of a metropolitan area's important industry clusters.
2. Compare that performance with the "expected" growth based on the estimated models of employment growth.
3. Identify and examine the specific industries that influenced the performance of these industry clusters.
4. Identify topics requiring further research to gain more detailed knowledge of local conditions.

The empirical implementation of the growth models will later be illustrated with three case studies of metropolitan areas: Charleston, South Carolina; Flint, Michigan; and Spokane, Washington.

Industry Clusters

Table 5.1 defines thirteen distinct industry clusters (plus one catchall category), based on the statistical extraction of common factors for 1986 as presented by Ó hUallacháin. Although these thirteen clusters are based on the twenty-one clusters he identified, the original statistical clustering results were not followed in every detail. Modifications were made largely for the sake of parsimony since one objective of the research was to identify a fairly small number of industry clusters in order to simplify and systematize the study of a local economy.

The most important deviation was to define a single manufacturing cluster. Since manufacturing did not cluster coherently in the initial factor analysis, a separate analysis of manufacturing was performed (see "Analyz-

TABLE 5.1

Industry Clusters in U.S. Metropolitan Areas

---

1. *Manufacturing Cluster*

   SIC[1] 20--Food and Kindred Products
   SIC   21--Tobacco Products
   SIC   22--Textile Mill Products
   SIC   23--Apparel and Other Textile Products
   SIC   24--Lumber and Wood Products
   SIC   25--Furniture and Fixtures
   SIC   26--Paper and Allied Products
   SIC   27--Printing and Publishing
   SIC   28--Chemicals and Allied Products
   SIC   29--Petroleum and Coal Products
   SIC   30--Rubber and Miscellaneous Plastics Products
   SIC   31--Leather and Leather Goods
   SIC   32--Stone, Clay, and Glass Products
   SIC   33--Primary Metal Industries
   SIC   34--Fabricated Metal Products
   SIC   35--Machinery Except Electrical
   SIC   36--Electric and Electronic Equipment
   SIC   37--Transportation Equipment
   SIC   38--Instruments and Related Products
   SIC   39--Miscellaneous Manufacturing Industries

2. *Financial and Legal Services Cluster*

   SIC   45--Transportation by Air
   SIC   47--Transportation Services
   SIC   48--Communications
   SIC   60--Banking
   SIC   61--Credit Agencies, Other than Banks
   SIC   62--Security, Commodity Brokers, and Services
   SIC   64--Insurance Agents, Brokers, and Services
   SIC   65--Real Estate
   SIC   67--Holding and Other Investment Offices
   SIC   81--Legal Services
          -----Auxiliary and Administrative: FIRE

3. *Business and Professional Services Cluster*

   SIC   73--Business Services
   SIC   89--Miscellaneous Professional Services

TABLE 5.1 (continued)
Industry Clusters in U.S. Metropolitan Areas

4. *Distribution Cluster*

   SIC   42--Trucking and Warehousing
   SIC   50--Wholesale Trade, Durable Goods
   SIC   51--Wholesale Trade, Nondurable Goods
   ------Auxiliary and Administrative: Wholesale Trade
   ------Auxiliary and Administrative: Retail Trade

5. *Health, Social Service, and Education Cluster*

   SIC   80--Health Services
   SIC   82--Education Services
   SIC   83--Social Services
   -----Government: State and Local
   SIC   41--Local and Interurban Passenger Transit

6. *Retail Trade Cluster*

   SIC   52–59--Retail Trade
   SIC   72--Personal Services
   SIC   75--Auto Repair, Services, Garages
   SIC   17--Special Trade Contractors

7. *Recreation Services Cluster*

   SIC   70--Motels and Other Lodging Places
   SIC   79--Amusement and Recreation Services
   SIC   84--Museums, Botanical, Zoological Gardens

8. *Wood Products Cluster*

   -----Agriculture, Forestry, and Fisheries
   SIC   24--Lumber and Wood Products Manufacturers
   SIC   52--Building Materials and Garden Supplies Retail

9. *Manufacturing Headquarters and Cultural Cluster*

   SIC   84--Museums, Zoos, and Botanical Gardens
   ------Auxiliary and Administrative: Manufacturing

10. *Construction Cluster*

   SIC   15--General Contractors
   SIC   16--Heavy Construction Contractors
   SIC   66--Combined Real Estate, Insurance
   ------Auxiliary and Administrative: Contract Construction

TABLE 5.1 (continued)

Industry Clusters in U.S. Metropolitan Areas

---

11. *Port Cluster*

    SIC   44--Water Transportation
    SIC   76--Miscellaneous Repair Services
    SIC   29--Petroleum and Coal Products
    SIC   47--Transportation Services

12. *Mining and Oil Cluster*

    -----Mining
    -----Auxiliary and Administrative: Mining
    SIC   46--Pipelines, Except Gas
    -----Auxiliary and Administrative: Transportation, Communication,
          and Public Utilities

13. *Apparel and Distribution Cluster*

    SIC   56--Apparel and Accessory Stores
    SIC   51--Wholesale Trade: Nondurable Goods
    SIC   23--Apparel and Other Textile Products

14. *Other Industries*

    SIC   40--Railroad Transportation
    SIC   49--Electric, Gas, and Sanitary Services
    SIC   63--Insurance Carriers
    SIC   78--Motion Pictures
    SIC   86--Membership Organizations
    -----Auxiliary and Administrative: Services
    -----Auxiliary and Administrative: Agriculture and Forestry
    -----Federal Government: Civilian
    -----Federal Government: Military

---

[1]Standard Industrial Classification.

ing Manufacturing"). The analysis used a two-level hierarchy of industry clusters, first grouping all manufacturing into one large cluster and then identifying smaller subclusters of manufacturing industries (Table 5.2). The resulting manufacturing subclusters preserve virtually all of the information on clusters of manufacturing industries contained in the original twenty-one clusters. One potential problem is the loss of information on the clustering of manufacturing industries with nonmanufacturing sectors. However, the original twenty-one clusters contained very few associations of this kind and the most important ones are preserved in Table 5.1. They include the following:

- SIC 24 Lumber and Wood Products (in cluster 8, Wood Products)
- SIC 29 Petroleum and Coal Products (in cluster 11, Port)
- SIC 23 Apparel and Other Textile Products (in cluster 13, Apparel and Distribution)

The consolidation of manufacturing industries eliminated nine of the factors identified by Ó hUallacháin. The remaining twelve original clusters were used, with the following alterations:

1. The retail trade cluster as defined here excludes federal government employment (civilian and military). Federal government employment is considered to be a separate sector for the purposes of analyzing a local economy. This decision was made because retail trade is an important part of any local economy, but the federal government has a significant presence in only a relatively small number of metropolitan areas. Also, federal employment is largely exogenous to the local economy, but retail trade is endogenous.
2. An industry must have had a factor loading of at least .30 to be included in a cluster.
3. Industries with negative factor loadings were not included in a cluster as defined here.
4. An industry was not included in a cluster even if its factor loading exceeded .30 if that industry had a very high factor loading in another cluster.

Of the thirteen clusters derived for this phase of the project, the most important nonmanufacturing clusters are clusters 2 through 6: financial and legal services; business and professional services; distribution; health, social services, and education; and retail trade. These are the largest clusters, and they exist in appreciable size in most Standard Metropolitan Statistical Areas (SMSAs). The remaining seven clusters (clusters 7 through 13) are either small or nonexistent in most SMSAs. However, these clusters are important to the economies of smaller groups of SMSAs. The analyst of a local economy should investigate whether any of these more specialized clusters are important to that local economy.

ANALYZING MANUFACTURING

As noted above, manufacturing industries did not cluster in any coherent way in the factor analysis performed on all seventy-eight sectors, so separate analyses were done of the twenty manufacturing industries. The first procedure was simply to compute the 20 × 20 matrix of simple correlations in

TABLE 5.2

Manufacturing Subclusters
(Based on Correlation Matrix)

1. *Food and Containers*

    SIC[1] 20--Food and Kindred Products
    SIC   32--Stone, Clay, and Glass Products

2. *Tobacco and Furniture*

    SIC   21--Tobacco Manufacturers
    SIC   25--Furniture and Fixtures

3. *Textiles and Apparel*

    SIC   22--Textile Mill Products
    SIC   23--Apparel

4. *Textiles and Furniture*

    SIC   22--Textile Mill Products
    SIC   25--Furniture and Fixtures

5. *Apparel and Leather*

    SIC   23--Apparel
    SIC   31--Leather and Leather Products

6. *Apparel and Jewelry*

    SIC   23--Apparel
    SIC   39--Miscellaneous Manufacturing

7. *Furniture and Fixtures*

    SIC   25--Furniture and Fixtures
    SIC   34--Fabricated Metal Products

8. *Printing and Supplies*

    SIC   27--Printing and Publishing
    SIC   39--Miscellaneous Manufacturing

9. *Petrochemicals*

    SIC   28--Chemicals and Allied Products
    SIC   29--Petroleum and Coal Products

10. *Chemical Products and Containers*

    SIC   28--Chemicals and Allied Products
    SIC   32--Stone, Clay, and Glass Products

TABLE 5.2   (continued)

Manufacturing Subclusters
(Based on Correlation Matrix)

---

11.   *Machinery I*

    SIC   30--Rubber and Miscellaneous Products
    SIC   34--Fabricated Metal Products
    SIC   35--Machinery Except Electronic

12.   *Metals*

    SIC   33--Primary Metal Products
    SIC   34--Fabricated Metal Products

13.   *Leather Products and Electronic Equipment*

    SIC   31--Leather and Leather Products
    SIC   36--Electric and Electronic Equipment

14.   *Sporting Goods*

    SIC   31--Leather and Leather Products
    SIC   39--Miscellaneous Manufacturing

15.   *Transportation Equipment*

    SIC   34--Fabricated Metal Products
    SIC   37--Transportation Equipment

16.   *Machinery II*

    SIC   35--Machinery, except Electrical
    SIC   36--Electric and Electronic Equipment

---

[1] Standard Industrial Classification.

employment shares. Of the 190 separate simple correlations, eighteen were *positive* and statistically significant at the .01 level. None of these simple correlations was *negative* and statistically significant at the .01 level. These eighteen simple correlations led to fifteen industry clusters of two industries each and one cluster of three industries. (The cluster of three industries has all three simple correlations statistically significant at the .01 level.) Table 5.2 shows these sixteen subclusters of manufacturing industries. With the exception of Leather Products and Electronic Equipment, all of these subclusters make good intuitive sense.

In addition, factor analysis of employment shares data for the twenty manufacturing industries generated four larger manufacturing industry clusters (Table 5.3). Note that these four industry clusters group some of the sub-clusters listed in Table 5.2. However, not all of the subclusters in Table 5.2 are included in the four industry clusters in Table 5.3.

Depending upon the composition of a local economy, an analysis of its manufacturing sector might focus on any of the following:

- The manufacturing sector as a whole.
- One or more manufacturing subclusters, as shown in Table 5.2.
- One or more larger manufacturing industry clusters, as shown in Table 5.3.
- A combination of manufacturing subclusters and clusters.
- Several individual manufacturing industries.

TABLE 5.3

Manufacturing Industry Clusters in the United States
(Metropolitan Areas)

1. *Apparel Cluster*

    SIC[1]   22--Textile Mill Products
    SIC   23--Apparel
    SIC   31--Leather and Leather Products
    SIC   39--Miscellaneous Manufacturing

2. *Machinery Cluster*

    SIC   35--Machinery Except Electrical
    SIC   36--Electric and Electronic Equipment

3. *Chemicals Cluster*

    SIC   28--Chemicals and Allied Products
    SIC   29--Petroleum and Coal Products
    SIC   32--Stone, Clay, Glass Products

4. *Furniture and Machinery Cluster*

    SIC   25--Furniture and Fixtures
    SIC   30--Rubber and Miscellaneous Products
    SIC   34--Fabricated Metal Products
    SIC   35--Machinery Except Electrical

[1]Standard Industrial Classification.

Modeling the Growth of a Local Industry or Industry Cluster

After selecting clusters for analysis, the next step was to specify a model of the growth of an industry cluster at the local level. The objective was to devise a simple model that could be estimated empirically so that predictions from the model can be used as benchmarks for comparing the performance of a subject metropolitan area.

Industry growth at the metropolitan or state level has been the topic of numerous empirical studies. The approach taken in this study is to develop a standard microeconomic model of employment *change* for an industry or cluster of industries in a metropolitan area. The approach is similar to that used recently by Crihfield (1989). Shapiro and Fulton (1985) also provide a review of labor demand models in the context of small regions or metropolitan areas. I believe that the best place to start in gaining an understanding of cluster growth is a basic neoclassical model of labor demand because (1) this approach has been used successfully at the national level by several researchers (with numerous modifications as summarized by Shapiro and Fulton, 1985); (2) only Crihfield (1989) and Shapiro and Fulton (1985) have explicitly used neoclassical theory to study industry employment growth at the metropolitan level; and (3) more studies along neoclassical lines are needed to test the validity of such an approach.

The model assumes initially that the industry is in equilibrium as it changes. This assumption is then relaxed and issues in the specification of disequilibrium growth paths are addressed. The basic approach followed is the neoclassical theory of derived demand for labor as first presented by Hicks (1963) in *The Theory of Wages* and subsequently extended by many others, including Muth (1964).

MODEL ASSUMPTIONS

The model is based on the following standard assumptions:

- The industry or industry cluster consists of a group of actual or potential producers of a single, homogenous product.
- These producers have identical production functions and use two inputs, labor and "nonlabor." Nonlabor is an aggregate input that includes capital (real estate and equipment), materials, and business services. This assumption of only two inputs simplifies the analysis; it is useful to think of nonlabor as an intermediate input that is produced using basic inputs. The cost of a unit of nonlabor is simply the price index for those basic inputs.

- All firms are assumed to be competitive in both product and input markets; prices, including both input and output prices, are taken as given.

Under these assumptions, the average cost curve is identical for each firm. Also, the assumed existence of identical potential producers implies that each firm operates at minimum average cost. If each firm has a unique output level for which average cost is a minimum, expansion of the industry comes about through the addition of new firms (assuming factor prices and technology remain constant). Thus, the production for the local industry is homogenous of degree one. If factor prices or technology change as a result of localization or urbanization economies (or other causes), firm sizes will change.

Two additional standard assumptions underlie the model:

- The local industry or industry cluster faces a demand with elasticity n that is less than perfectly elastic. This assumption is made because it is unreasonable to assume that an industry in a single metropolitan area could sell unlimited amounts of output at some constant price. Transportation, communication, and information costs limit the size of the market area.
- Localization economies, urbanization economies, and technical change shift the industry production function. Henderson (1988) notes that localization economies can arise from economies of intraindustry specialization, labor market economies in searching for workers with specific training, increased speed of adoption of new technologies, and scale economies in providing public inputs needed by the particular industry. Urbanization economies are external to the industry and arise from operating in larger overall product and input markets.

This model in percentage change form implies that

$$dlnL = (-k_N\sigma + k_L n)\, dlnP_L + dlnZ + [k_N(\sigma + n)]dlnP_N - (1+n)\delta. \quad (1)$$

The notation is as follows:

$$
\begin{array}{ll}
L & = \text{labor} \\
k_N,\ k_L & = \text{shares of nonlabor and labor} \\
\sigma & = \text{elasticity of substitution of labor for nonlabor} \\
n & = \text{elasticity of demand for output} \\
P_L,\ P_N & = \text{prices of nonlabor and labor} \\
Z & = \text{variable that shifts the demand for output} \\
\delta & = \text{rate of technical change}
\end{array}
$$

These are the conventional results for the elasticity of derived demand. The first term states that dlnL will rise when $dlnP_L$ falls because $\sigma > 0$ and $n < 0$. The second term states that L and Z will increase by equal percentages; labor demand increases proportionately with demand, other things being equal. The third term states that a reduction in P_N will increase L if $\sigma + n < 0$ or if the elasticity of substitution is smaller (in absolute terms) than the elasticity of demand. A reduction in the price of other inputs does not necessarily increase employment; the output effect must outweigh the substitution effect. Finally, the last term indicates that technical change will increase employment if the elasticity of demand exceeds one in absolute terms (elastic demand). The output effect must exceed the tendency to reduce labor as technology improves. Localization and urbanization economies are included in the general category of technical change. *In summary, equation (1) states that percentage employment change depends on contemporaneous percentage changes in input prices, demand, and technology (including localization and urbanization economies).*

ADJUSTMENTS TO THE MODEL

Consideration should be given to the possibility that employment in an industry cluster is not always in equilibrium so that current employment change may also reflect adjustments to past events or expected future events. This possibility is particularly important because the model is to be estimated for the time period 1983 to 1986, a period of recovery from the recession of 1981 to 1982. The most current data available were used because the pace of economic change and restructuring has been rapid in the late 1970s and early 1980s.

As reported in the *Economic Report of the President* (Council of Economic Advisors, 1990), employment in manufacturing in the United States reached its peak in 1979 at 21.04 million, or 23.4 percent of total employment. Manufacturing employment dropped 12.4 percent to 18.43 million in 1983; by 1988, it had recovered to only 19.52 million, or 18.4 percent of total employment. The recent absolute decline in manufacturing employment, coupled with large employment increases in other sectors, appears to mark the period of the late 1970s and early 1980s as a watershed period. In earlier periods, manufacturing employment had increased slightly or remained constant from business cycle peak to business cycle peak. Among the factors that may have contributed to this departure from past trends are the second energy price shock in 1979, the decline in international competitiveness of U.S. industry, and the twin deficits (in the federal budget and the balance of payments). Since the period of approximately 1979 to 1982 appears to be a watershed period, my interest is in devising a model for the purpose of studying the period *since* 1982. I hope to develop methods for examining how metropolitan economies have functioned in the post-1982 period. Studies that use earlier data, such as Crihfield's (1989) and Wheat's (1986) study of the 1963–77 period, may not provide reliable results for the period of the 1980s. Interest in the 1983–86 period requires that allowance be made for the possibility that events before 1983 influenced employment change after 1983.

Shapiro and Fulton (1985) note that studies of labor demand at the national level have uncovered two possible sources of disequilibrium: (1) partial adjustment to changes in desired employment levels and (2) labor hoarding in response to either a decline in labor demand or slow growth in labor demand that is not considered permanent. Firms may only partially adjust to changes in desired employment levels because rapid adjustment requires costly hiring and training activity as well as large wage increases. Labor hoarding in a downturn can occur because of contractual commitments, aversion to the loss of specific skills and high subsequent training costs, morale and public relations factors, and unwillingness to incur reorganization costs. Labor hoarding during a period of slow growth involves the anticipation of more rapid demand growth in the near future. Contractual commitments may be made and specific training accomplished so the firm is ready for the expected upturn in demand.

The standard approach is to assume a partial adjustment model of the form

$$y_t - y_{t-1} = \beta(y_t^* - y_{t-1}),$$

where y_t is the actual level of the input at time t, y_t^* is its desired level based on conditions at time t, and β is an adjustment coefficient. The adjustment coefficient may be between zero and one, indicating partial adjustment toward the desired level of y, or the adjustment coefficient may be greater than one, which would indicate that the industry "overshoots" the desired level of y during the time period under examination. This corresponds to the notion of labor hoarding in a period of slow growth if y_t^* is greater than y_{t-1}. In fact, this last case is the one supported by the empirical tests reported below.

This model can be adapted to the employment change model represented by equation (1). First, assume that the partial adjustment model is expressed in exponential form, or

$$y_t \div y_{t-1} = (y_t^*/y_{t-1})^\beta.$$

In logarithmic form, this becomes

$$\ln y_t = \beta \ln y_t^* + (1 - \beta) \ln y_{t-1}.$$

Similarly,

$$\ln y_{t-1} = \beta \ln y_{t-1}* + (1 - \beta) \ln y_{t-2}.$$

These equations imply that

$$\ln y_t - \ln y_{t-1} = \beta(\ln y_t* - \ln y_{t-1}*) + (1 - \beta)(\ln y_{t-1} - \ln y_{t-2}). \quad (2)$$

The left-hand side of equation (2) is simply dlnL in finite difference form. The term $(\ln y_t* - \ln y_{t-1}*)$ is simply the right-hand side of equation (1) in finite difference form, and $(\ln y_{t-1} - \ln y_{t-2})$ is the lagged value of dlnL in finite difference form. Consequently, the disequilibrium model for employment change is

$$\ln L_t - \ln L_{t-1} = \beta[(-k_N\sigma + k_L n)(\ln P_{L,t} - \ln P_{L,t-1})]$$
$$+ \beta(\ln Z_t - \ln Z_{t-1})$$
$$+ \beta(\sigma + n)(\ln P_{N,t} - \ln P_{N,t-1})$$
$$- \beta(1 + n)\delta_t$$
$$+ (1 - \beta)(\ln L_{t-1} - \ln L_{t-2}). \quad (3)$$

Employment change is a function of contemporaneous changes in input prices, demand, and technology; proportion β of these effects is recorded in the same time period. Employment change is a function of lagged employment *change* (not the employment level). The coefficient of lagged employment change is $(1 - \beta)$, so the β parameter can be identified. Furthermore, if the coeffcient of lagged employment growth is not statistically significantly different from zero, this means that full adjustment has taken place over the time period of the analysis and that labor hoarding is not present.

It is important to recognize that the basic model represented by equation (3) is a model of *percentage change* in employment and that the variables on the right-hand side of the equation are also in terms of *changes*. This is the implication of a model that views a local industry or industry cluster as generally tending to be in equilibrium most of the time. Assuming the industry exists at all in the SMSA, *changes* in that industry result from *changes* in the variables that influence the demand and supply of that industry. As Crihfield (1989) argues, this modeling approach permits us to avoid having to measure the numerous variables that influence the employment *level* of the local industry. Variables that change are important in the model. However, empirical implementation requires the use of proxy variables for some changes. For example, dummy variables for regions are used as proxies for demand growth at the regional level; the initial employment level in the industry or industry cluster is used to test for the presence of localization economies. The empirical models contain a relatively small number of variables partly because relatively few variables changed appreciably over the 1983–86 period examined.

DATA SOURCES AND ECONOMETRIC METHODS

The data for the empirical tests were taken from two U.S. Department of Commerce sources: the *County Business Patterns* series of the U.S. Bureau of the Census and the *Regional Economic Information System* of the Bureau of Economic Analysis (BEA). *County Business Patterns* provides data by detailed industry category at the county level on employment covered by the Social Security system, total payrolls, and the number of establishments. From the county data, we assembled totals for each SMSA, using the Census Bureau's 1980 SMSA definitions. Employment data for some counties are not disclosed for some smaller industries so a method developed by Gardocki and Baj (1985) was used to estimate the missing data. The BEA data were used to compile SMSA totals for population, real per capita income, and government employment (again using the 1980 SMSA definitions). Data were assembled for three years: 1980, 1983, and 1986.

The econometric model, which was estimated for each of six sectoral clusters, consisted of four simultaneous equations:

- A *labor demand* equation based on equation (3)
- An equation for *change in wage rates*
- An equation for *population growth*
- An equation for the *change in real per capita income*

The four variables treated as jointly dependent were the percentage changes in employment, wages, population, and real per capita income. In practice, only the labor demand equation was estimated by the two-stage least squares (2SLS) method. Lagged values of the wage change, population change, and change in real per capita income were used to help construct predicted values of the percentage changes in wages, population, and real per capita income. These predicted variables were then used in the labor demand equation. The labor demand equation did not include lagged wage changes, lagged population changes, or lagged change in real per capita income. Preliminary results obtained by using ordinary least squares (OLS) were compared with the 2SLS results. Simultaneity bias was evident in the OLS results. Consequently, we used 2SLS as the estimation method for all of the results reported below.

Empirical Results for Nonmanufacturing

Table 5.1 identified the following major clusters of nonmanufacturing industries:

- Financial and Legal Services
- Business and Professional Services
- Distribution
- Health, Social Services, and Education
- Retail Trade

Each of these clusters was modeled in accordance with equation (3) in order to identify the basic economic forces that caused employment to change from 1983 to 1986. Data from the 150 largest SMSAs were used. Each of these clusters is considered in turn.

FINANCIAL AND LEGAL SERVICES

Table 5.4 presents the results of the regression analysis of 1983–86 employment growth in the financial and legal services cluster. The demand shift variables included were population growth in the SMSA, growth in real per capita personal income, and employment growth outside the financial and legal services cluster. Regional dummy variables were included to capture demand change at the regional level. Employment in the financial and legal services cluster in 1983 (natural log) was included to test for the possibility that a larger employment cluster will experience more rapid (or slower) growth—a test for the effects of localization economies on employment growth.

The results can be summarized easily: Employment in the financial and legal services cluster was driven by local population growth, per capita income growth, and employment growth in other local industries. Employment growth due to other factors was greater in the northeastern region (the omitted region dummy) than elsewhere. The t value for the coefficient of per capita real income appeared to be low, but it was statistically significant at the .05 level for a one-tail test. The other estimated coefficients were not statistically significant. In particular, the effect of the wage change was zero. This result may simply mean that the SMSA wage does not provide a good measure of wage change in this cluster.

The key elasticities in the model—the elasticities of employment in the

TABLE 5.4

Two-stage Least Squares
Regression Analysis of Employment Change in the
Financial and Legal Services Cluster: 1983–1986
(Department Variable Is Percent Change)

Intercept	–2.11
	(0.26)
Lagged change in employment (%)	–.10
	(.76)
*Wage change (%)	.15
	(.72)
*Population growth (%)	.94
	(2.65)
*Real income per capita (% change)	.66
	(1.63)
Employment in cluster in 1983 (In)	.35
	(.50)
Employment growth not in cluster (%)	.74
	(6.40)
Midwest	–6.69
	(2.70)
South	–8.29
	(2.86)
West	–10.99
	(3.35)
Sample Size (126)	

Unsigned t values are in parentheses. Jointly dependent variables are denoted by *.

financial and legal services cluster with respect to population, per capita real income, and employment—are all plausible in magnitude. The results show that growth in local population generates a demand for financial and legal services approximately in equal proportion (elasticity of .94). Per capita real income growth generates demand in somewhat smaller proportion (elasticity of .66), and the elasticity with respect to increases in local employment in other industries is .74.

BUSINESS AND PROFESSIONAL SERVICES

The empirical results for the business and professional services cluster (Table 5.5) are substantially different from the results for the financial and legal services cluster. First of all, the coefficient of lagged employment

TABLE 5.5

Two-stage Least Squares
Regression Analysis of Employment Change in the
Business and Professional Services Cluster: 1983–1986
(Dependent Variable Is Percent Change)

		Long-run Effect
Intercept	33.28	
	(2.40)	
Lagged change in employment (%)	–.31	
	(2.92)	
*Wage change	.10	.08
	(.23)	
*Population growth	–.55	–.42
	(.78)	
*Real income per capita (% change)	1.09	.83
	(1.42)	
Employment in cluster in 1983 (In)	–2.76	–2.11
	(2.12)	
Employment growth not in cluster (%)	1.88	1.44
	(7.73)	
Midwest	11.07	
	(2.94)	
South	8.68	
	(1.54)	
West	–1.30	
	(.19)	
Sample Size (150)		

Unsigned t values are in parentheses. Jointly dependent variables are denoted by *.

change was statistically significantly different from zero and negative. The negative coefficient means that SMSAs that had larger percentage growth in the cluster during 1980 to 1983 had *lower* growth in the subsequent period of 1983 to 1986—a finding that is consistent with labor hoarding during a period of slow growth. This means that the long-run effects of the various variables are *smaller* than the coefficients listed in column 1 of Table 5.5 These long-run effects are listed in column 2.

The results in Table 5.5 show that, as one would expect, employment in business and professional services was driven primarily by *employment* in other sectors rather than by consumers directly (that is, population or real per capita income). This particular long-run elasticity was estimated to be 1.44.

Also, employment growth was *lower* in SMSAs with a larger business and professional services cluster in 1983. This finding is consistent with Henderson's (1988) notion of localization economies as shifts in the production function. Given equal increases in demand (as included in the model), larger clusters of business and professional services were able to satisfy that demand with *less* employment growth. Finally, the results show that employment growth was greatest in the Midwest, other things being equal.

DISTRIBUTION

The model for the distribution cluster (Table 5.6) used manufacturing employment growth as a demand shifter instead of total employment growth outside the cluster. The purpose of the distribution cluster is, after all, to distribute manufactured products. As with the business and professional services cluster, the coefficient of lagged employment growth was *negative* and statistically significant. Labor hoarding was taking place in this cluster as well. The long-run effects are shown in column 2 of Table 5.6. The empirical results turn out largely as one would expect. Population and per capita income growth call forth employment in the distribution cluster to handle *imports* to the SMSA, and manufacturing employment growth in the SMSA generates employment growth in the distribution cluster to distribute the goods to consumers (both inside and outside the SMSA). Finally, employment growth in this cluster was less in the West than in the other regions.

HEALTH, SOCIAL SERVICES, AND EDUCATION

The results for the health, social services, and education cluster, shown in Table 5.7, can be summarized very simply. Employment in this cluster was, as one would expect, driven by population. The long-run elasticity was estimated to be .79. The wage rate variable was negative and statistically significant, but no other variable in the model (except for lagged employment change) had a coefficient that attains statistical significance. The largest component of this cluster is health services. Since most people are covered by health insurance, per capita income turned out not to be an important factor in employment growth over the three-year period of 1983 to 1986. (The results of a separate regression analysis run for Health Services—SIC 80—confirm this finding.)

TABLE 5.6

Two-stage Least Squares
Regression Analysis of Employment Change in the
Distribution Cluster: 1983–1986
(Dependent Variable Is Percent Change)

		Long-run Effect
Intercept	–6.49	
	(.67)	
Lagged change in employment (%)	–.33	
	(2.80)	
*Wage change (%)	.27	.20
	(1.13)	
*Population growth (%)	.93	.70
	(2.29)	
*Real income per capita (% change)	1.63	1.23
	(3.59)	
Employment in cluster in 1983 (ln)	.25	.19
	(.28)	
Employment growth in manufacturing	.46	.35
	(4.51)	
Midwest	–5.60	
	(1.82)	
South	–1.56	
	(.44)	
West	–9.47	
	(2.51)	
Sample Size (125)		

Unsigned t values are in parentheses. Jointly dependent variables are denoted by *.

RETAIL TRADE

The final nonmanufacturing cluster modeled is the retail trade cluster (Table 5.8). Retail trade employment responds to population and per capita income growth as expected (with rather large elasticities of 1.16 and 1.67, respectively). The elasticity of employment with respect to the wage rate was estimated to be − .43, and a larger retail trade cluster in 1983 was associated with slower employment growth.

TABLE 5.7

Two-stage Least Squares
Regression of Employment Change in the
Health, Social Services, and Education Cluster: 1983–1986
(Dependent Variable Is Percentage Change)

		Long-run Effect
Intercept	5.77	
	(1.25)	
Lagged change in employment (%)	−.22	
	(2.34)	
*Wage change (%)	−.29	−.24
	(3.04)	
*Population growth (%)	.96	.79
	(6.83)	
*Real income per capita (% change)	.18	.15
	(1.11)	
Employment in cluster in 1983 (ln)	−.02	−.02
	(.04)	
Midwest	−1.61	
	(1.40)	
South	−1.15	
	(.90)	
West	−.60	
	(.40)	
Sample Size (141)		

Unsigned t values are in parentheses. Jointly dependent variables are denoted by *.

Empirical Results for Manufacturing

A similar regression model was estimated for total manufacturing. The dependent variable in the model was percentage change in manufacturing employment from 1983 to 1986. The variables on the right-hand side of the equation were the following:

- Lagged percentage change in employment (1980 to 1983)
- Percentage change in the real wage (jointly dependent)
- Population growth percentage (jointly dependent)
- Percentage change in real per capita personal income (jointly dependent)

TABLE 5.8

Two-stage Least Squares
Regression Analysis of Employment Change in the
Retail Trade Cluster: 1983–1986
(Dependent Variable Is Percentage Change)

Intercept	7.22
	(1.36)
Lagged change in employment (%)	–.08
	(.76)
*Wage change (%)	–.43
	(3.72)
*Population growth (%)	1.16
	(4.95)
*Real income per capita (% change)	1.67
	(8.91)
Employment in cluster in 1983 (ln)	–1.04
	(2.26)
Midwest	1.67
	(1.11)
South	5.03
	(3.20)
West	2.02
	(1.02)
Sample Size (149)	

Unsigned t values are in parentheses. Jointly dependent variables are denoted by *.

- Natural log of employment in manufacturing in 1983
- Share of local manufacturing employment in declining sectors
- Percent change in federal government procurement for 1984 to 1986
- Region dummies

The first four variables were the same ones used in the other models discussed above. The base year (1983) employment level was included to test for localization economies.

The other variables were used to capture variations in export demand growth. It was hypothesized that export demand growth depends upon the region in which the SMSA is located, industry mix, and the growth in federal government procurement spending. Industry mix is the proportion of SMSA manufacturing employment in the following "declining" industries:

SIC 20	Food and Kindred Products
SIC 21	Tobacco Manufacturers
SIC 22	Textile Mill Products
SIC 23	Apparel
SIC 28	Chemicals and Allied Products
SIC 29	Petroleum and Coal Products
SIC 31	Leather and Leather Products
SIC 33	Primary Metals

The regression results for this model are shown in Table 5.9. The empirical results are quite satisfactory.

TABLE 5.9

Two-stage Least Squares
Regression Analysis of Total Manufacturing Employment Change:
1983–1986
(Dependent Variable Is Percentage Change)

Intercept	−.26
	(.03)
Lagged change in employment (%)	.03
	(.40)
*Wage change (%)	−.71
	(2.18)
*Population growth (%)	.84
	(2.00)
*Real income per capita (% change)	.81
	(2.24)
Employment in manufacturing in 1983 (ln)	.31
	(.50)
Share of employment in declining industries in 1983	.18
	(3.90)
Growth in federal procurement, 1984–86 (%)	.04
	(2.62)
Midwest	5.25
	(1.99)
South	.43
	(1.50)
West	5.24
	(1.53)
Sample Size (263)	

Unsigned t values are in parentheses. Jointly dependent variables are denoted by *.

Assessing the Development Status of a Metropolitan Area

The foregoing model results can be used to undertake a preliminary assessment of the development status of a metropolitan area. In outline form, the steps to be followed are these:

1. Data collection.
2. Identification of all important industry clusters and recent trends of those clusters.
3. Computation of the expected growth rates of these industry clusters over the 1983–86 period, using the equations previously estimated for the 150 largest SMSAs.
4. Comparison of actual and expected growth rates for these clusters; measurement of local industry cluster performance relative to expectation.
5. Identification of a research agenda to determine possible causes of good or poor performance.

This procedure is illustrated below with case studies of three metropolitan areas.

SPOKANE, WASHINGTON

The Spokane SMSA is located in east-central Washington. Table 5.10 shows the basic facts about employment in Spokane. The top panel displays employment levels for manufacturing and the five other industry clusters that were analyzed. The "Other" category is all other employment. The second panel shows percentage changes in employment over a three-year period and the third panel displays location quotients for the industry clusters. The location quotient is the percentage of local employment accounted for by a particular cluster relative to the corresponding figure for the nation. A location quotient of 100 means that the local and national percentages for the clusters are equal. The bottom panel displays the local percentages upon which the location quotients are based.

These basic data show the effects of the recession of the early 1980s and the subsequent recovery (up to 1986). Employment was particularly volatile in manufacturing and in business and professional services.

The location quotients reveal the areas of specialization of the Spokane economy. Spokane is not a manufacturing town. Its manufacturing location quotient is only 67. Spokane's areas of specialization are health, social services, and education; distribution; and the "Other" category. In 1986, the

TABLE 5.10
Spokane, Washington

	1977	1980	1983	1986
Total Employment	115,217	135,670	127,869	144,312
Manufacturing	16,133	18,583	15,503	17,260
Retail	25,060	30,204	28,001	31,360
Financial and Legal Services	8,331	10,564	9,964	11,660
Business and Professional				
Services	4,665	5,103	4,442	5,808
Distribution	11,245	12,999	12,132	12,510
Health, Education, Social Services	28,862	34,312	33,595	38,659
Other	20,921	23,905	24,232	27,055
Employment Growth Rates (%)				
Overall		17.8	−5.7	12.9
Manufacturing		15.2	−16.6	11.3
Retail		20.5	−7.3	12.0
Financial and Legal Services		26.8	−5.7	17.0
Business and Professional Services		9.4	−13.0	30.8
Distribution		15.6	−6.7	3.1
Health, Education, Social Services		18.9	−2.1	15.1
Other		14.3	1.4	11.6
Location Quotients				
Overall	100.0	100.0	100.0	100.0
Manufacturing	60.9	62.4	66.8	67.0
Retail	113.7	115.0	109.6	105.8
Financial and Legal Services	101.6	104.5	89.4	98.4
Business and Professional				
Services	96.9	77.6	64.5	60.5
Distribution	121.9	119.9	119.7	107.6
Health, Education, Social Services	113.4	116.5	117.6	122.1
Other	110.2	105.5	108.3	111.9
Percent of Total Employment				
Manufacturing	14.0	13.7	12.1	12.0
Retail	21.8	22.3	21.9	21.7
Financial and Legal Services	7.2	7.8	7.8	8.1
Business and Professional Services	4.0	3.8	3.5	4.0
Distribution	9.8	9.6	9.5	8.7
Health, Education, Social Services	25.1	25.3	26.3	26.8
Other	18.2	17.6	19.0	18.7

largest components of the 27,055 jobs comprising "Other" employment were the following:

Federal civilian	4,408
Federal military	6,697
Membership organizations	3,868
Recreation services cluster	2,662

These sectors accounted for 65 percent of "Other" employment. The rest was scattered among several other sectors.

Federal government employment of 11,105 (including military jobs) accounted for 7.7 percent of employment in the Spokane metropolitan area. Federal employment has been increasing as follows:

Federal Government Employment

	1977	1980	1983	1986
Civilian	4,113	4,262	4,260	4,408
Military	5,281	5,431	6,341	6,697

Clearly, military employment has boosted the Spokane economy, particularly in the early 1980s.

The next step is to use the models of cluster growth estimated earlier to compare actual with expected growth for Spokane's main employment clusters over the 1983–86 period. Table 5.11 shows these comparisons. Note that both business and professional services and distribution performed poorly

TABLE 5.11

Actual and Predicted Employment Growth: 1983–1986
Spokane SMSA

	Actual Growth %	Predicted Growth %	Estimated Residual	Confidence Bands Lower Limit	Confidence Bands Upper Limit
Retail	13.80	18.62	−4.82	4.55	32.69
Financial and Legal Services	11.51	11.70	−0.18	−4.33	27.72
Business and Professional Services	30.75	48.00	−17.25	12.07	83.92
Distribution	3.12	13.27	−10.16	−8.43	34.98
Health, Social Services, and Education	15.07	9.18	5.89	0.48	17.89
Manufacturing	11.33	5.88	5.45	−16.97	28.73

compared to the expected growth. Manufacturing as well as health, social services, and education performed somewhat better than expected (growing more than 10 percent over three years). As shown by the location quotients in Table 5.10, health, social services, and education is one area of specialization for Spokane and this sector has done fairly well. However, the distribution cluster, once a strength, has been weakening in recent years.

Table 5.12 identifies the sources of growth in health, social services, and education. Health services is the industry in this cluster with the greatest employment growth over 1983 to 1986. This industry added 2,400 jobs (a 21 percent increase over three years). Moreover, social services experienced a large percentage increase (58 percent).

Table 5.13 reveals that the disappointing performance of the distribution cluster can be traced to wholesale trade in durables. Employment in this industry did not recover from its steep decline during the 1980–83 recession.

This brief assessment of Spokane's development potential can be summarized as follows:

1. Employment in the reference SMSAs increased by 12.8 percent from 1983 to 1986 while jobs in Spokane increased 14.4 percent over this period.
2. Spokane's areas of specialization are the distribution cluster; the health, social services, and education cluster; and federal employment (including the military).
3. The health, social services, and education cluster provided an economic stimulus, primarily because of growth in health services.
4. The distribution cluster performed poorly because of the failure of wholesale trade in durables to recover from the recession of the early 1980s.

TABLE 5.12

Health, Social Services, and Education Cluster
Spokane SMSA

	Employment Levels by Year			
SIC	1977	1980	1983	1986
80--Health Services	9,328	11,322	11,518	13,919
82--Education Services	1,135	2,317	2,422	2,642
83--Social Services	1,265	1,649	1,602	2,524
41--Transit	415	467	487	444
State and Local	16,719	18,557	17,566	19,130

TABLE 5.13

Distribution Cluster: Spokane SMSA

		Employment Levels by Year		
SIC	*1977*	*1980*	*1983*	*1986*
42--Trucking	1,531	1,564	1,385	1,615
50--Wholesale Trade,				
Durable	5,696	6,873	5,680	5,630
51--Wholesale Trade,				
Nondurable	3,332	3,190	3,923	4,405
------Auxiliary and				
Administrative: Wholesale	104	680	558	235
Auxiliary and				
Administrative: Retail	582	692	586	625

5. The federal government also had an important direct influence on the Spokane economy.

The assessment suggests that Spokane's economic development planners should include more detailed studies of health services, wholesale trade in durables, and the military on their research agenda.

CHARLESTON, SOUTH CAROLINA

The Charleston–North Charleston SMSA is on the seacoast and is known for its military bases. Table 5.14 shows the basic employment data. Employment growth in the Charleston economy slowed during the recession of 1980 to 1983 to 1.8 percent per year. Nevertheless, Charleston's employment increased 5.5 percent over this period while employment in all SMSAs dropped 1.6 percent. From 1983 to 1986, Charleston's employment increased 15.4 percent, slightly exceeding the national figure of 12.8 percent.

The Charleston economy relies directly on the federal government. Employment in the "Other" category of 75,411 in 1986 was 35.6 percent of total employment. Some 53,490 of "Other" employment comprised federal government jobs, including 34,366 military jobs. Given the size of this federal sector, Charleston really does not specialize in any of the employment clusters we have studied, but Table 5.14 reveals that some industry clusters have displayed rapid employment growth. Also, the direct reliance on the federal government has been diminishing. Indeed, it was the decline in federal employment (-1.5 percent from 1983 to 1986) that held

TABLE 5.14

Charleston-North Charleston, South Carolina

	1977	1980	1983	1986
Total Employment	150,450	174,136	183,659	211,941
Manufacturing	17,139	19,264	18,085	20,526
Retail	26,302	32,936	33,624	43,718
Financial and Legal Services	5,944	8,056	8,429	10,941
Business and Professional Services	2,868	3,889	4,928	9,251
Distribution	7,472	8,965	8,725	10,494
Health, Education, Social Services	31,419	36,364	37,431	41,600
Other	59,306	64,662	72,437	75,411
Employment Growth Rates (%)				
Overall		15.7	5.5	15.4
Manufacturing		12.4	−6.1	13.5
Retail		25.2	2.1	30.0
Financial and Legal Services		35.5	4.6	29.8
Business and Professional Services		35.6	26.7	87.7
Distribution		20.0	−2.7	20.3
Health, Education, Social Services		15.7	2.9	11.1
Other		9.0	12.0	4.1
Location Quotients				
Overall	100.0	100.0	100.0	100.0
Manufacturing	49.5	50.4	54.3	54.3
Retail	91.4	97.7	91.6	100.4
Financial and Legal Services	55.5	62.1	52.6	62.9
Business and Professional Services	45.6	46.1	49.8	65.6
Distribution	62.1	64.4	59.9	61.4
Health, Education, Social Services	94.6	96.2	91.2	89.5
Other	239.3	222.4	225.5	212.3
Percent of Total Employment				
Manufacturing	11.4	11.1	9.8	9.7
Retail	17.5	18.9	18.3	20.6
Financial and Legal Services	4.0	4.6	4.6	5.2
Business and Professional Services	1.9	2.2	2.7	4.4
Distribution	5.0	5.1	4.8	5.0
Health, Education, Social Services	20.9	20.9	20.4	19.6
Other	39.4	37.1	39.4	35.6

Charleston's employment growth down. The shares of local employment in retail and consumer services, financial and legal services, and business and professional services increased noticeably from 1983 to 1986. In fact, Table 5.15 shows that actual employment growth for 1983 to 1986 exceeded expected growth by large amounts in these three industry clusters, as well as in manufacturing.

Using data from *County Business Patterns*, one can study each of the four strong growth clusters in more depth. The results of these investigations are summarized below.

The manufacturing cluster was led by strong performance in transportation equipment. Employment in this industry increased from 1,532 in 1983 to 3,095 in 1986. As one would expect, employment in fabricated metals increased also. However, this industry is small—the employment levels were only 386 in 1983 and 671 in 1986. Charleston also benefited from an increase in auxiliary and administrative employment in manufacturing—up from 339 in 1983 to 1,129 in 1986.

The retail trade cluster grew across the board, but the biggest gains were recorded in eating and drinking places, up 31.1 percent from 1983 to 1986; food stores, up 23.8 percent; miscellaneous retailing, up 25.05 percent; personal services, up 23.1 percent; and special trade contractors, up 44.1 percent.

The financial and legal services cluster (which includes air transportation) had strong growth in air transportation of 52.3 percent, in credit agen-

TABLE 5.15

Actual and Predicted Growth: 1983–1986
Charleston SMSA

	Actual Growth %	Predicted Growth %	Estimated Residual	Confidence Bands Lower Limit	Upper Limit
Retail	30.86	20.07	10.79	6.18	33.97
Financial and Legal Services	28.60	21.85	6.75	6.04	37.67
Business and Professional Services	87.72	56.95	30.77	21.43	32.48
Distribution	20.28	18.59	1.68	–2.73	39.92
Health, Social Services, and Education	11.14	11.43	–0.29	2.85	20.02
Manufacturing	13.50	4.99	8.51	–17.64	27.61

cies other than banks of 48.9, and in real estate of 45.0 percent. Legal services employment increased 26.9 percent. It would be useful to determine whether Charleston is exporting some of these services outside the SMSA.

Business and professional services exhibited an employment increase of 87.7 percent from 1983 to 1986. Business services increased from 3,595 jobs in 1983 to 7,091 jobs in 1986, a jump of 97.2 percent. Professional services was not too far behind, with an increase from 1,333 to 2,160 jobs (62 percent). These trends call for further research to find out what is happening in this cluster in more detail.

We also expected that the port cluster would be important to Charleston. Table 5.16 shows the employment levels in the industries in this cluster. The 4,690 jobs in the port cluster made up 2.2 percent of total employment in 1986. Table 5.16 shows that employment increased steadily from 1977 to 1983 but that this trend was reversed as employment dropped from 5,336 jobs in 1983 to 4,690 jobs in 1986. The decline came in the water transportation industry itself (SIC 44). This drop would also merit further investigation.

One other industry is worth noting. Membership organizations gained 879 jobs from 1983 to 1986, to reach an employment level of 2,917 in 1986.

This brief look at the Charleston economy has yielded the following conclusions:

1. Charleston is heavily dependent on federal employment, but direct dependence declined during 1983 to 1986.
2. Four industry clusters in the private economy displayed great vitality. These clusters are manufacturing, retail trade, financial and legal services, and business and professional services.
3. Each of these four clusters has its leading industries, and an economic development research agenda should include more detailed studies of these important industries.

TABLE 5.16
Employment in the Port Cluster
Charleston SMSA

SIC	1977	1980	1983	1986
44--Water Transportation	1,718	2,046	2,554	1,772
76--Miscellaneous Repair Services	669	683	830	928
29--Petroleum and Coal Products	499	335	250	250
47--Transportation Services	1,089	2,010	1,702	1,740
Total	3,975	5,074	5,336	4,690

4. Employment in the federal government and in the port cluster declined during 1983 to 1986. The reasons for these outcomes need to be determined.
5. The transformation of the Charleston economy to a more diverse and modern SMSA was well under way during 1983 to 1986.

FLINT, MICHIGAN

Flint is well known as an auto manufacturing town, the location of a number of large General Motors (GM) plants. Flint's fortunes are closely tied to those of the domestic auto industry, and the area's lack of diversity is a serious problem given that GM is facing an increasingly competitive environment in the United States and around the world. It is useful to try to determine Flint's development potential in sectors other than autos. At the outset, it should be recognized that the analytical system developed in this report may not be capable of shedding much light on events that are strongly influenced by one company such as GM. Cyclical trends in the auto industry appear in the data, and the corporate restructuring being undertaken by GM will also appear as an exogenous force acting on the Flint economy. Thus, it is evident that the research agenda for a place such as Flint must include detailed studies of the auto industry and, to the extent possible, acquisition of information on GM's actions and plans.

Table 5.17 contains the basic employment data for the Flint SMSA in the same format that was used for Spokane and Charleston. The strong effect of the 1981–82 recession is apparent—employment dropped 14.4 percent from 1980 to 1983. The employment decline for all SMSAs was only 1.6 percent over this period. By 1986, employment in Flint had rebounded to 99 percent of its 1980 level, but employment in all SMSAs in 1986 was 10.9 percent above the 1980 level. Although the employment totals for Flint in 1980 and 1986 are roughly equal, the industry composition is quite different. Manufacturing employment was off by 11,073 jobs, so the share of manufacturing in total employment dropped from 40.3 percent to 35.0 percent. Meanwhile, there was significant employment growth in retail trade, business and professional services, and "Other" employment.

The heavy concentration in manufacturing is seen in the location quotient figures. A manufacturing location quotient of 196.1 for 1986 is surely one of the largest among metropolitan areas of medium and large size. The location quotients for the other industry clusters are very low (45.3 to 68.5) or are close to 100 in the cases of the retail trade cluster and the health, social services, and education cluster. A fundamental question for Flint is why— with such a large traditional export base sector—the local economy is not much larger. Is there something about the presence of GM that actually in-

TABLE 5.17

Flint, Michigan

	1977	1980	1983	1986
Total Employment	186,545	195,710	167,528	193,723
Manufacturing	82,755	78,827	62,739	67,754
Retail	33,508	37,137	31,451	40,964
Financial and Legal Services	7,681	9,069	7,760	8,151
Business and Professional Services	3,643	3,973	3,757	8,508
Distribution	10,457	10,320	9,704	10,697
Health, Education, Social Services	37,483	43,422	40,654	42,938
Other	11,018	12,962	11,463	14,711
Employment Growth Rates (%)				
Overall		4.9	−14.4	15.6
Manufacturing		−4.7	−20.4	8.0
Retail		10.8	−15.3	30.2
Financial and Legal Services		18.1	−14.4	5.0
Business and Professional Services		9.1	−5.4	126.5
Distribution		−1.3	−6.0	10.2
Health, Education, Social Services		15.8	−6.4	5.6
Other		17.6	−11.6	28.3
Location Quotients				
Overall	100.0	100.0	100.0	100.0
Manufacturing	192.8	183.5	206.5	196.1
Retail	93.9	98.1	93.9	102.9
Financial and Legal Services	57.8	62.2	53.1	51.2
Business and Professional Services	46.7	41.9	41.6	66.0
Distribution	70.0	66.0	73.1	68.5
Health, Education, Social Services	91.0	102.2	108.6	101.0
Other	35.9	39.7	39.1	45.3
Percent of Total Employment				
Manufacturing	44.4	40.3	37.4	35.0
Retail	18.0	19.0	18.8	21.1
Financial and Legal Services	4.1	4.6	4.6	4.2
Business and Professional Services	2.0	2.0	2.2	4.4
Distribution	5.6	5.3	5.8	5.5
Health, Education, Social Services	20.1	22.2	24.3	22.2
Other	5.9	6.6	6.8	7.6

hibits growth in other industries? The data suggest a need for further research along these lines.

The local dominance of GM can be seen in the *County Business Patterns* employment data. Of 63,629 manufacturing jobs in Genesee County in 1986, fully 51,159 (80 percent) were in transportation equipment and at least 5,000 more were in fabricated metals.

Table 5.18 shows the actual and expected employment growth figures for 1983 to 1986. The retail trade cluster increased by 9 percent more than expected, and the business and professional services cluster jumped 64 percent more than expected. The latter cluster started with a small base of 3,757 jobs in 1983 and grew to 8,508 jobs in 1986. The other clusters performed roughly as expected.

The next step is to look into the specific sources of employment growth in the retail and business and professional services clusters. Growth in the retail trade cluster was primarily the result of growth in retail trade itself (SIC 52–59) and in special trade contractors (SIC 17). The latter industry is cyclical, of course. Special trade contractors added 1,396 jobs in Genesee County from 1983 to 1986 (Genesee County contains 94 percent of the Flint SMSA retail trade cluster). Employment growth in retailing was strong in all sectors, but the largest component of growth in terms of the number of jobs was in eating and drinking places in Genesee County, which increased from 8,668 jobs in 1983 to 10,727 jobs in 1986. This strong growth in retailing suggests that Genesee County may be attracting consumer dollars from a larger area—or at least doing a better job of holding on to its own consumer dollars. The sources of this growth should be investigated more fully.

TABLE 5.18

Actual and Predicted Growth: 1983–1986
Flint SMSA

	Actual Growth %	*Predicted Growth %*	*Estimated Residual*	*Confidence Bands*	
				Lower Limit	*Upper Limit*
Retail	27.56	18.43	9.13	4.29	32.56
Financial and Legal Services	9.81	14.08	–4.27	–1.94	30.10
Business and Professional Services	126.46	62.60	63.86	26.64	98.56
Distribution	10.23	9.75	0.49	–11.96	31.45
Health, Social Services, and Education	5.62	8.20	–2.58	–0.50	16.89
Manufacturing	7.99	11.46	–3.47	–11.48	34.41

It was in the business and professional services cluster that the Flint SMSA really displayed rapid growth. Jobs in business services (SIC 73) in Genesee County increased from 2,779 in 1983 to 6,218 in 1986, a jump of 124 percent. Many types of business services showed appreciable employment increases. The main contributors to growth were personnel supply services, computer and data processing services, management and public relations, and other business services not elsewhere classified. The data processing industry was also an important factor in growth. Additional studies are needed to determine whether this growth was real or if it may have resulted from a reclassification of people employed by GM in 1983 to a different SIC code, for example. Further investigations might focus on the significance of growth in the computer and data processing sector.

In addition to business services, Genesee County employment in professional services (SIC 89) jumped from 817 to 2,073 over the 1983–86 period. The largest component in this growth was in engineering services. These jobs may be closely related to the auto industry; this hypothesis should be checked.

This brief examination of the Flint economy suggests the following summary points:

1. Employment in Flint is dominated by manufacturing, but this dominance is declining.
2. The sources of employment growth include retail trade and business and professional services.
3. Growth in the retail trade cluster suggests that Flint is doing better at attracting consumer dollars.
4. Growth in business and professional services (SIC 73 and 89) may partly reflect corporate restructuring by GM, but some of that growth appears to be real.
5. A more comprehensive understanding of the Flint economy calls for a closer examination of the auto industry in general and GM in particular.

These three case studies illustrate the insights into a local economy that can be gained from the use of the analytical method summarized in this chapter. The method uses a set of industry clusters, which simplifies the study of a local economy. Sources of employment growth greater than the expected amount are then pinpointed within clusters. This analytical system carries the analyst only so far, of course; local knowledge must be brought to bear on the industries pinpointed by the analysis. The value of the system lies in suggesting the specific topics to which local knowledge must be applied.

References

Bureau of Economic Analysis. *Regional Economic Information System.* Washington, D.C.: U.S. Government Printing Office, 1980, 1983, 1986.

Council of Economic Advisors. *Economic Report of the President.* Transmitted to the Congress February 1990 together with the Annual Report of Economic Advisors. Washington, D.C.: U.S. Government Printing Office, 1990.

Crihfield, J. "A Structural Empirical Analysis of Metropolitan Labor Demand." *Journal of Regional Science* 29 (1989): 347–371.

Gardocki, A., and D. Baj. *A Method for Estimating Undisclosed Data in County Business Patterns.* De Kalb, Ill.: Northern Illinois University, 1985.

Henderson, J. V. *Urban Development: Theory, Fact and Illusion.* New York: Oxford University Press, 1988.

Hicks, J. R. *The Theory of Wages.* 2nd ed. London: Macmillan, 1963.

McDonald, J. F., B. Ó hUallacháin, and T. M. Beam. *Assessing the Development Status of Metropolitan Areas.* Final Report to the U.S. Department of Commerce, Economic Development Administration, Project #99-07-13719. Evanston, Ill.: NCI Research, 1989.

Muth, R. F. "The Derived Demand for a Productive Factor and the Industry Supply Curve." *Oxford Economic Papers* 16 (1964): 221–234.

Shapiro, H., and G. Fulton. *A Regional Econometric Forecasting System.* Ann Arbor: University of Michigan Press, 1985.

U.S. Bureau of the Census. *County Business Patterns.* Computer tapes. Washington, D.C.: U.S. Government Printing Office, 1980, 1983, 1986.

Wheat, L. F. "The Determinants of 1963–77 Regional Manufacturing Growth: Why the South and the West Grow." *Journal of Regional Science* 26 (1986): 635–659.

PART III

Empirical Analysis of Key Sectors

WILLIAM B. BEYERS

6 *Producer Services and Metropolitan Growth and Development*

The American economy has been an enormous job generator over the past several decades, successfully absorbing the "baby boomers" into the ranks of the employed. However, the recent pattern of job growth has been controversial from a sectoral and occupational standpoint. Employment in the goods-producing sectors has stagnated nationally at the same time as the structure of employment within the goods-producing sectors has tended to become more white collar. Simultaneously, the various services have accounted for almost all the job growth, a trend that has often been viewed skeptically because of the tendency for many of these jobs to be part-time and low wage. Still, this view of the services as a whole is too simplistic. We are beginning to appreciate the highly differentiated nature of the service economy and the important changes in the nature of work within all segments of the economy.

This paper reports on some of these trends. First, we present some data on national employment trends followed by forecasts of expected employment change to the end of the century. These data reveal the differing rates of growth of service industries and lead us to focus on one rapidly growing segment—the producer services. This paper reviews recent research that attempts to explain why the producer services have grown so rapidly. Next, we analyze changes in the geographical distribution of the producer services and reasons for variations in the rate of growth of these services among regions. We conclude with some policy implications associated with the anticipated strong growth of the producer services.

National Employment Trends

Over the 1977–86 decade, the U.S. economy expanded by 19.3 million jobs; 18.6 million of these jobs were created in the various services. Table 6.1 shows employment change by broad industrial sector in the United States over this time period. The extractive-transformative sector, which accounted for about 30 percent of the jobs in America in 1977, was the source of almost no new jobs between 1977 and 1986. Services and government were the source of almost all new jobs in this time period, and one category of services, the producer services, accounted for almost one-third of new jobs.

The classification scheme used in this table is one that has been developed over the past several decades to better reflect the market orientation of various industries (Noyelle and Stanback, 1984). The extractive-transformative sector includes industries that extract raw materials from the earth, oceans, or atmosphere; that grow botanical or biological products; or that process these commodities into physical goods. The movement of products of these industries to intermediate markets or to final consumers is considered the function of the distributive sectors while retailing delivers final products to household consumers. The nonprofit and mainly consumer sectors also have strong final markets. In contrast to most of the other services, the producer services tend to have businesses and governments as their principal clients. These are "intermediate" services—services used to make other services or products of the extractive and transformative sectors. Data will be presented below that show variations in the market orientation of various producer services.

The data in Table 6.1 are now history. However, the U.S. Department of Labor (DOL) has prepared forecasts to the year 2000 based on careful assessments of expected changes in the labor force and the aggregate economy. Industry output was estimated using projections of final demand in conjunction with an adjusted version of the 1977 U.S. input-output model. Analyses of changing ratios of employment per unit of output by sector were then used to project employment. Finally, analyses of changing occupational patterns within industries were used to project employment by occupation (DOL *Projections 2000*, 1988).

These DOL projections suggest continued strong growth of services employment. Table 6.2 shows anticipated changes in employment from 1986 through the year 2000. The estimate for the year 2000 shown here is the midrange estimate of employment prepared by DOL. The extractive-transformative sector is anticipated to continue its proportional decline, from 25 percent to 20 percent of total employment. Service and government employment is anticipated to rise to 80 percent of total employment, and almost 30 percent of new jobs are anticipated to occur in the producer services.

The occupational structure of the changing economy also reflects this continuing shift toward the services. Table 6.3 shows forecasts of employment by occupation from 1986 to 2000. (The minor differences in total employment in 1986 in Tables 6.2 and 6.3 are due to differing sources for these data series.) These data show strong absolute and percentage growth in executive and managerial, professional, technical, sales, and "other service workers." Occupations expected to exhibit slow growth are administrative support (including clerical); precision production, craft, and repair; and operators, fabricators, and laborers.

When the sectoral data and occupational data presented in Tables 6.2 and 6.3 are considered jointly, it is possible to see how the occupational structure of particular industries differs and how they are expected to change (DOL, *Projections 2000*, 1988). These data reveal that producer services employment structures are dominated by professional, technical, executive/managerial, and clerical workers. However, they also reveal a tendency for these same occupational categories to expand employment within the transformative sectors, even though aggregate sectoral employment is anticipated to decrease. In effect, the transformative sectors have had and are anticipated to have a growing white-collar component. For example, employment in manufacturing is projected to decline by 830,000 jobs, but managerial, professional, and technical employment is expected to expand by 370,000 (DOL, *Projections 2000*, 1988). These new workers are expected to be engaged in types of producer service work within manufacturing firms. Thus, the employment data on expansion of producer services employment understate the expansion in the overall number of people engaged in producer services work.

Producer services sectors differ substantially in terms of total employment and rates of growth. Table 6.4 shows employment in 1974 and 1985, absolute change in employment, and percentage change in employment for thirty-nine producer services sectors. Aggregate growth of these sectors was 60 percent—more than double the overall national employment growth rate of 29 percent for the 1974–85 period (a slightly different time period from that shown in Table 6.1), yet within the producer services, some sectors experienced especially strong growth, whether measured in percentage or absolute terms. These large, rapidly growing sectors included personnel supply; computing and data processing; legal services; management, consulting, and public relations; accounting; services to transportation; administrative and auxiliary (A&A) in the finance–insurance–real estate sector; and equipment rental. Each of these sectors grew by at least 100,000 jobs and more than doubled their employment between 1974 and 1985.

A number of other sectors had growth rates well above the producer services average but did not grow quite as fast as the services just mentioned. These sectors were also large sources of job growth. They included architec-

TABLE 6.1

Change in Employment in the United States
May 1977 to May 1986
(thousands)

Sector	May 1977	May 1986	Change	Percent Change
Extractive and Transformative				
Agriculture	3,500 Est.	3,400 Est.		
Mining	843	786		
Construction	3,859	5,001		
Manufacturing	19,469	19,173		
Total	27,671	28,360	689	2.5
Distributive				
Transportation, Communication, Utilities (TCU)	4,576	5,267		
Wholesale	4,351	5,858		
Total	8,927	11,125	2,198	24.6
Retail	13,816	17,903	4,087	29.6
Nonprofit				
Health	4,676	6,534		
Education	1,339	1,404		
Total	6,015	7,937	1,922	32.0
Producer Services				
Finance, Insurance, Real Estate (FIRE)	4,477	6,255		
Business Services	2,223	4,738		
Legal Services	395	720		
Membership Organization	579 Est.	620		
Miscellaneous Professional Services	953	1,289		
Social Services	750 Est.	1,427		
Total	9,377	15,049	5,672	60.5

TABLE 6.1 (continued)

Change in Employment in the United States
May 1977 to May 1986
(thousands)

Sector	May 1977	May 1986	Change	Percent Change
Mainly Consumer Services				
Hotels	1,063	1,373		
Personal Services	809	1,114		
Repair Services	703	1,089		
Motion Pictures and				
Amusement	826	1,217		
Membership Organizations	871	898		
Total	4,272	5,691	1,419	33.2
Private Households	1,344	1,339	–5	–0.4
Nonfarm Self-employed and				
Unpaid Family Workers	6,451	8,086	1,635	25.3
Government				
Federal	2,728	2,935		
State	3,365	3,984		
Local	9,249	10,144		
Total	15,342	17,063	1,721	11.2
Total	93,215	112,552	19,337	20.7

Source: U.S. Department of Labor, *Employment and Earnings* (1986 data).

ture and engineering, security brokerages, and services A&A offices. Some sectors showed large percentage rates of growth but somewhat smaller absolute job gains. These sectors included research and development (R&D) labs; mining A&A; transportation, communication, and utilities (TCU) A&A; mailing, stenographic, and reprographic services; and other professional services. Another group of sectors had large absolute job gains and grew at about the average rate of growth for producer services as a whole. These sectors included insurance agents, retail A&A, credit agencies other than banks, building services, holding and investment companies, advertising, detective and protective services, other business services, noncommercial educational and scientific organizations, and commercial testing laboratories. There were

TABLE 6.2

Projected Change in Employment by Sector
(Thousands of Jobs)

Sector	1986	2000	Change	Percent Change
Extractive and Transformative				
Agriculture	3,400	2,917		
Mining	786	724		
Construction	5,001	5,794		
Manufacturing	19,173	18,160		
Total	28,360	27,595	–765	–2.7
Distributive				
TCU	5,267	5,719		
Wholesale	5,858	7,266		
Total	11,125	12,985	1,860	16.7
Retail	17,903	22,702	4,799	26.8
Nonprofit				
Health	6,534	9,774		
Education	1,404	1,620		
Total	7,937	11,394	3,457	43.6
Producer Services				
FIRE	6,255	7,917		
Business Services	4,738	8,121		
Legal Services	720	1,267		
Membership Organizations	620	690		
Professional Services	1,289	1,647		
Social Services	1,427	2,124		
Total	15,049	21,766	6,717	44.6
Mainly Consumer Services	5,691	7,302	1,611	28.3
Private Households	1,339	1,215	–124	–9.3
Nonfarm Self-employed and Unpaid Family Workers	8,086	9,742	1,656	20.5
Government				
Federal	2,935	3,000		
State and Local	14,128	15,329		
Total	17,063	18,329	1,266	7.4
Total	112,552	133,030	20,478	18.2

Source: U.S. Department of Labor, *Employment and Earnings* (1986 data);
U.S. Department of Labor, *Projections 2000*, 1988.

TABLE 6.3

Projected Change in Employment by Occupation
(Thousands)

Occupation	*1986*	*2000*	*Change*	*Percent Change*
Executive and Managerial	10,583	13,616	3,033	28.7
Professional	13,538	17,192	3,654	27.0
Technical	3,726	5,151	1,425	38.2
Sales	12,606	16,334	3,728	29.6
Administrative Support, Including Clerical	19,851	22,109	2,258	11.4
Other Service Workers	16,555	21,962	5,407	32.7
Precision Production, Craft, and Repair	13,924	15,590	1,666	12.0
Operators, Fabricators, and Laborers	16,300	16,724	424	2.6
Private Households	981	953	–28	–2.7
Farm, Forestry, and Fisheries	3,556	3,393	–163	–4.6
Total	111,623	133,030	21,407	19.2

Source: U.S. Department of Labor, *Projections 2000*, 1988.

also some slowly growing producer services, although these slow-growth sectors had large absolute job gains: banking, insurance carriers, and real estate. A few small sectors actually declined.

The Rapid Growth of the Producer Services

The rapid growth of producer services has started to attract the attention of scholars in the United States and in other advanced economies for a variety of reasons. Evidence is mounting that these sectors have a relatively strong traded component, both in international and in interregional markets. As a recognized part of a region's economic base, they become the target of regional development efforts (Beyers and Alvine, 1985; Feketekuty, 1988). The producer services also tend to have pay scales comparable to manufacturing industry and well above pay scales in service sectors, such as retailing and hotels. An example of the intensified interest in the producer services is the recently published National Academy of Engineering study of technology in the services (Guile and Quinn, 1988). This wide-ranging and insightful

TABLE 6.4

Employment Growth — Producer Services

SIC	Sector	1974 Employ- ment	1985 Employ- ment	Change	Percent Change
098	Resources Adm./Aux.	1,532	2,236	704	46.0
149	Mining Adm./Aux.	69,439	142,170	72,731	104.7
179	Construction Adm./Aux.	14,768	20,093	5,325	36.1
399	Manufacturing Adm./Aux.	1,142,079	1,277,928	35,849	11.9
4700	Transportation Services	132,979	277,845	144,866	108.9
497	Transport./Commun./ Utilities Adm./Aux.	100,690	194,646	93,956	93.3
519	Wholesale Administrative/ Auxiliary	223,551	291,164	67,613	30.2
599	Retail Adm./Aux.	508,608	772,426	263,818	51.9
6000	Banking	1,189,511	1,580,727	391,216	32.9
6100	Other Credit Agencies	442,580	742,598	300,018	67.8
6200	Security/Commodity Brokers	183,639	335,481	151,842	82.7
6300	Insurance Carriers	1,110,830	1,249,393	138,563	12.5
6400	Insurance Agents	344,555	552,637	208,082	60.4
6500	Real Estate	843,462	1,143,284	299,822	35.5
6600	Combined Real Estate and Insurance	30,249	24,349	−5,900	−19.5
6700	Holding and Investments	114,937	193,102	78,165	68.0
679	Finance, Insurance, Real Estate Adm./Aux.	58,905	167,167	108,262	183.8
7310	Advertising	113,405	183,540	70,135	61.8
7320	Consumer Credit Agencies/ Collections	63,981	72,672	8,691	13.6
7330	Mailing, Reproduction, and Stenographic	91,862	189,445	97,583	106.2
7340	Building Services	378,053	604,890	226,837	60.0
7350	News Syndicates	6,160	7,492	1,332	21.6
7360	Personnel Supply Services	355,452	862,863	507,411	142.8
7370	Computing and Data Processing	147,999	513,274	365,275	246.8
7391	R&D Labs	68,590	141,569	72,979	106.4
7392	Management/Consulting/ Public Relations	177,106	510,980	333,874	188.5
7393	Detective Agcy./Protective Services	248,206	412,373	164,167	66.1
7394	Equipment Rental/Lease	76,183	218,342	142,159	186.6
7395	Photofinishing Labs	53,924	75,365	21,441	39.8
7396	Trading Stamp Services	1,378	1,134	−244	−17.7

TABLE 6.4 (continued)

Employment Growth — Producer Services

SIC	Sector	1974 Employ- ment	1985 Employ- ment	Change	Percent Change
7397	Commercial Testing Laboratories	25,076	42,902	17,826	71.1
7399	Business Services nec	210,561	368,118	157,557	74.8
8100	Legal Services	317,669	683,721	366,052	115.2
8600	Membership Organizations	996,828	1,547,022	550,194	55.2
8910	Engineering/Architectural	343,124	672,958	329,834	96.1
8920	Noncommercial Education/ Research Org.	46,824	70,220	23,396	50.0
8930	Accounting/Auditing	191,446	404,861	213,415	111.5
8990	Other Services nec	14,036	144,255	130,219	927.8
899	Services Adm./Aux.	125,755	241,880	116,125	92.3
	Total	10,565,932	16,937,122	6,371,190	60.2

Note: Adm./Aux. refers to the administrative and auxiliary offices of firms in the referenced sector. For example, Mining Adm./Aux. would include the administrative and auxiliary offices of firms engaged in the mining business. The term "nec" refers to services "not elsewhere classified."

Source: *County Business Patterns* data tapes.

study examines producer services development processes and points to some challenges facing the global competitiveness of the American economy in the delivery of these services. In the following discussion, we touch on some of these recent findings.

A variety of explanations have been offered for the rapid growth of the producer services, including (1) the continuing division of labor, (2) externalization of functions, and (3) innovation in the types of services offered and technological change in the way services are performed, resulting in greater use of these services in the production process.

The division of labor argument stems from fundamental models of economic systems in which producers must make decisions about the scope of the firm (the range of functions to be contained within it) and the scale (size) of the firm. Scale is related to the structure of costs for components of the production process, in particular, their tendency to exhibit economies or diseconomies of scale. In the case of processes subject to economies of scale, it is visualized that firms would wish to exploit these scale economies to enlarge their market. Traditionally, however, the cost to consumers of purchasing from distant sellers has placed a constraint on this expansion process, leading to economist Adam Smith's famous dictum, "The division of labor is limited by the extent of the market." Hence, in many ways, the organization of production reflects the most profitable or least-cost outcomes as far as bundling together particular processes in specific firms (solving the problem of scope), given the market area served by these firms.

In some ways the externalization argument is a continuation of the preceding argument. Let us assume that a firm with internal accounting and legal services departments discovers that freestanding accounting and legal services firms would provide the same services at a lower cost. From a cost minimization perspective, the firm would lower its costs by externalizing the purchases of these services. According to this line of thought, as economic systems enlarge over time, producers are able to continue exploiting scale economies. Often this leads to basic reorganization of the scope of firms, with a different collection of functions internalized and a new division of labor. This pattern of change could lead to more specialized producers or to more generalized firms.

The arguments just presented do not explicitly incorporate the influence of changes in technology or changes in concepts of service products upon the process of externalization or the continuing division of labor. However, it is important to recognize that the technology used in service industry productive processes has been subject to considerable change in recent years. In particular, advances in telecommunications and information processing technologies have made it possible to engage in types of service functions not previously possible. This has allowed sellers to innovate in the range of services they offer and in the way in which they accomplish service industry work processes (for example, research a legal brief or prepare an accounting balance sheet). Scholars who focus on the influence of technological change upon service production processes and products argue that these innovations have allowed changes in the scale and scope of both producer service firms and the firms using their services.

Changing information processing and telecommunications technologies have strongly affected the market extension process in producer services. These advances have permitted the transmission of producer service work products to more distant clients at lower costs, through telephonic networks of all types, fax machines, and so on. At the same time, they have facilitated the reorganization of producer service firms into office networks, often in a national or international organizational structure. Reduced regulatory barriers have likewise facilitated this process of change. At present, these changes at the international scale may be having very important impacts on the American producer services sector. Subcontracting relationships are also made easier by new telecommunications and information processing technologies. Whether of an enduring nature or formed on an ad hoc project-by-project basis, flexible specialization processes analogous to those observed in many lines of manufacturing appear to be developing in producer services.

ASSESSING SOURCES OF PRODUCER SERVICES GROWTH

Each of the different processes just described could lead to relative growth of the producer services. If externalization of functions previously performed in-house has occurred on a massive scale, this could explain relatively rapid producer services growth. If the general growth of the economy has allowed specialization processes to lead to a larger freestanding producer services sector, this too could explain the observed rapid growth. If technical change has affected the inputs vital to the production processes of producer services, if firms in this part of the economy have changed their service offerings in response to the opportunities presented by technological innovation, and if purchasers of these services have responded with increased demand for these new service products, then this could also explain the relatively rapid growth of producer services.

Research has addressed these alternative explanations at both the macro scale and the micro scale (Guile and Quinn, 1988). At the macro scale, industry input-output data and data on the occupational structure of various industries have been used to evaluate the relative importance of externalization processes (Kutscher, 1988). Survey research has been more limited than macro analysis. However, the picture that has begun to emerge is as follows.

The producer services (and some other services) have become much more capital intensive in recent years, primarily as a result of adapting various telecommunications and information processing technologies. These technologies do not appear to have had a dramatic impact on productivity in the producer services as a group, in part because in the process of using these new technologies, producer service firms have changed what they offer customers (Kendrick, 1988). At the same time, these technologies have allowed more and more specialization—either to exploit scale economies via narrower ranges of functions (scope) or as new concepts of service functions have crystallized (Quinn, 1988). Falling transportation costs for both people and information have permitted the exploitation of more distant markets (Beyers and Alvine, 1985), and businesses in all parts of the economy appear to have chosen to use these services to a greater extent in the production process, effectively changing their business practices in the process. For example, external consultants are used more frequently to help in research design, advertising, financial management, market development, and so on (Quinn, 1988). Recent advances in telecommunications and information processing technologies have made it possible to decouple both the production and delivery of service work from centralized locations. Nevertheless, research suggests a strong continuing need for face-to-face contacts in the production and distribution process, supporting highly agglomerated spatial patterns (Beyers, 1989). Further development of telecommunications networks will probably lead to more "telework" in the future and assist in market extension processes, but producer services work will still have a strong human contact component.

Detailed statistical analyses of occupations prevalent in producer services firms have been carried out at the national level, in conjunction with analyses of changing demand structures in input-out models. This work, conducted by the Bureau of Labor Statistics (BLS), suggests that less than half of the growth of employment in the producer services is attributable to the overall growth of the gross national product (GNP). Also, changes in the structure of final consumer demand were found to have had a negligible impact on output of producer services. Employment in producer service occupations in manufacturing has increased simultaneously with growth in outside purchases of these services by manufacturers. This leads to the conclusion that changing business practices—specifically, a changing division of labor driven by a dynamic technological environment—have been a major factor in the expansion of the producer services in recent years (Table 6.5).

Regional Employment Trends in Producer Services

From a regional perspective, the U.S. economy has experienced quite different trends in employment change in recent years. Figure 6.1 shows

TABLE 6.5

Sources of Industry Output Growth, 1972–1985
(Average annual change, in percent)

| | | Output Change Explained by: | | |
| | | | Composition of | |
	Actual Change	GNP Growth	Final Demand	Business Practices
Producer Services	6.0	2.6	0.1	3.3
All Services	2.9	2.6	0.1	0.2

Source: R. E. Kutscher, "Growth of Services Employment in the United States," 1988.

FIGURE 6.1

Growth in Total Employment, 1974–1985

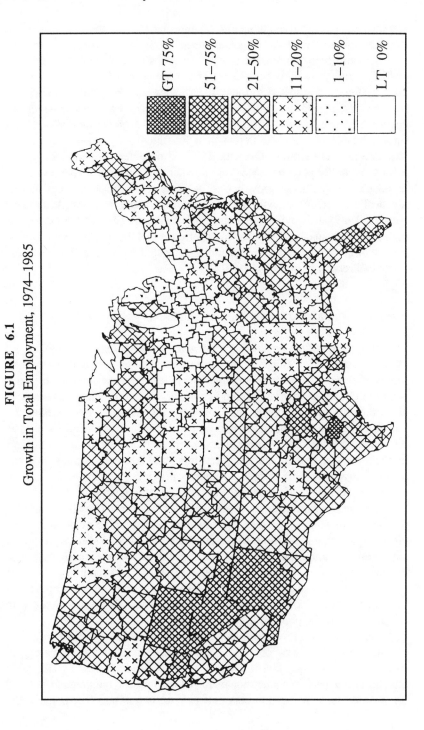

GT 75%

51–75%

21–50%

11–20%

1–10%

LT 0%

employment change over the 1974–85 time period for the 183 Bureau of Economic Analysis (BEA) economic areas. These are urban-focused regions with Standard Metropolitan Statistical Areas (SMSAs) as their core and non-SMSA territory as their periphery. The more than 3,000 counties in the United States are assigned to these 183 regions according to whether more people commuted to the central city in the BEA economic area in which the county is grouped than to an adjacent county. Although the time period used for Figure 6.1 is slightly different than for Table 6.1, trends in change in structure are very similar. Over the 1974–85 time period, national employment grew by 29 percent: SMSA employment growth was 30 percent while non-SMSA employment growth was 24 percent. Producer services had an identical 60 percent growth rate in both SMSA and non-SMSA territory (Beyers, 1989). It is evident in Figure 6.1 that many parts of the Northeast, upper Great Plains, and Appalachia experienced relatively slow employment growth or employment decline. In contrast, most of the West and much of the South had relatively rapid growth.

PRODUCER SERVICES LOCATIONAL TENDENCIES

The metropolitan locational tendencies of the producer services are clearly illustrated in Table 6.6, which presents location quotients for various producer services. Location quotients are index numbers showing the concentration of an activity in a region in comparison to a benchmark region. In Table 6.6, the metro (SMSA) and nonmetro (non-SMSA) territories of the United States are the regions of interest and the nation as a whole is used as the benchmark. An index greater than 1 suggests relatively higher concentration while an index less than 1 suggests industrial concentration less than the national average. This simple technique provides a convenient way of describing regional variations in the distribution of industries.

Metropolitan location quotients in 1974 were above 1 in almost all sectors shown in Table 6.6, indicating a relative concentration of producer services employment in metropolitan areas. However, several sectors do show a significant nonmetropolitan presence: banking, other credit agencies, insurance agents, consumer credit agencies, legal, and accounting. Most of these are producer services with mixed business, government, and household consumer markets, often supplied by small offices distributed broadly in accordance with the population of the country.

Concentration in metropolitan areas was still evident in 1985; nine out of ten producer services jobs were found in SMSAs, although in the aggregate only five out of six jobs (83 percent) were located in SMSAs. Still, Table 6.6 shows a general tendency for metropolitan location quotients to fall and for nonmetropolitan location quotients to rise. It was noted earlier that the overall employment growth rate in metropolitan and nonmetropolitan areas was the same in the producer services: 60 percent between 1974 and 1985. However, overall employment grew more slowly in nonmetropolitan areas than in metropolitan areas. Thus, the producer services represented a slightly larger share of total employment in nonmetropolitan areas in 1985 than in 1974. This in turn contributed to an increase in the magnitude of nonmetropolitan producer services location quotients. The result of this compositional effect was also to reduce slightly the magnitude of producer services location quotients in metropolitan territory, although for most sectors this change did not significantly diminish the pattern of metropolitan dominance. In addition to this underlying compositional effect, in a number of sectors, the nonmetropolitan location quotient rose more sharply, reflecting some deconcentration of activity from metropolitan areas.

To summarize, although the producer services as a whole are primarily located in SMSAs, several sectors are well represented in the economic structure of non-SMSA territory. These sectors include banking, credit agencies other than banks, insurance agents, real estate agents, membership organizations, legal services, and, to a lesser extent, accounting services. Most producer service sectors tended to become slightly less concentrated in SMSAs over the 1974–85 time period (Beyers, 1989).

The producer services are also unevenly distributed among BEA economic areas. Only about one-sixth of the BEA economic areas have a producer services employment share above the national average, and these places tend to be the locales of the nation's largest metropolitan areas. There was no aggregate change in the number of BEA economic areas with above-average employment shares in the producer services over the 1974–85 time period. Figure 6.2 shows location quotients for the BEA economic areas in 1985 and Figure 6.3 shows changes in location quotients between 1974 and 1985. Figure 6.2 shows the strong tendency of producer services to be differentially concentrated in the nation's largest cities while Figure 6.3 shows that there has been some tendency toward deconcentration of these sectors.

Even among the largest of places, some deconcentration has occurred. The following areas exhibited relatively slow growth in producer services employment (although they still experienced a 35 percent gain between 1974 and 1985): New York, Chicago, Cleveland, Detroit, Pittsburgh, Philadelphia, Milwaukee, Hartford, and Buffalo. In contrast, places with relatively rapid gains in producer services employment (collectively experiencing a 95 percent gain over the 1974–85 time period) included Los Angeles, Dallas–Fort Worth, San Francisco, Washington, D.C., Phoenix, Houston, Tampa–St. Petersburg, Anchorage, Atlanta, Orlando, San Diego, Denver, Boston, Seattle, Austin, Sacramento, and Miami.

The differences in the development experiences of the largest metropoli-

TABLE 6.6

U.S. Producer Services Location Quotients,
Metropolitan and Nonmetropolitan Territory
(1974 and change, 1974–85)

		1974 LQ		Change in LQ	
SIC	Sector Name	Metro	Nonmetro	Metro	Nonmetro
4700	Transportation Services	1.13	.37	–.02	.08
6000	Banking	1.0	.99	–.02	.10
6100	Other Credit Agencies	1.06	.73	.01	–.04
6200	Security/Commodity Brokers	1.19	.09	–.02	.07
6300	Insurance Carriers	1.15	.25	–.02	.06
6400	Insurance Agents	1.05	.77	–.01	.03
6500	Real Estate	1.10	.49	–.01	.04
7310	Advertising	1.17	.19	–.01	.01
7320	Consumer Credit Agencies/ Collections	1.05	.74	–.02	.08
7330	Mailing, Reproduction, and Stenographic	1.15	.27	–.01	.02
7340	Building Services	1.14	.34	–.02	.07
7350	News Syndicates	1.12	.03	–.05	.21
7360	Personnel Supply Services	1.17	.19	–.01	.00
7370	Computing/Data Processing	1.17	.16	–.01	.03
7391	R&D Labs	1.13	.35	–.02	.09
7392	Management/Consulting/ Public Relations	1.16	.23	–.02	.08
7393	Detective Agcy./Protective Services	1.18	.13	–.04	.13
7394	Equipment Rental/Lease	1.10	.50	–.04	.18
7395	Photofinishing Labs	1.12	.41	–.02	.08
7396	Trading Stamp Services	1.08	.59	–.12	.60
7397	Commercial Testing Laboratories	1.13	.39	–.06	.28
7399	Business Services nec	1.12	.41	.00	–.03
8100	Legal Services	1.06	.73	.02	–.11
8910	Engineering/Architectural	1.12	.42	.00	–.03
8920	Noncommercial Education/ Research Org.	1.13	.35	–.03	.00
8930	Accounting/Auditing	1.06	.71	–.02	.07
8990	Other Services nec	1.10	.51	–.04	.20
098	Primary Admin.	.80	1.95	.32	–1.58
149	Mining Admin.	1.01	.94	–.01	.03
179	Construction Admin.	1.18	.15	–.01	.02
399	Manufacturing Admin.	1.13	.38	.01	–.07

TABLE 6.6 **(Continued)**

U.S. Producer Services Location Quotients, Metropolitan and Nonmetropolitan Territory (1974 and change, 1974–85)

		1974 LQ		Change in LQ	
SIC	Sector Name	Metro	Nonmetro	Metro	Nonmetro
497	Transport./Commun./				
	Utilities Admin.	1.16	.20	–.02	.06
519	Wholesale Adm.	1.15	.26	–.04	.17
599	Retail Adm.	1.15	.27	–.01	.00
679	Finance, Insurance, Real				
	Estate Adm.	1.15	.26	.00	–.04
899	Services Adm.	1.14	.32	.01	–.09

Note: Adm. refers to the administrative offices of firms in the referenced sector. The term "nec" refers to services "not elsewhere classified."

Source: Computed from *County Business Patterns* data tapes.

tan places, as well as other BEA economic areas, can be partially explained by the fast or slow growth of key traded sectors in these regions, including manufacturing, agriculture, mining, government, and service industries. Other contributing factors include (1) differences in rates of growth of interregional trade in producer services destined for consumption in intermediate and final markets, (2) increases in demand for these services as inputs in the production process by businesses (as discussed earlier), and (3) increases in final demands for producer services by household consumers and governments (Beyers, 1989).

Over the 1974–85 time period, the large metropolitan places with slow growth in the producer services also experienced greater decline in manufacturing employment than the nation as a whole (a loss of 21 percent versus the national average loss of 4 percent). In contrast, the group of large metropolitan areas that had rapid growth in the producer services had employment growth of 21 percent in manufacturing. These data suggest that the overall growth rate of the producer services in particular BEA economic areas has been functionally related to the health of the local economic base. Input-output data on producer services markets help explain structural mechanisms leading to these differing regional experiences, as shown in Table 6.7. These data show that the producer services have a sectorally diversified market base. Some sectors, such as banking and legal services, are strongly oriented to final markets while others are primarily dependent upon intermediate mar-

FIGURE 6.2
Producer Services Location Quotients (LQs), 1985

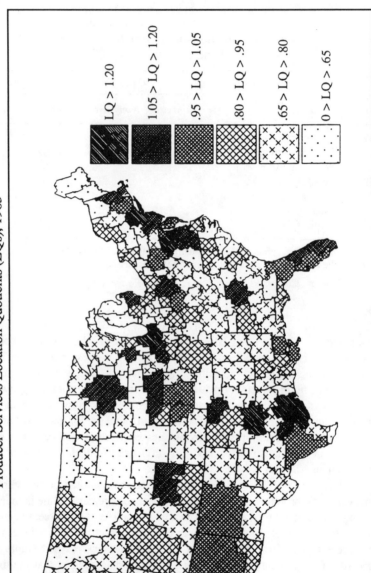

LQ > 1.20

1.05 > LQ > 1.20

.95 > LQ > 1.05

.80 > LQ > .95

.65 > LQ > .80

0 > LQ > .65

FIGURE 6.3

Change in Location Quotients (LQs), 1974–1985—Producer Services

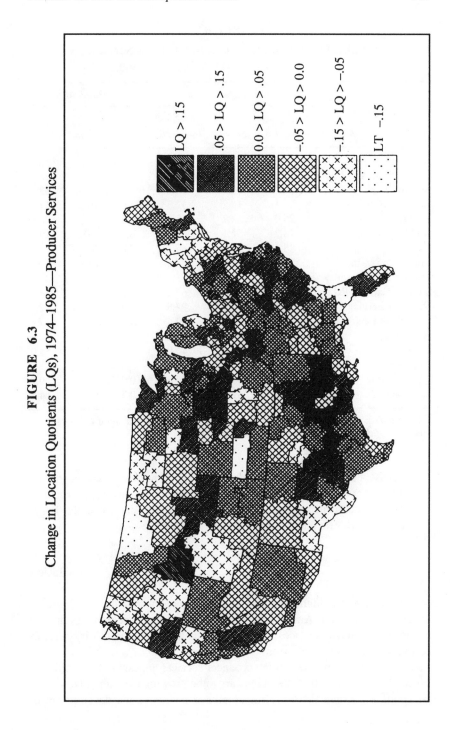

LQ > .15

.05 > LQ > .15

0.0 > LQ > .05

−.05 > LQ > 0.0

−.15 > LQ > −.05

LT −.15

TABLE 6.7

Market Orientation for Selected Producer Services,
U.S. Economy, 1977

| | Intermediate Sales | | | Final Sales | | |
	Extractive & Transform.	Service	Total Intermed.	PCE	Gvmt.	Total Final
Banking	18.6%	22.9%	41.5%	50.9%	7.2%	58.5%
Other Credit Agencies	11.7	12.9	24.6	75.3	0	75.4
Securities	9.2	37.4	46.6	43.8	8.6	53.4
Insurance Carriers	14.1	18.2	32.3	67.6	0.5	67.7
Real Estate	25.2	28.7	53.9	33.6	2.7	46.1
Building Services	28.2	52.1	80.3	8.9	10.6	19.7
Temporary Help	35.6	32.0	67.6	7.6	24.7	32.4
Computer Services	37.0	46.8	83.8	0.0	16.1	16.2
Management Consult./						
Pub. Relations, R&D	34.7	30.9	65.6	0.0	27.8	34.5
Detective Service	48.4	49.2	97.6	0.6	1.2	2.4
Equipment Rental	67.6	24.8	92.4	4.1	3.4	7.6
Advertising	49.6	47.6	97.2	0.1	2.7	2.8
Legal	13.3	30.7	44.0	46.6	7.9	56.0
Architecture/						
Engineering	82.6	7.7	90.3	0.0	1.7	9.8
Accounting	36.0	49.5	85.5	0.5	3.9	14.5

Source: U.S. Bureau of Economic Analysis, *The Detailed Input-Output Structure of the U.S. Economy, 1977*, 1984.

kets. These national input-output data provide important evidence of the strength of services markets for producer services output. This structural relation was confirmed in survey data developed for studies of the Puget Sound region (Beyers and Alvine, 1985).

Conclusion

This paper has highlighted the importance of the rapidly growing producer services in the American economy. What should regional policy be toward the producer services? In thinking about this question, it is useful to consider some key findings from recent research.

The traded component of the producer services appears to be significant, especially in larger cities, and it appears to be growing over time. New capital goods and organizational structures have facilitated the development of more specialized producer services able to tap more distant markets. The advent of modern telecommunications and information processing technologies, coupled with human creativity in the design and use of these technologies, has been critically important in this process. However, it is clear that even within given sectors, such as banking, in a given community there will be highly differentiated firms. Some firms focus primarily on local markets, others primarily on external markets, and some are split in their market focus. It was found that the growth rate of the producer services was either rapid or slow, reflecting growth or decline in the overall economic base and the degree of stimulation of local intermediate or final demands. The overall magnitude of this linkage has grown as there is greater proportional use of producer services.

It would appear as though regional development policy toward the producer services ought to embrace factors that would (1) help a region's economic base remain vital, (2) develop high-quality infrastructure in the telecommunications field, and (3) support the education and training system needed to provide workers with the skills needed in the more technical, professional, and managerially oriented economy that appears to be coming in this country. In addition, support for research that continues the evolution and development of information processing and telecommunications technologies, as well as support for the creative application of these technologies in industries in various communities, would appear to be high priorities. This would include assistance in marketing for small "niche" firms, allowing them to engage in the market extension process needed to take advantage of new possibilities for economies of scale in the provision of services. It would also include a clear recognition that while many regional economies are shifting in composition toward a greater service component, the vitality of the strongly traded goods-producing sectors is still critically important in the successful development of regional economies.

References

Beyers, W. B. *The Producer Services and Economic Development in the United States: The Last Decade.* Final Report prepared for the Economic Development Administration, Technical Assistance and Research Division. Washington, D.C.: U.S. Department of Commerce, 1989.

Beyers, W. B., and M. J. Alvine. "Export Services in Post Industrial Society." *Papers of the Regional Science Association* 57 (1985): 33–45.

Feketekuty, G. *International Trade in Services: An Overview and Blueprint for Negotiations.* Cambridge: Ballinger, 1988.

Guile, B., and J. B. Quinn, eds. *Technology in Services: Policies for Growth, Trade, and Employment.* Washington, D.C.: National Academy Press, 1988.

Kendrick, J. "Productivity in Services." In *Technology in Services: Policies for*

Growth, Trade, and Employment. Eds. B. R. Guile and J. B. Quinn. Washington, D.C.: National Academy Press, 1988.

Kutscher, R. E. "Growth of Services Employment in the United States." In *Technology in Services: Policies for Growth, Trade, and Employment.* Eds. B. R. Guile and J. B. Quinn. Washington, D.C.: National Academy Press, 1988.

Noyelle, T. J., and T. M. Stanback. *The Economic Transformation of American Cities.* Totowa, N. J.: Rowman & Allenheld, 1984.

Quinn, J. B. "Technology in Services: Past Myths and Future Challenges." In *Technology in Services: Policies for Growth, Trade, and Employment.* Eds. B. R. Guile and J. B. Quinn. Washington, D.C.: National Academy Press, 1988.

U.S. Bureau of Economic Analysis. *The Detailed Input-Output Structure of the U.S. Economy, 1977.* Washington, D.C.: U.S. Government Printing Office, 1984.

U.S. Department of Labor. *Projections 2000.* Bulletin 2302. Washington, D.C.: U.S. Government Printing Office, 1988.

TRUMAN A. HARTSHORN and PETER O. MULLER

7 *The Suburban Downtown and Urban Economic Development Today*

A recent survey by the American Institute of Architects indicated that the most profound impact on the built environment in the twenty-first century will come from the urbanization of the suburbs.[1] Indeed, this process is already well under way. The suburban downtowns now evolving in all larger U.S. metropolitan areas promise to become even more comprehensive and specialized in terms of function and organization in the future. Increasingly, they will serve as the focal points of the metropolitan landscape. As has been the case with planned residential communities, which typically outperform their competition in terms of build-out rates and value, these suburban centers are likely to emerge as the strongest retail and office centers in metropolitan areas, but as yet we have only a weak understanding of their function and impact—not to mention the policy issues that must also be addressed.

Transportation as City Shaper

The classic models of urban structure, such as the ring, sector, and multiple nuclei conceptualizations,[2] emphasize the primary role of the central business district (CBD) as the commercial center of the city. These models reflect the form of the city shaped by the rail and streetcar technology of the late nineteenth and early twentieth centuries. The compact, pedestrian-oriented, high-rise form of the CBD reflects this historical circumstance that resulted in a premium placed on front footage. Today we know that these

147

models no longer work to explain metropolitan growth and change, but we do not yet have adequate replacements.

The automobile and associated highway-based transportation improvements following World War II dramatically changed accessibility patterns within U.S. metropolitan areas. The decline of the downtown area's monopoly on location is perhaps the most significant development, in urban form, that has occurred in the twentieth century. We now hear observers talking about the decline or even the end of location as an important factor in community development as the automobile and arterial highway offer relatively uniform accessibility in all directions.[3] We not only have multiple choices in choosing among metropolitan areas for business locations, including the corporate headquarters decision, but also multiple choices within metropolitan areas as the transportation infrastructure to service high-order commercial development becomes more ubiquitous.

Indeed, commercial activity intensified in suburban areas as developers seized the opportunity to take advantage of the transportation accessibility offered by key intersections of radial arteries and circumferential highways. At these sites, suburban downtowns have emerged over the past two decades that now rival and even outperform their center-city antecedents in terms of office space, retail sales, and even hotel/entertainment facilities. Just as high-rise office buildings gave the CBD a dramatic skyline identity earlier in this century, the postmodern corporate trophy architecture emerging in the suburbs is helping to define today's outlying centers.

We now have what Vance has called *urban realms*[4] evolving around each of these major suburban centers (Figure 7.1). Each realm, including the CBD, has its own role in the metropolitan economy, but none is dominant nor necessarily destructive to the others. Each has its own market niche. The CBD, for example, has increasingly become a government office center, a hotel/convention district, and the commercial hub for in-town residents in a growing number of cities. At the same time, the suburban downtown can be thought of as the transaction center for the postindustrial metropolis. It is where corporate and yuppie America increasingly works, shops, and lives.

The office has become the factory of the information age and the primary anchor of the suburban downtown. Among the most widely heralded suburban downtowns in America today, one must include Tyson's Corner near the Washington, D.C., beltway in Fairfax County, Virginia; South Coast Metro in Orange County, California; Schaumburg in the suburban Chicago market; Perimeter Center on Atlanta's north side; and City Post Oak in Houston. Each of these centers claims a large professional office employment base and noteworthy regional malls. In addition, several other downtowns with similar business mixes are also evolving in these and other major metropolitan areas.

FIGURE 7.1

Urban Realms in Relation to Metropolitan Downtown
in the Polycentric Metropolis

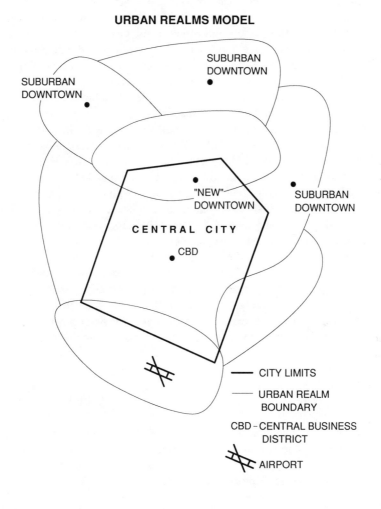

URBAN REALMS MODEL

Source: Hartshorn and Muller, 1989.

Not all suburban downtowns claim the same roles. Back-office functions dominate in some centers, high-technology research and development (R&D) activity prevails in others, and other types of commercial or producer services are found in yet another group. The New Jersey waterfront across the Hudson River from Manhattan provides a dramatic example of an emerging concentration of back-office activity. The sleek new office towers that are supplanting derelict manufacturing sites in that area attract the routine computer-based operations of Wall Street firms relocating from Manhattan. These buildings offer larger floor plans in comparison to the older cramped facilities in the Wall Street financial district, as well as good accessibility to the suburban New Jersey residential/commercial market.

Major metropolitan areas support multiple downtowns because of the growing demand for retail and office space that cannot be confined to a single or a few locations in a rapidly evolving consumer society. Greater affluence and buyer discrimination demand that the retail market become more highly differentiated in terms of market niches. Several levels of this retail activity are now housed in the suburban downtown in addition to the regional mall. In the Cumberland-Galleria downtown in greater Atlanta, for example, five retail market segments exist: (1) Cumberland Mall regional shopping center, (2) The Galleria specialty mall, (3) Akers Mill mass goods shopping center anchored by a K-Mart and Mervyns, (4) a festival marketplace, and (5) a major arterial highway strip dominated by automobile dealerships.

Office functions have also multiplied in these centers. William B. Beyers's article in this volume (chapter 6) analyzes the dramatic growth of the producer services market, an important segment of the commercial market housed in these centers. In addition, a growing hotel function and restaurant assemblages serve the needs of both the business and residential communities.

Definitions and Criteria

When a new phenomenon emerges, professionals often have a difficult time agreeing on the appropriate appellation. In this instance, a plethora of terms have been suggested to identify the activity, but no consensus has emerged among the descriptors, which include:

- nucleation
- megacenter
- minicity
- suburban activity center
- urban subcenter
- suburban business district (SBD)

- suburban employment center (SEC)
- urban core
- urban village
- edge city

The last of the terms in the list, *edge city*, was coined by geographic journalist Joel Garreau,[5] writer with the *Washington Post*. An intriguing adaptation of this thinking has been used to classify growth along the I-78 corridor westward from the Newark International Airport to Allentown-Bethlehem, Pennsylvania. That area has been described as the last major urban development frontier in the Northeast in the twentieth century.[6] No fewer than five edge cities are emerging in that corridor. Brief mention of the *urban village* concept is also warranted.[7] That term, which has been used to describe and guide growth in emerging nucleations in Phoenix and elsewhere, is a misnomer in that it misrepresents "the geographical and the truly high order of economic function characteristic of these suburban cores."[8]

The reference here is to the highest order of these centers, those with the largest employment concentrations and the best-developed market areas. That is why they should be thought of as downtowns and why most of the terms listed above do not apply. Our definition of these downtowns therefore includes several minimal criteria:

1. A regional shopping center of 1 million square feet;
2. Three or more high-rise office buildings housing at least one Fortune 1,000 corporate headquarters or regional headquarters;
3. Office space of 5 million or more square feet;
4. Two or more major chain hotels with four hundred or more rooms each; and
5. An employment base of 50,000 or more.

Toward a Process Model of Development

In thinking through the process of change that has restructured metropolitan form in the forty-five years since World War II, the authors developed a five-stage descriptive model of suburban economic-spatial development.[9] This model is built on the work of Erickson and Baerwald,[10] as well as others who also have undertaken longitudinal studies of the suburban space-economy. The five stages of development that we identified were the following:

- Stage 1 Bedroom community
- Stage 2 Independence

- Stage 3   Catalytic growth
- Stage 4   High-rise/high-technology
- Stage 5   Mature town center

The *bedroom community* stage evolved in many suburban areas after World War II as the pent-up demand for housing, the availability of plentiful financing for single-family housing construction, and greater dependence on the automobile converged to create a tremendous building boom. In areas noted for early adaptations to the automobile, such as Los Angeles, considerable suburban residential expansion occurred before the war. A popular, if dated, mind-set is that single-family housing still provides the sole raison d'être for suburbs, but as subsequent stages of growth unfolded, housing became one of the many functions of the suburban landscape.

By the middle 1950s, high-order retailing came to the suburbs in the form of the regional mall. The office park and freeway-oriented industrial park also evolved in this period. No longer did the suburbanite depend solely on the central city for employment, as jobs generated *independence* for the area.

As growth continued into the 1960s and 1970s, the housing market matured in these areas in terms of both variety and price and commercial investments multiplied. This *catalytic growth* stage typically involved both diversification and intensification of land-use activity. The hotels and restaurant market came of age at that time, as did the midrise office function.

The rapid growth of the postindustrial service economy in the 1980s spawned yet another phase of growth in the *high-rise/high-technology* stage of development. The high-rise office tower accommodated the growing middle and upper-middle management functions associated with corporate headquarters expansion. High-technology R&D activity also discovered corridors leading to and from these emerging downtowns during the decade.

In the most robust of these downtowns, such as Reston in Virginia, South Coast Metro in Orange County, Las Colinas in Dallas, and others, we have now entered a fifth *mature town center* phase of growth as cultural, social, and recreation activities find their proper niche in these markets. The future will likely bring more changes, including a maturing of the political/governmental function, but overall, the future city is here—the polycentric metropolis.

Policy Issues

Despite their diversity and newness, suburban downtowns face an uncertain future because of a lack of understanding of their role and significance. The public generally finds these centers both exciting and practical, hence, their rapid acceptance. Problems arise, however, as development of infrastructure, particularly transportation systems, fails to keep pace.[11] Local government fiscal problems, a mismatch in housing affordability that requires many workers to commute long distances, and density issues compound the infrastructure shortcomings and have contributed to the increasing clamor for growth controls in these areas, especially in California.

To manage and provide for quality future growth in these centers, we need to be more sensitive to the policy issues facing these areas today. It must be recognized at the outset that many exist in a political limbo. Often they have grown up in unincorporated suburban areas without the benefit of coordinated local government guidance. Often positioned astride local political boundaries, such as county lines or magisterial districts, many of these downtowns possess no identifiable political constituency that could help resolve problems such as traffic congestion. These areas often face an identity crisis, to the extent that some even lack a separately identifiable postal address, as is the case with Tyson's Corner outside Washington, D.C., and Perimeter Center in Atlanta.

Transportation Mismatch

In the future, the unique and complex transportation needs of these areas will require special attention. While many middle and upper-level management personnel working in these centers live in adjacent residential communities and have relatively short work trips, a growing share of workers must travel long distances to these centers. At least three groups of workers face long-distance commuting:

1. Skilled workers living in other suburban locations;
2. Inner-city lesser-skilled clerical and blue-collar workers; and
3. Lesser-skilled clerical and blue-collar workers living on the rural fringe.

We will now consider the needs of each of these commuter flows.

The *crosstown suburb-to-suburb commuting flow* via beltways and arterials experiences the most congestion of any work-trip type of our cities today. The growing trends toward dual career households and higher job turnover rates among professionals continue to cause the trip to lengthen, but highway capacity increases have not kept pace in the suburbs. Now that the federal role in highway construction has diminished, responsibility has increasingly shifted to local areas, but typically neither the fiscal capacity nor the political will exist to fill the breach. To overcome this vacuum, privatization has grown rapidly in the form of impact fees and other exactions levied on new developments by local governments to finance new highway capacity.

Community Improvements Districts (CIDs) offer another source of local funding. In this instance, property owners agree to tax themselves to pay off bonds issued to fund transportation improvements. Developers increasingly recognize that improved access will permit increased density in their projects, and they are ready to become more involved in financing these improvements in the future. Toll roads, such as the North Dallas Tollway or the Georgia 400-Extension now under construction in Atlanta, provide yet another financing alternative certain to grow in popularity in the future.

Another transportation strategy worthy of increased attention involves better management of the existing capacity. Local traffic management associations, for example, seek to obtain better performance from the existing street system through trip reduction programs such as car-pool and van-pool programs. Today there are only about one hundred such associations nationwide, but the number is growing rapidly, particularly in California, where growth control issues have created the greatest need for action.[12] It is likely that these organizations will evolve into comprehensive administrative organizations in the future, essentially retaining their identity as private rather than public agencies. Indeed, many already provide day-care services, parking, and other management functions.

Inner-city lesser-skilled clerical and blue-collar workers face a difficult *reverse-trip commute* to suburban downtowns. Bus transit service itself is typically poor to suburban downtowns from central city locations, but many such trips must be made by transit due to the lack of an automobile. Moreover, this trip type is the most rapidly growing metropolitan flow today. Initiatives are now being taken in many metropolitan areas to provide direct access for the inner-city disadvantaged workers to suburban employment centers using vans and buses due to the scarcity of public transit service. These programs are supported by a mix of public and private funds as well as by the fare box. In some cases, tenant associations of public housing projects operate and manage these systems.[13]

The other lesser-skilled work-trip flow, referred to as an *extended commute*, occurs from the rural fringe. This flow of rural workers occurs by automobile, often a car pool, from an area not previously incorporated within the metropolitan labor market. Laborers from rural West Virginia, for example, are now within commuting distance of suburban Loudoun County, Virginia, and the mushrooming commercial development in the vicinity of Dulles Airport in metropolitan Washington, D.C.

Housing Mismatch

These suburban centers now possess well-defined labor markets and trade areas. Case studies reveal that the most successful of these downtowns are located on the high-income sides of the metropolitan area—to the west in the case of Houston, to the north in Atlanta, and to the south-southwest in the case of Denver.[14] In fact, these centers grew in these locations because corporate decision makers lived there and could minimize commuting time, have easy access to sporting and golf clubs, and enjoy other life-style amenities.

As these centers grew, the demand for blue-collar service, construction, and clerical jobs mushroomed along with the rest, but moderate-cost housing opportunities in the vicinity of the new jobs were conspicuously absent for this segment of the labor force. Their work-trip problems have been discussed above.

Housing density must increase in these areas in the future to combat rising costs and help alleviate housing and transportation mismatches. Increased densities not only help contain sprawl but also tend to accommodate a wider range of household incomes. Higher residential densities decrease work-trip lengths and help build the critical mass necessary for a secondary mode of transportation in and around the downtown area, such as an automated light rail system. Density also imparts prestige and urbanity when handled properly. Taken together, these factors promote a better balance of housing and jobs.

What we need in the future is visionary growth management that promotes the mixing of uses and balanced development. Housing and employment must be more carefully linked, as they are already in California.

Visions for the Future

Suburban downtowns have been very successful in reshaping urban form and in providing skilled jobs commensurate with the ongoing transition to an information-based service economy. Each metropolitan area seems to be experiencing similar stages in the emergence of these centers. There is, however, ample latitude in this development process for centers in each area to reflect the character of their local economy—energy in the case of Houston, a national service economy in the case of Atlanta, and a diversified manufacturing, defense, and pharmaceutical base in the case of Philadelphia.

Despite their overwhelming success, these centers have magnified several mismatches in the metropolitan economy. The transportation mismatch has been addressed here, as has the jobs and housing mismatch experienced by the central city worker and, to a lesser degree, the clerical and blue-collar rural fringe resident.

Local development policies for suburban downtowners must remain flexible and amenable to increased densities as market forces dictate such land-use intensification. With property foresight, master plans for suburban centers should be able to accommodate expansion with minimal problems— provided that lead times can be sustained and public-private cooperation nurtured. Higher commercial densities and, to a lesser degree, higher residential densities are compatible with maintaining and enhancing quality-of-life opportunities in the suburbs. Performance standards for developments and land-use buffering will also be needed, along with more generous set-aside agreements for public open space. Similarly, more attention must be focused on future pedestrian needs in these areas. Indeed, the retrofitting now going on in existing centers has focused on this problem.

Negative reactions to ongoing suburban development have been most visible and forceful in areas that lack long-range master plans and are suffering severe infrastructure inadequacies, but as the situation in California amply demonstrates, growth does not stop when controls are imposed, although infrastructure improvements may well slow down. The control solution only leads to a larger problem. Indeed, agglomeration economies are continuing to gain strength in our larger urban areas.

Privatization, density, and the automobile will continue to be the controlling factors shaping suburban growth. The public is generally satisfied with the process and life-style associated with these developments, but the prospect of more growth management looms ever larger on the horizon.[15] So this is our challenge: to create progressive economic development policies and programs that will permit these business hubs and their metropolitan areas to continue to grow and evolve.

Notes

1. Olson and Kurent, 1988.
2. Harris and Ullman, 1945, pp. 7–17.
3. Shulman, 1989.
4. Vance, 1977.
5. Garreau, 1988, pp. 48–55.
6. Byrne, 1989.
7. Leinberger and Lockwood, 1986, pp. 43–52.
8. Muller, 1989.

9. The original four-stage model was reported in Hartshorn and Muller, 1986. See also Hartshorn and Muller, 1989.

10. Erickson, 1983; Baerwald, 1978.

11. An extended discussion of suburban mobility and the transportation crisis can be found in Cervero, 1986, 1989.

12. Association for Commuter Transportation, 1989.

13. Schmidt, 1989.

14. Hartshorn and Muller, 1989; Muller, 1989.

15. The state of Florida, for example, is now in the process of implementing a concurrency regulation requiring that new infrastructure capacity simultaneously accompany new development, and a 1989 Planning Act in Georgia now requires more local comprehensive planning.

References

Association for Commuter Transportation. *Transportation Management Association Directory.* Washington, D.C.: 1989.

Baerwald, T. J. "The Emergence of a New Downtown." *Geographical Review* 68 (1978): 308–318.

Byrne, T. E. "The Edge City as a Paradigm: Remodeling the I–78 Corridor." Monograph. New York: Solomon Brothers, September 1989.

Cervero, R. *America's Suburban Centers: The Land Use–Transportation Link.* London: Unwin Hyman, 1989.

———. *Suburban Gridlock.* New Brunswick: Rutgers University, Center for Urban Policy Research, 1986.

Erickson, R. A. "The Evolution of the Suburban Space Economy." *Urban Geography* 4 (1983): 95–121.

Garreau, J. "Edge Cities." *Landscape Architecture* (December 1988): 48–55.

Harris, C., and E. Ullman. "The Nature of Cities." *Annals of the American Academy of Political and Social Science* 242 (1945): 7–17.

Hartshorn, T. A., and P. O. Muller. "Suburban Business Centers: Employment Implications." Report to the U.S. Department of Commerce, Economic Development Administration, Project No. RED–808–G–84–5 (99–7–13616). Washington, D.C.: Economic Development Administration, 1986.

———. "Suburban Downtowns and the Transformation of Metropolitan Atlanta's Business Landscape." *Urban Geography* 10 (1989): 375–395.

Leinberger, C., and C. Lockwood. "How Business is Reshaping America." *The Atlantic* 258 (October 1986): 43–52.

Muller, P. O. "The Transformation of Bedroom Suburbia into the Outer City: An Overview of Metropolitan Structural Change Since 1947." In *Suburbia Reexamined.* Ed. B. M. Kelly. Contributions in Sociology, No. 78. New York: Greenwood Press, 1989.

Olson, R., and H. Kurent. *Trends Shaping Architecture's Future.* Study produced for the American Institute of Architects by the Institute for Alternative Futures, Alexandria, Va., 1988.

Schmidt, W. E. "Projects Link Inner Cities, Jobless to Suburban Work Opportunities." *New York Times* (October 25, 1989).

Shulman, D. "The End of Location." *Real Estate Report.* New York: Solomon Brothers, 1989.

Vance, J. E., Jr. *This Scene of Man: The Role and Structure of the City in the Geography of Western Civilization.* New York: Harper's College Press, 1977.

PART IV

Policy and Metropolitan Economic Development

RODNEY A. ERICKSON

8 Enterprise Zones: Lessons from the State Government Experience

Enterprise zones (EZs) have been a hotly debated economic development policy tool during the 1980s (Hall, 1982; Massey, 1982; Taylor, 1981).
The British geographer Peter Hall (1977) is generally credited with sowing
the seed for the idea whereby decayed urban "wastelands" would be opened
to the initiatives of private enterprise in the near absence of governmental
planning and regulation. In 1981, the Thatcher government in England
transformed the original concept into a somewhat different EZ policy in
which geographically targeted areas characterized by socioeconomic distress
and derelict land have been provided with publicly funded inducements to
attract and retain businesses. The espoused benefits of EZs have included the
new private investment that would be attracted, the jobs for zone residents

The author wishes to thank Susan W. Friedman and Richard E. McCluskey for
their collaboration and assistance in the completion of this research. Michael Savage,
Janice Knutson, and Robert Brever of the U.S. Department of Housing and Urban
Development provided assistance in data processing and acquisition. Dan Dabney of
the Economic Development Administration provided valuable comments on an earlier
draft of this paper. This chapter is based, in part, upon research by the author and
Susan W. Friedman previously published in *Environment and Planning C: Govern-
ment and Policy* (1990) © Pion, Ltd. and in *Enterprise Zones: New Directions in
Economic Development*, Roy E. Green, editor (1990), © Sage Publications, Inc.
Reprinting of selected tables and information by permission of Pion, Ltd. and Sage
Publications, Inc. Full citations to these publications appear in the references to this
chapter; see Erickson and Friedman, 1990a, 1990b, 1990c.

that would accompany the influx of capital, the taxes that would be paid as the zones redevelop, and the sense of neighborhood and community spirit that would be engendered in the revitalization process.

In the United States, the EZ concept was originally championed as an urban redevelopment tool by Stuart Butler (1979, 1980, 1981) of the conservative Heritage Foundation. Proposals for federal EZ legislation were introduced in the U.S. Congress early in the Reagan administration. The bills were essentially packages of tax incentives for businesses and residents to stabilize and improve economic and social conditions in geographically small zones of metropolitan areas. Despite bipartisan introduction and at least tacit support from both conservatives and liberals, the bills went nowhere in the atmosphere of fiscal crisis created by the burgeoning federal deficit.

The first federal EZ legislation was finally passed as Title VII (Enterprise Zone Development) of the Housing and Community Development Act of 1987 [Public Law 100–242]. This legislation authorized the Secretary of Housing and Urban Development (HUD) to designate not more than one hundred EZs across the nation. These zones were to be situated in the most distressed locations of metropolitan (and some nonmetropolitan) locations, although "redevelopment potential" of the areas was to be considered in the implementation phase. The Secretary of HUD and, in certain cases, the Secretary of Agriculture were authorized to waive departmental regulations, promote coordination between existing programs, and expedite consideration of requests for assistance within the zones. However, the legislation lacked any federal tax incentives for the zones, and HUD Secretary Jack Kemp suspended implementation of the legislation pending action on proposed new initiatives.

Despite the absence of any federal EZ program for much of the 1980s, state legislatures encountered much less opposition to EZs and pressed ahead with their own versions beginning in 1982. Currently, thirty-seven states and the District of Columbia have legislation or an executive order authorizing some form of EZs or related (geographically targeted) program. Because the EZ concept remains somewhat fuzzy in principle—let alone in its specific implementation—it is not surprising that a quick perusal of state programs reveals policy differences among the states. Once again, the states are serving as the "laboratories of democracy." The lessons that are emerging from the state experience should not be lost on the federal government, where legislative hearings and interest in the EZ approach continue.

The purpose of the research reviewed here was to examine the program structure and effectiveness of state government–designated EZs and to conduct a comparative analysis of EZs across those states with active programs.[1] The research examined similarities and differences in program thrusts, including legislative intent, designation criteria for zones, and the nature of incentives for business development. The study used data on EZs and their host communities in a large number of states. The analysis related business investment in the zones to state program structures and, where possible, to the local tax gains and losses related to EZ developments.

Critical Issues in State EZ Policies

Proponents of the EZ concept have argued that this geographically targeted development policy can produce positive effects in urban areas and neighborhoods suffering from social and economic distress (Butler, 1979; Kemp, 1982). It is significant that the concept was transformed in its implementation from its original, predominantly "free-enterprise" approach to one in which government actions and public subsidies have been given the central role. EZ supporters believe that modest tax and other incentives targeted to relatively small geographic areas will provide a sufficient catalyst for businesses to invest in such zones and that the small public costs required to turn the zones around will be more than recouped in future tax payments as the area is revitalized. Although most of the academic literature has argued against the assertions of EZ proponents, the concept continues to attract the attention of policymakers. Perhaps this interest stems from EZs' intriguing "enterprise" label, the targeted approach, the lack of much solid empirical evidence against EZs in past academic research, and a desire among state government officials to offer a set of development incentives competitive with other states that already have zones.

There has been considerable debate concerning the geographic dimensions of EZs, including the actual location of zones themselves (Sternlieb, 1981). It has been argued that very large zones may substantially dilute the limited public resources for incentives; as a result, there would be little observable change and the essential grass-roots support and initiative for revitalization would be lost (Butler, 1979, 1980). Others have argued that the designation of zones in the most severely depressed areas is a typically counterproductive "worst first" economic policy since such zones have an unlimited capacity to absorb resources without making the zones markedly more attractive (Gunther and Leathers, 1981).

Perhaps the most common debate has centered around the question of where new firms and investment in the zones would originate. Obviously, if zone investment comes from establishments that have relocated from other areas, then EZ programs foster a "zero-sum game" in which development is merely transferred from one area to another. In this case, the value of the EZ program would have to be based on the benefits of redistributing economic activities to other supposedly more distressed areas. Thus, the question of whether zone incentives attract new businesses, encourage existing ones to expand, or stave off closures or contractions is critically important.

Policy debate has also focused on the capacity of EZ incentives to measurably alter the costs of doing business in depressed areas (Dabney, 1989). A majority of academics believe that tax credits and incentives, particularly those aimed at reducing capital costs, fail to significantly influence business location decisions (Alexander Grant and Company, 1981; Davis and DiPasquale, 1982; Jacobs and Wasylenko, 1981; U.S. General Accounting Office, 1988; Witthans, 1984). Mier and Gelzer (1982) argue that this skepticism is especially relevant at the state level because state taxes constitute only a fraction of business operating costs. Some also fear that tax incentives could not only fail to achieve EZ program goals but might produce negative impacts by reducing local tax revenues available for public infrastructure and service provision (Hawkins, 1984; Sternlieb, 1981). Furthermore, tax incentives that favor corporate income and property tax relief at the expense of incentives to hire zone residents or disadvantaged labor may simply provide windfall profits for businesses without generating many new jobs.

Other critics of EZ programs have charged that the zones will be ineffective in generating manufacturing or other higher-paying jobs. They argue that many depressed areas have greater opportunities for redevelopment through nonmanufacturing activities, such as retailing, services, or distribution, and that policies should be focused on these opportunities, even though they may not generate jobs as highly paid as in manufacturing. For these nonmanufacturing activities, tax credits for new capital investment or the elimination of taxes on goods used in production processes may be of relatively little value.

There has also been concern regarding the balance of incentives for business and labor. Many state EZ programs are thought to be biased in favor of capital-intensive activities. Some analysts worry that large footloose branch facilities of major corporations may be attracted by EZ tax credits, that they may hire few zone area and disadvantaged residents, and that they would generally exploit the program to their own advantage at the expense of the local zone community (Jacobs and Wasylenko, 1981). Conversely, others, including Goldsmith (1982a, 1982b) and Humberger (1982), fear the development of sweatshops and labor deskilling in EZs, with a consequent reduction of living standards of zone area residents.

EZ policies often have direct costs in terms of subsidies provided, such as labor training costs or infrastructure improvements. They always have indirect costs in the form of taxes foregone for both state and (usually) local governments, as well as opportunity costs from unrealized alternative public investments. On the other hand, new investment may, at least in the longer run, contribute new sources of tax revenues that may overshadow the public expenditures or revenues foregone by state and local governments.

The Structures of State EZ Programs

State EZ programs do not vary greatly in their principal objectives. However, our contacts in late 1989 with EZ administrators representing thirty-nine programs in thirty-seven states[2] and the District of Columbia indicate that the legislative intent of the programs was not simply economic development. All are targeted programs requiring some distress measures for zone designation, and most indicate a concern for health, safety, and welfare in addition to economic development. Job creation is mentioned as a goal in more than half of the programs, and it is often linked either explicitly or implicitly to zone residents. Only a few of the program statements of intent mention neighborhood revitalization and community development as explicit goals of the EZ authorization. Another aim occasionally expressed is to promote a broadly based collaboration between government, business, labor, and community organizations.

DESIGNATION CRITERIA AND INCENTIVES

Despite their similar intents and the relative lack of controversy surrounding their implementation, the structures of state EZ programs vary enormously. From contacts with state EZ administrators, we determined whether or not a given program used any of seven typical zone designation criteria and twelve incentives (Table 8.1).

The seven designation criteria were unemployment measures, minimum and/or maximum population size limits for the zones, measures of population decline, a poverty-level measure, a measure based on median income, some accounting for the number of welfare recipients, and a measure of abandoned buildings or property tax arrearages.

The twelve incentives chosen included (1) five investment incentives (property tax credits, franchise tax credits, sales tax credits, investment tax credits, and other significant employer tax credits), (2) four labor incentives (a credit per job created; a selective hiring credit requiring either zone residence or some measure of poverty, unemployment, or disadvantage; a job training tax credit; and a tax credit for employees), and (3) three finance incentives (a linked investment fund, preferential treatment for Industrial Development Bond [IDB] allocation, and any refundable credits, that is, those allowing cash back if there is insufficient tax liability). We did not include separate categories for capital gains exemptions, depreciation allowances, and free ports since these are very atypical of the state programs.

We also gathered information from state EZ program managers on

TABLE 8.1
Criteria and Incentives for the State EZ Programs
(as of November 1989)

State	Unemployment	Min.–Max. Pop.	Pop. Decline	Poverty Level	Median Income	Welfare Assistance	Buildings	TOTAL	Property	Franchise	Sales	Investment	Other Employer	TOTAL	Job	Selective Hire	Training	Employee	TOTAL	Investment Fund	IDB Preference	Refunds	TOTAL
	Designation Criteria								Investment Credits						Labor Credits					Finance			
Alabama	I	–	I	I	I	I	–	10	–	x	x	x	–	3	Ch	Ch	x	–	2	–	–	–	0
Arizona	C	mi	–	C	–	–	C	4.5	–	–	–	–	–	0	–	x	–	–	1	–	–	–	0
Arkansas	I	–	–	I	–	I	–	6	–	–	x	–	–	1	x	Ch	–	–	1.5	–	x	–	1
California$_{(N)}$[a]	R	mi	–	R	R	–	C	11.5	–	–	x	x	–	2	–	x	–	x	2	x	x	–	2
California$_{(W)}$[a]	R	mi	–	R	R	–	C	11.5	–	–	x	x	–	2	–	x	–	–	1	–	x	–	2
Colorado	C	ma	–	–	C	–	–	3.5	L	–	x	x	–	2	x	–	–	–	1	x	–	x	1
Connecticut	C	–	–	C	–	C	–	3	x	–	x	–	x	3	x	Ch	x	–	2.5	–	–	–	1
Delaware[b]		–	–	–	–	–	–		L	L	–	x	x	2	x	–	x	–	1	–	–	–	0
District of Columbia[c]	C	–	C	C	C	–	C[d]	5	x	–	x	–	x	2	–	x	–	–	1	x	x	–	2
Florida[e]	I	–	–	I	I	I	I	10	L	–	–	x	x	3	–	x	–	–	1	–	L	–	0
Georgia	C	–	–	C	–	–	–	2	x	L	–	–	–	1	–	–	–	–	0	–	–	–	0
Hawaii	C	–	–	C	C	–	–	2	–	–	x	–	x	1	–	Ch	–	–	0.5	–	–	–	0
Illinois	C	–	C	C	C	–	–	4	L	–	–	x	x	3	Ch	x	–	–	1.5	–	x	–	1
Indiana	R	x	–	R	–	–	–	9	x	–	x	x	x	3	–	x	–	x	2	x	–	–	1
Kansas	C	ma	C	–	C	–	C	5.5	–	–	x	x	–	2	x	x	–	–	2	–	–	–	0

State	C1	C2	C3	C4	C5	C6	C7	C8	C9	C10	C11	C12	C13	C14	C15	C16	C17	C18	C19	C20	C21
Kentucky	0	–	–	–	0.5	–	Ch	–	2	x	–	–	L	6	C	–	C	–	C	R	–
Louisiana	0	–	–	–	1.5	–	Ch	x	1	–	–	x	–	3	–	C	C	–	–	C	–
Maryland	1	–	–	x	2	–	x	x	1	–	–	x	x	5	C	–	C	C	C	C	–
Michigan	0	–	–	–	0	–	–	–	3	x	–	–	x	6	–	–	R	–	–	R	–
Minnesota	1	x	–	–	1	–	–	x	2	–	–	x	x	5.5	C	–	C	C	–	C	mi
Missouri	2	x	–	x	3	–	x	x	3	x	x	x	x	10	C	–	R	–	–	R	x
Nevada	0	–	–	–	0.5	–	–	–	0	–	–	–	L	3	–	R	–	R	C	C	–
New Jersey	1	–	x	–	2	–	Ch	x	3	x	x	x	–	9	R	–	–	R	–	R	–
New York	2	–	x	x	2	–	x	x	3	x	x	x	L	10.5	–	C	–	–	R	R	mi
Ohio	0	–	–	–	2	–	x	–	2	x	–	–	L	8	C	–	C	–	C	C	x
Oklahoma	0	–	–	–	0	–	x	Ch	1	–	x	–	x	2	C	C	C	–	–	C	–
Oregon^f	0	–	–	–	0.5	–	–	–	1	–	–	–	–	–	–	–	–	–	–	–	–
Pennsylvania	2	–	x	x	0	–	–	x	0	x	–	–	x	4	–	–	I	C	C	C	–
Rhode Island	0	–	–	–	2	x	–	x	2	–	–	x	L	2	–	–	C	C	–	C	mi
Tennessee	0	–	x	x	1.5	–	–	–	1	–	–	x	–	5.5	C	–	C	C	C	C	–
Texas	2	–	–	–	0.5	–	Ch	x	1	–	x	–	L_g	6	C	–	C	–	–	R	–
Utah	0	–	x	x	2	–	Ch	x	0	–	–	x	L	4	–	–	R	–	–	C	mi
Vermont	2	–	x	–	2	–	x	Ch	2	x	–	x	L	5.5	–	–	C	–	C	C	–
Virginia	1	–	–	–	1	–	x	Ch	2	x	–	x	–	2	–	–	C	–	–	C	–
West Virginia	0	x	–	–	1	–	–	–	3	x	x	–	–	3	C	C	C	–	–	C	x
Wisconsin	1	–	–	–	1	–	x	x	–	–	–	–	–	6	–	–	C	–	–	C	–

Other Geographically Targeted Programs:

State	C1	C2	C3	C4	C5	C6	C7	C8	C9	C10	C11	C12	C13	C14	C15	C16	C17	C18	C19	C20	C21
Maine^h	(1)	–	–	(x)	(1)	–	–	(x)	0	–	–	–	–	7	C	C	C	–	–	C	x
Mississippi	1	–	–	x	1	–	–	x	1	–	–	x	–	4	–	–	–	–	–	x	–
South Carolina	0	–	–	–	1	–	–	x	0	–	–	–	–	4	–	–	–	–	–	C	–

167

TABLE 8.1 (Continued)

Criteria and Incentives for the State EZ Programs
(as of November 1989)

KEY

	Criteria		Incentives	Values for Totals
				For Criteria:
C	considered	Cn	a condition of another credit or of business eligibility	$C = 1$, $I = 2$, $R = 3$
I	part of an index			full pop. (x) = 3
R	required			mi or ma = 1.5
ma	just population maximum	L	local option	*For Incentives:*
mi	just population minimum			x = 1
				Cn = 0.5
				L = 0

Notes:

a $CA_{(N)}$ and $CA_{(W)}$ are California's Nolan and Waters EZ programs.

b   Specific "target areas" are identified in the legislation.

c   The initial three zones for the District of Columbia were specified in the legislation.

d   Specified as the lack of owner-occupied housing.

e   Zones can also qualify on the basis of the Community Conservation index and if they are eligible for an Urban Development Action Grant or a Community Development Block Grant, or if they are a Neighborhood Strategy Area.

f   Legislation in 1989 left designation requirements open.

g   Some franchise tax reduction is effective in 1991 for certain projects.

h   The Maine program has no tax credits. It uses job opportunity grants contingent upon the creation of new "quality jobs." There are also "flexible grants" allocated to zones for use in staff support, special projects, and so on.

Source: Erickson and Friedman (1990c).

issues of regulatory relief, marketing, and coordination with other programs. Although the basic EZ concept espouses a minimization of governmental controls, we found very little regulatory relief in practice. The regulatory relief that is used tends to be procedural rather than substantive. Most of the states reported that an effort had been made to coordinate the EZ program with other federal programs, such as Urban Development Action Grants (UDAG), Community Development Block Grants (CDBG), and various Economic Development Administration (EDA) initiatives. Although the majority of states reported some efforts to market the zones, most marketing was done at the local level, occasionally with some state assistance.

DIMENSIONS OF PROGRAM STRUCTURE

A number of statistical techniques were used to explore the dimensions of EZ program structure. Our basis for classification differs from some others (for example, Brintnall and Green, 1988) in that the aim is to provide a tool for assessing the economic effectiveness of particular program designs rather than to characterize management styles and implementation.

One dimension identified in the statistical analyses was a distinction between those programs that include a sizable number of designation criteria and program incentives and those that offer few of each. A significant correlation exists between the number of criteria and the number of incentives. Early experiments with multidimensional scaling also indicated that the programs could be ranked along a small-scale versus large-scale dimension.[3] States offering many incentives tend to pay more attention to the designation process, perhaps to limit public expenditure. One can also detect a regional breakdown in which most states from Appalachia, the Deep South, and some western states, as well as Oklahoma, Virginia, and Hawaii, fall into the small-scale category. Industrial states from the Northeast, some midwestern states, and the additional states of California and Florida tend to fall into the large-scale category.

The correlations linking the zone designation criteria with the incentives used point to two possible kinds of programs. The strongest correlations occurred between the use of a poverty-level criterion and the labor-oriented incentives of selective hiring and employee tax credits. The poverty criterion was also correlated with the criteria for unemployment and welfare assistance. In contrast, the population criterion was correlated with the financial incentives of an investment fund, refundable credits, and, to a somewhat lesser extent, investment tax credits.

These findings suggest that some programs are more targeted to disadvantaged workers and others are more concerned with encouraging investment and economic development. Further support for this distinction comes from principal components analyses for the criteria. We selected the three criteria of poverty, unemployment, and welfare assistance along with the incentives of selective hiring and employee tax credits as indicators of a social welfare orientation. Indicators for economic development included the population criterion along with the incentives of investment tax credits, investment funds, and refundable tax credits. These indicators were weighted according to whether the criteria are considered or required and whether selective hiring is a full incentive or just a condition of another incentive or of business eligibility. The raw scores for states were converted into percentiles for subsequent empirical analysis (Table 8.2). These dimensions do not divide the programs into two distinct groups because some programs can be characterized by both orientations.

Additional classifactory dimensions are derived from the literature on EZs. The original division between investment, labor, and finance incentives was used as the basis of a classification scheme to label the programs according to their economic orientation. In the third program dimension, each of the investment, labor, and finance incentives was weighted in terms of its size, the respective state tax burdens, and duplication with other state incentives, all of which vary considerably from state to state (Table 8.2). More than half of the states have more investment incentives than either of the other two types. Clear labor or finance orientations are much less common.

An additional dimension included in our typology is a categorization of programs on the basis of the number of active zones (Table 8.3). Programs that include much of the state, such as Louisiana, Kansas, and Arkansas, may well have very different impacts from programs that are effectively limited to one city, as in Michigan, Georgia, and Nevada. A grouping of these data demonstrated that more than half of the active programs had fewer than twenty zones.

One final aspect of program structure distinguishes between Pennsylvania's administratively authorized program and the others, which are all legislated programs. Because the Pennsylvania program was authorized by executive order and not legislation, it relies on the state's line agencies to coordinate, package, and target many preexisting state economic development incentives to EZ-designated areas.

Enterprise Zone Development and Comparative Policy Dimensions

Reported below are the results of an empirical analysis of zone effectiveness and policy dimensions based on a HUD survey of local EZ coordinators undertaken in two rounds during 1985 and 1987. The survey includes information on 357 EZs located in 186 communities across seventeen states. All of these states had operational EZ programs by 1984; the

TABLE 8.2

Economic Orientation of State EZ Incentives, November 1989
(arranged in descending order of number of incentives)

MISSOURI	*DISTRICT OF COLUMBIA*	*VERMONT*	*LOUISIANA*
I I I I I I	I I I I	—	I I
F F F F	F F F F	F F	—
L L L L L L	L L	L L L L	L L L
NEW YORK	*WISCONSIN*	*VIRGINIA*	*TENNESSEE*
I I I I I I I	I I I I I I	I I I I	I I
F F F F	F F	F F	—
L L L L	L L	L L	L L
CONNECTICUT	*COLORADO*	*ARKANSAS*	*PENNSYLVANIA*
I I I I I I I	I I I I	I I	—
F F	F F	F F	F F F F
L L L L L	L L	L L L	—
CALIFORNIA$_{(N)}$ ^{a}	*FLORIDA*	*TEXAS*	*HAWAII*
I I I I	I I I I I I	I I	I I
F F F F	—	F F F F	—
L L L L	L L	L	L
INDIANA	*KANSAS*	*DELAWARE*	*OREGON*
I I I I I I	I I I I	I I I I	I I
F F	—	—	—
L L L L	L L L L	L L	L
NEW JERSEY	*MARYLAND*	*MICHIGAN*	*ARIZONA*
I I I I I I	I I	I I I I I I	—
F F	F F	—	—
L L L L	L L L L	—	L L
ILLINOIS	*MINNESOTA*	*UTAH*	*GEORGIA*
I I I I I I	I I I I	I I	I I
F F	F F	—	—
L L L	L L	L L L L	—
ALABAMA	*OHIO*	*WEST VIRGINIA*	*OKLAHOMA*
I I I I I I	I I I I	I I I I	I I
—	—	—	—
L L L L	L L L L	L L	—
CALIFORNIA$_{(W)}$ ^{a}	*RHODE ISLAND*	*KENTUCKY*	*NEVADA*
I I I I	I I I I	I I I I	—
F F F F	—	—	—
L L	L L L L	L	L

Key: Type of Incentive — I = Investment; F = Finance; L = Labor

Notes: a. (N) and (W) represent California's Nolan and Waters programs, respectively.

Totals from Table 8.1 doubled to make whole numbers, i.e., each letter represents one-half incentive.

Source: Legislation, program information, and state EZ coordinators, 1989.

TABLE 8.3

Number of Active Enterprise Zones (November 1989)

| | | Number of Zones | | |
No Zones	1–4	5–19	20–74	> 75
Arizona	Maine	California$_{(N)}$[1]	Alabama	Arkansas
Hawaii	Michigan	California$_{(W)}$[1]	Delaware	Kansas
Rhode Island	Nevada	Colorado	Florida	Louisiana
West Virginia	Tennessee	Connecticut	Illinois	Ohio
	Vermont	Georgia	Missouri	
		Indiana	Oklahoma	
		Kentucky	Oregon	
		Maryland	Pennsylvania	
		Minnesota	Texas	
		New Jersey		
		New York		
		Utah		
		Virginia		
		Wisconsin		

[1]CA$_{(N)}$ and CA$_{(W)}$ represent California's Nolan and Waters EZ programs, respectively.

Source: Erickson and Friedman (1990c).

zones included in the survey had been operating for one to five years, with an average of two years at the time the local coordinators were surveyed. The data set includes baseline information on the host community and the EZ area, the business incentives offered by the community, indicators of new economic activity since EZ designation, and the business establishments making new investments (or reversing decisions to close or contract) in the zones. In addition, data on establishments investing in the EZs following designation were provided for 2,014 businesses.

Baseline descriptive statistics for the 186 communities in the survey indicate that both the host communities and the EZs suffered from significant social and economic distress (Table 8.4). The host communities are typically characterized by slow population growth or decline. The average host community had more than 19 percent of its families living in poverty in 1979, double the national average. The average of median family income levels among the host communities was 82 percent of the national average (U.S. Department of Commerce, Bureau of the Census, 1983a). Minority residents represented an average of 24.6 percent of the host community population in comparison to a 16.2 percent share of nonwhite persons in the nation in 1980 (U.S. Department of Commerce, Bureau of the Census, 1983b). However,

TABLE 8.4

Characteristics of Host Communities and
State-designated Enterprise Zones at Designation

Variable	Host Community			Enterprise Zone		
	Mean	*Median*	*n*	*Mean*	*Median*	*n*
Population (Thousands)	94.9	30.0	152	14.5	4.5	241
Population Change, 1970–80 (%)	6.8	4.8	140	–2.5	–1.7	110
Unemployment (%)	10.8	10.4	139	16.0	14.4	197
Median Family Income ($ Thousands)	16.4	15.7	139	11.5	11.5	168
Families in Poverty (%)	19.3	14.5	136	32.4	29.3	167
Minority (%)	24.6	20.0	142	44.3	45.0	175
Land Use						
Residential (%)	38.5	36.8	116	32.5	30.0	213
Commercial (%)	8.9	6.8	116	15.3	10.0	213
Industrial (%)	9.0	6.0	116	18.1	10.0	213
Open Space (%)	30.0	20.0	116	26.6	15.0	213
Other (%)	31.9	21.2	116	7.6	0.0	213
Number of Enterprise Zones (Excluding Louisiana)	1.5	1.0	169	NA	NA	NA

Source: Based upon HUD survey data as reported in Erickson and Friedman (1990a) and Erickson et al. (1989).

the typical EZ was substantially more distressed than the community in which it is located (see Table 8.4). While some communities have multiple zones—especially in Louisiana, which has hundreds of EZs—nearly 80 percent have only one zone (see Table 8.4).

The wide variation among zones is reflected in the substantial differences between the means and medians for some variables. In many cases, the median is more indicative of the typical zone or host community. The median size of EZs is less than two square miles with about 4,500 residents, with a land-use base more heavily oriented to commercial and industrial uses than the host community as a whole. The median number of business establishments was 105 and median employment was 2,000 at the time of zone designation.

INVESTMENT AND JOB CREATION IN THE ZONES

Our findings concerning the extent of zone development following designation indicate that the EZ programs were not the panacea for economic distress claimed by some proponents. However, notable improvements occurred in many zones. As often occurs with public intervention, there is a limited set of high performers and a multitude that have achieved far less success.

The typical zone experienced the additional investment of several new and expanding businesses, although, not unexpectedly, less success was registered in staving off planned closures and contractions.[4] These new investments resulted in a median of 175 and an average of 464 jobs gained per zone between the time of designation and survey response, a period of about two years on the average (Table 8.5).[5] Average new capital investment in the zones totaled nearly $23.4 million between the time of zone designation and the time of questionnaire completion. Median investment was significantly lower, at $4.5 million, providing evidence of the substantial role of a relatively few high-performance zones on average measures. More than 30 percent of the sixty-six zones for which baseline employment data were available experienced gross annual job growth rates after designation that were higher than estimated gross job changes in the national economy.[6]

The survey data indicate that there was an average of nearly nine new establishments formed, more than nine expansions of existing establishments, and less than two closures or contractions prevented. Once again, the median values are substantially lower. The investment-per-job figures indicate that apprehensions that EZs would lead to a labor-intensive sweatshop environment are not well founded, especially when one considers that expansion jobs and jobs saved—which together constitute a significant share of the EZ increase—generally require less capital per worker than jobs due to new establishments.[7] In addition, zone residents filled many of these new jobs; unemployed and low-income workers received lesser, although still significant, shares (see Table 8.5).

Firms investing in the zones were neither large businesses nor existing businesses previously located somewhere outside the EZ (see Table 8.5). The average increase was forty-six jobs per establishment with a median of ten. New firms (26.4 percent) and the expansions of existing establishments (54.8 percent) accounted for most of the new investment decisions. Branch facili-

TABLE 8.5

New Business Activity in Enterprise Zones after Designation

Variable	By Zone			By Establishment		
	Mean	Median	n	Mean	Median	n
New Establishments	8.6	3	141	NA	NA	NA
Expansions of Existing Establishments	9.3	3	134	NA	NA	NA
Closures Prevented	1.9	1	31	NA	NA	NA
New Hires	332.9	134	212	34.7	10	1,403
Jobs Saved	571.8	122	48	169.4	25	95
Total Jobs Created or Saved	463.9	175	213	46.0	10	1,403
Total Investment ($ Thousands)	23,446.3	4,500	203	3,491.9	145	1,711
Investment Per Job Created/Saved ($ Thousands)	105.9	25.9	196	83.3	17.6	1,403
Ratio of Real Property Investment to Total Investment	0.56	0.60	81	0.55	0.60	317
Ratio of Jobs Provided for Zone Residents to Total Jobs Created/Saved	0.61	0.68	31	NA	NA	NA
Ratio of Jobs Provided for Low-income Persons to Total Jobs Created/Saved	0.52	0.44	33	NA	NA	NA
Ratio of Jobs Provided for Unemployed Persons to Total Jobs Created/Saved	0.48	0.36	28	NA	NA	NA

Source: Based upon HUD survey data as reported in Erickson and Friedman (1990a) and Erickson et al. (1989).

ties made larger investments and hired more workers than others, but they were still relatively small employers and generated less than 8 percent of the investment decisions. Relocations represented only 9.1 percent of the investing establishments. Larger numbers of jobs were generally saved as a result of closures or contractions prevented, but they were far more infrequent than other types of investment decisions. Concerns that service businesses would flock to the zones were also not substantiated; manufacturing firms dominated the set of investing businesses, representing nearly 73 percent of all job gains. Judging by this extensive set of EZ performance data, some of the major fears of EZ opponents do not appear to be well founded.

A COMPARATIVE ANALYSIS OF STATE PROGRAM VARIABLES

In order to assess EZ program effectiveness across states, we constructed two variables: (1) the number of establishments per year in which firms made investments in the zones after designation and (2) the number of jobs created or saved per year by firms investing in the EZ following designation. Absolute rather than percentage changes were used because low baseline values in some small zones can falsely create the impression of dramatic growth; in addition, size effects are controlled with other variables in the analysis.

Changes in investment and jobs in the zones were related to seven state program variables that we were able to derive from our data.[8] The first variable used indicated whether or not the state has taken an active role in marketing the zone. The second variable was the absolute number of incentives offered by the state.[9] The third variable was a social welfare index based on designation criteria and labor-oriented incentives reflecting a program slanted toward improving poverty, unemployment, and welfare conditions. The fourth variable was an index of the number of zones designated per state. The fifth was the absolute number of criteria used in zone designation. The sixth variable indicated whether or not the EZ program was a legislated or administratively ordered one (the Pennsylvania variable). The seventh policy variable was the length of time between EZ designation and date of reported zone performance.

In addition to these state policy variables, a set of nine variables was derived to control for different EZ size and situation (local environment) conditions. These included the baseline residential population of the zone, the area size of the zone, whether or not the zone was located in a Sunbelt state, whether or not the zone was located in a Metropolitan Statistical Area (MSA), the EZ's baseline unemployment rate, its poverty level, its share of residents who are members of a minority group, the baseline share of the EZ's land area that was in industrial use, and the percentage employment change experienced in the MSA or the county (if a nonmetropolitan EZ) over the time period comparable to zone operation.

Based on correlation and multivariate statistical procedures, including ordinary and stepwise regression analysis, we have found that several state policy variables are directly related to EZ performance. On the basis of these analyses, it seems that EZs in states that designate a large number of zones do not perform as well as those in states that target a small number of areas. There is statistical evidence that a larger number of investment or job creation incentives in the EZ package is a positive inducement for firms to locate, expand, or retain operations in the zones. Thus, it may be that tax incentives—the principal form of inducements to invest in the zones—are a significant element in zone redevelopment when they are a substantial proportion of the firm's investment. In addition, the Pennsylvania approach was strongly associated with zone employment gains. This suggests that other states consider how this approach could be used in their situations to coordinate and target the financial and infrastructure resources of disparate state line agencies for EZ redevelopment. The social welfare variable proved to be an inconsistent policy variable. State help in marketing the zones may be a necessary—though it was certainly not a sufficient—condition for higher zone performance. Finally, the length of time the zone was operational bore no relationship to performance; in short, there are many older EZs in which little redevelopment has yet occurred.

Among the size and environmental situation control variables, there were also some interesting findings. Zone performance was not related to general regional economic conditions, casting doubt on some limited previous suggestions that EZ growth would only occur in healthier areawide economies (Jones et al., 1985). EZ growth was also positively related to zones with a prevailing industrial land-use character. Among the zone distress conditions, higher minority population share proved to be no impediment to zone investment and job gains, at least within the levels characteristic of the sample zones. Sunbelt EZs did not experience higher growth rates, again related to the lack of influence of general economic conditions. Indeed, the relatively better performance of the Frostbelt states may be a reflection of the larger-scale EZ programs and more aggressive approach that characterizes many of these non-Sunbelt states. Proponents of EZs for nonmetropolitan areas will find little in our results to support the use of zones in this setting.

HIGH-PERFORMANCE ZONES

As a follow-up to the statistical analysis reported above, we identified the twenty highest residual zones in both the investment analysis and the employment analysis. Eliminating overlap, this yielded a total of thirty-two high-performing zones. These so-called "high-performance zones" represented ones that had achieved much greater success with the EZ program than our analyses would have predicted; they were also widely spread across the states represented in the survey. From this group, we selected zones that averaged ten or more firms per year investing in the zone with 150 or more jobs created or saved per year. We were able to conduct telephone interviews with twenty-one local EZ coordinators represented in this subset of zones. The discussions revealed a clear pattern of four principal factors in success: (1) None of these zones could be described as "irretrievably derelict," (2) the EZ program enhanced the area's visibility and made a marginal, but definitely catalytic, contribution in conjunction with other development programs, (3) the zone incentive package was significant enough to attract the attention of businesses and focused on one or a few major incentives, and (4) strong local participation of both municipal and business interests contributed to success.

PROGRAM COSTS

Data concerning the public sector costs of the programs were very limited in the HUD survey. Information from four states (Illinois, Kentucky, Ohio, and Virginia) suggests that the local tax costs of the EZ program are quite small in relation to job gains and are in the general magnitude of costs noted in other case studies of state EZ programs (Rubin and Wilder, 1989).[10] Indeed, in most of the cases where data were available, it appears that the added local tax revenues derived from greater EZ investments were sufficient to offset the estimated tax losses. Some states have also targeted their CDBG funds to EZs. There were no data available concerning the costs of state incentives used in the study zones; however, the state policy tools typically used in EZ programs are generally considered to be relatively low-cost inducements.

Lessons from the State Enterprise Zone Experience

Overall, the results of our study indicate that many state-designated EZs have achieved notable successes in revitalizing economically distressed areas. While the exact causal role played by the EZ program remains open to question, considerable evidence—both quantitative and qualitative—suggests that in instances where higher investment and job gains have been recorded, EZs played a catalytic role. The local EZ coordinators surveyed generally believe that zone incentives alone play a limited part in revitalizing the EZs but that zone designation in conjunction with the incentives focuses public resources and business attention on the zones, thereby creating a favorable climate for economic development. Thus, it may be unrealistic to expect EZs—or any single incentive in and of itself—to have anything other than a marginal effect on business location; yet by giving a marginal competitive edge to the EZ, the policy can stimulate new business activity and job creation.

Many of the fears of EZ opponents regarding the types of development in the zones are not supported by analysis of the extensive HUD data set. Zone incentives are apparently not strong enough to induce any large-scale relocation of existing establishments into the zones; most zone gains came from expansions and new firm formations. Large establishments did not dominate the EZ changes nor do typical levels of investment per job suggest sweatshop industries. A widespread attraction of low-level service activities into the zones has not occurred. Indeed, the substantial role of manufacturing industry in zone investment and job creation suggests that EZs may want to consider plant expansions to take advantage of surplus labor and lower wage, land, and other costs in zone locations. Of particular note is the finding that zone area residents filled a majority of the new jobs and that unemployed and poverty-level persons also received significant shares.

Our comparative statistical analysis of investment and job gains indicates that EZ performance is significantly related to some program variables. We would argue that state EZ programs should (1) develop eligibility criteria that limit the number of zones to a relatively small and manageable set; (2) adopt a package of incentives broad enough to appeal to a wide range of business types, from which localities can showcase a few substantial incentives for businesses in targeted sectors; (3) tailor designation criteria to focus on distressed areas that are not beyond potential economic turnaround; and (4) explore the possibility of directing state-line agency activities to the zones in a more coordinated and targeted fashion. In general, states and localities do not appear to have expended much of their resources on their EZ programs, administering them largely through existing agencies.

Clearly, the states have experimented with a wide variety of different EZ program structures and there are lessons here for the federal government. The EZ approach cannot be a freestanding one; it must be part of a larger development package that involves the programs of several line agencies. The EZ incentives must be sufficiently attractive to achieve visibility for the area and the development package but not so large as to induce "pirating" of existing establishments from other areas or a depressed property market around the perimeter of the zones (Erickson and Syms, 1986). Identifying this balance point is not a trivial matter. Designating the one hundred most distressed areas as EZs, as intended by the 1987 federal EZ legislation, may well have resulted in designation of EZs that were beyond the capability of any program to revitalize. Similarly, there is little evidence to suggest that rural zones will achieve much success with an EZ program. Finally, any federal EZ program will be only as effective as the government is successful in enlisting the support and cooperation of a broad range of interests within local communities.

Notes

1. The original report of this research may be found in Erickson et al., 1989.

2. The State of California is unique in having two different EZ programs, each of which is named for its legislative sponsor.

3. Multidimensional scaling is a statistical technique used to identify dimensions that are "hidden" in data matrices, especially when scaled data are involved.

4. More detailed analysis and discussion of zone investment and job gains may be found in Erickson and Friedman (1990a) and Erickson et al. (1989).

5. Our findings concerning EZ effectiveness must be cautiously interpreted. The HUD data were reported by local EZ coordinators and, like any survey, are subject to potential inaccuracies. However, our many contacts with respondents led us to believe that considerable effort was made to provide accurate information. It must also be noted that our information covers EZ programs through either late 1985 or early 1987, when many zones were still relatively new. The most serious problem is that of attribution or causality, knowing which zone businesses made investments as a result of the EZ programs. Only a study of the motives of business managers could ever achieve unequivocal attribution, and such a study is, of course, impossible.

6. National gross employment growth rates during the time periods corresponding to zone operation were estimated by incorporating a closures and contractions factor derived from Birch (1979) to inflate net job change figures.

7. The HUD data for zones do not break out expansion jobs within the "new hires" category. However, data from the establishments section of the survey as reported below indicate that expanding establishments accounted for a majority of the new investment decisions reported for the zones.

8. Further detail concerning the definition and construction of state policy and control variables may be found in Erickson et al., 1989. See also, Erickson and Friedman (1990b) for a complete discussion of the results of the analysis.

9. Unfortunately, it proved to be impossible to derive a specific variable for tax incentives. The substantial interstate differences in tax structures were the principal reason precluding such a measure.

10. See Erickson and Friedman (1990a) for a more detailed discussion of program costs.

References

Alexander Grant and Company. *Analysis of Selected Investment Incentives and the Enterprise Zone Concept*. Final Report submitted to the Economic Development Administration. Chicago: Alexander Grant, 1981.

Birch, D. L. *The Job Generation Process*. Cambridge: MIT Program on Neighborhood and Regional Change, 1979.

Brintnall, M., and R. Green. "Comparing State Enterprise Zone Programs: Variations in Structure and Coverage." *Economic Development Quarterly* 2 (February 1988): 50–68.

Butler, S. *Enterprise Zones: A Solution to the Urban Crisis?* Washington, D.C.: Heritage Foundation, 1979.

_____. *Enterprise Zones: Greenlining the Inner Cities*. New York: Universe Books, 1981.

_____. *Enterprise Zones in the Inner City*. Washington, D.C.: Heritage Foundation, 1980.

Dabney, D. Y. "Enterprise Zones and Their Relationship to Business Location Decisions." Ph.D. dissertation. Department of Economics, University of Texas at Austin, 1989.

Davis, O., and D. DiPasquale. "Enterprise Zones: New Deal, Old Deal, or No Deal?" *Cato Journal* 2 (Fall 1982): 391–406.

Erickson, R. A., and S. W. Friedman. "Enterprise Zones I: Investment and Job Creation of State Government Programs in the United States." *Environment and Planning C: Government and Policy* 8 (August, 1990a): 251–267.

_____. "Enterprise Zones II: A Comparative Analysis of Zone Performance and State Government Policies." *Environment and Planning C: Government and Policy* 8 (November 1990b): 363–378.

_____. "Comparative Dimensions of State Enterprise Zone Policies." In *Enterprise Zones: New Directions in Economic Development*. Ed. R. E. Green. Newbury Park, Calif.: Sage Publications, 1990c.

Erickson, R. A., and P. M. Syms. "The Effects of Enterprise Zones on Local Property Markets." *Regional Studies* 20 (February 1986): 1–14.

Erickson, R. A., S. W. Friedman, and R. E. McCluskey. *Enterprise Zones: An Evaluation of State Government Policies*. Final report prepared for the U.S. Department of Commerce, Economic Development Administration. Washington, D.C.: U.S. Government Printing Office, 1989.

Goldsmith, W. "Bringing the Third World Home." *Working Papers for a New Society* 9 (March–April 1982a): 25–30.

_____. "Enterprise Zones: If They Work We're in Trouble." *International Journal of Urban and Regional Research* 6 (September 1982b): 435–442.

Gunther, W., and C. G. Leathers. "Urban Enterprise Zones: Can They Work in the United States?" *Texas Business Review* 55 (July–August 1981): 149–151.

Hall, P. "Enterprise Zones: A Justification." *International Journal of Urban and Regional Research* 6 (September 1982): 416–421.

_____. "Green Fields and Grey Areas." In *Proceedings of the Royal Town Planning Institute Annual Conference*. London: Royal Town Planning Institute, 1977.

Hawkins, B. "The Impact of the Enterprise Zone on Urban Areas." *Growth and Change* 15 (January 1984): 35–40.

Humberger, E. "The Enterprise Zone Fallacy." *Rain* 8 (April 1982): 16–17.

Jacobs, S., and M. Wasylenko. "Government Policy to Stimulate Economic Development: Enterprise Zones." In *Financing State and Local Governments in the 1980's: Issues and Trends*. Eds. N. Walzer and D. L. Chicoine. Cambridge: Oelgeschlager, Gunn, and Hain, 1981.

Jones, S. A., A. R. Marshall, and G. E. Weisbrod. *Business Impacts of State Enterprise Zones*. Report prepared for the U.S. Small Business Administration. Cambridge: Cambridge Systematics, 1985.

Kemp, J. "A Case for Enterprise Zones." *Nation's Business* 70 (November 1982): 54–56.

Massey, D. "Enterprise Zones: A Political Issue." *International Journal of Urban and Regional Research* 6 (September 1982): 429–434.

Mier, R., and S. E. Gelzer. "State Enterprise Zones: The New Frontier?" *Urban Affairs Quarterly* 18 (September 1982): 39–52.

Rubin, B., and M. E. Wilder. "Urban Enterprise Zones: An Analysis of Employment Impacts and Fiscal Incentives." *Journal of the American Planning Association* 55 (Autumn 1989): 418–431.

Sternlieb, G. "Kemp-Garcia Act: An Initial Evaluation." In *New Tools for Economic Development: The Enterprise Zone, Development Bank, and RFC*. Eds. G. Sternlieb and D. Listokin. New Brunswick, NJ: Rutgers University, Center for Urban Policy Research, 1981.

Taylor, J. "The Politics of Enterprise Zones." *Public Administration* 59 (Winter 1981): 421–439.

U.S. Department of Commerce, Bureau of the Census. *1980 Census of Population: General Social and Economic Characteristics: U.S. Summary*. Washington, D.C.: U.S. Government Printing Office, 1983a.

_____. *1980 Census of Population: U.S. Summary*. Washington, D.C.: U.S. Government Printing Office, 1983b.

U.S. General Accounting Office. *Enterprise Zones: Lessons from the Maryland Experience*. Washington, D.C.: U.S. General Accounting Office, 1988.

Witthans, F. W. "Will Enterprise Zones Work?" *Journal of Small Business Management* 22 (July 1984): 9–17.

RICHARD FLORIDA and DONALD F. SMITH, JR.

9 Venture Capital's Role in Economic Development: An Empirical Analysis

Introduction

"Venture capital," "innovation," and "entrepreneurship"—these are the new buzzwords of economic development policymaking. The success stories of California's Silicon Valley and the Route 128 area around Boston contrast sharply with the alternate realities of plant closings, the decline of mass-production industry, and the social dislocation left in their wake. Today, our premier high-technology regions stand almost alone as models of economic renewal and growth. Indeed, the combination of economic restructuring and burgeoning interlocality competition for jobs and resources threatens to transform public intervention from economic development strategy into political imperative, regardless of applicability or merit. Given this context, it is not surprising that public policymakers and others concerned with the viability of this nation's cities, states, and regions have become enamored with venture capital's role in economic development.

Venture capital plays an important role in technological innovation and economic development. Venture capital has played a catalytic role in the formation of new technologies and, indeed, entirely new industries, with three-quarters of all investment going to high-technology sectors. The

Special thanks are due to Martin Kenney for his role in helping to formulate many of the issues dealt with in this research. We are grateful for the research assistance provided by an extremely capable group of graduate students: Hodjat Ghadimi, Mark Clark, and Elizabeth Sechoka.

revolutionary innovations of venture capital–backed start-ups, such as Fairchild, Intel, Digital Equipment Corporation, Apple Computer, Cray Computer, Sun Microsystems, and Genentech, have set in motion waves of industrial restructuring and economic renewal. Many of these "breakthrough" companies and technologies would not have been launched, nor attained commercial success so quickly, without the financial backing and managerial expertise of venture capitalists (Florida and Kenney, 1990).

For the purposes of this study, venture capital is defined as capital that is provided by institutional venture funds, including private venture capital limited partnerships and venture funds affiliated with banks, financial institutions, and large industrial corporations (Charles River Associates, 1976; Venture Economics, 1983; Wilson, 1985). This type of capital differs from other forms of finance capital in that institutionalized venture capitalists provide equity rather than debt financing and frequently take an active role in the management of the enterprises they finance (Bean et al., 1975; Bullock, 1983; Kozmetsky et al., 1985; U.S. Congress, 1984b). The venture capital pool increased more than sixfold during the 1980s, from less than $5 billion to more than $30 billion. The amount of venture capital invested annually also increased steadily during these years—from $1.1 billion in 1980 to $3.9 billion in 1987 (Venture Economics, *Venture Capital Journal*, various issues). Venture capital investments have typically outperformed more traditional financial investments, such as corporate stocks. According to a study done by Horseley Keogh and Associates (1986), the returns generated by venture capital funds during the mid-1980s were more than five times greater than the returns on corporate stocks that comprise the Standard and Poor 500.

This chapter summarizes a two-year research project on venture capital and economic development (Florida, Kenney, and Smith, 1990). The research addressed three questions. First, where is venture capital invested? Second, why is venture capital invested where it is? Third, what is the effect of venture capital on economic development—under what conditions does venture capital enhance the economic development potentials of particular areas? In order to answer these questions, the research developed a microlevel data base on venture capital investment. The data base was compiled from information reported in *Venture Capital Journal*[1] between January 1984 and December 1987, representing roughly 40 to 45 percent of all venture investments made during that period. The data base contains microlevel information on venture capital firms, venture capital investments, and the companies that received those investments. The data enabled us to undertake detailed analyses of venture capital investment (and coinvestment) flows at the metropolitan, state, and regional levels.

The research findings indicate that venture capital investments mainly flow to established high-technology centers, such as Silicon Valley and Route

128. While venture capitalists in these areas tend to invest locally, venture capitalists in New York and Chicago mainly export their capital to the established centers of high technology. These findings suggest that venture capital is relatively mobile and, furthermore, that venture capitalists are quite proficient in locating and channeling funds to investment opportunities where they exist. Thus, public policy measures that seek to stimulate high-tech economic development simply by overcoming regional "capital gaps" in the supply of venture capital are not likely to succeed, given the tendency of venture capital investment to flow toward areas with the highest potential return (for example, established concentrations of high-tech industry).

Venture Capital and High Technology: The Research Literature

The conventional wisdom assumes that the supply of venture capital is an important determinant of the ability of regions and metropolitan areas to generate high-technology economic development. This is reflected in public policy measures designed to stimulate high-tech development by increasing the local pool of venture capital. These policies are based on the rationale that the existence of imperfections or "gaps" in the supply of venture capital makes it difficult for certain cities and regions to generate high-tech development.

It has been difficult to assess this issue because research on the location of high-tech industry and the formation of high-tech centers neglects venture capital's role in the formation and functioning of such centers. Markusen and colleagues (1986) attribute the regional agglomeration of high-tech industry to a variety of attraction factors, such as research universities, access to air transport, presence of high-skilled labor, and so forth. However, their models do not include a venture capital variable. Others have suggested that a technological infrastructure comprised of high-tech businesses, universities, specialized labor pools, suppliers, vendors, and consultants is an important prerequisite for high-tech development (Dorfman, 1983; Malecki, 1987; Miller and Cote, 1985; Stohr, 1986; U.S. Office of Technology Assessment, 1984). Scott and Storper (1988) argue that high-tech regions represent new forms of "flexible production complexes" comprised of tightly linked groups of small and medium-size manufacturing firms, suggesting that the high transaction costs and information-intensive nature of high-tech activity require companies to locate close to one another and cooperate as a production complex. This research stream, though, also fails to take adequate account of venture capital's role in high-tech complexes.

The research literature on the economic development implications of venture capital is far less developed. Most of this research relies heavily on aggregate data that provide an inadequate picture of investment flows at the state or metropolitan level and from which it is hard to generalize findings. In addition, most of this work is hampered by a poor understanding of the industry itself, based upon anecdotes and secondhand stories.

The majority of this research focuses on the question of venture capital supply. This work indicates that venture capital is highly concentrated in just a few areas, notably New York, Chicago, Boston, and San Francisco, but for the most part, it does not provide answers as to why this is so. This literature shows little understanding of the differences among the venture capital centers (Leinbach and Amrhein, 1987; McNaughton and Green, 1986). Moreover, this literature suggests that venture capital has a stimulative effect on high-tech industry. This is partly true, at best. On the one hand, some high-tech centers, such as North Carolina's Research Triangle, have very little in the way of venture capital (being comprised mainly of high-tech branch plant operations; Luger, 1984). On the other hand, a number of venture capital centers, such as New York and Chicago, have generated very little in the way of high-tech development. Research by Florida and Kenney (1988a) indicates that venture capital supply is concentrated in three types of areas: those with high concentrations of financial institutions (for example, New York and Chicago), those with high concentrations of high-tech businesses (for example, Silicon Valley), and those with both (for example, the Boston Route 128 area).

The literature on venture capital investment is less extensive. Leinbach and Amrhein (1987) used aggregate data on venture capital investments for one year to analyze regional variations in venture capital investment. Based on this, they conclude that the Pacific Southwest, New England, and the Gulf Coast/Southwest regions attract the greatest volume of investment. Unfortunately, their analyses obscure many of the most interesting state- and metropolitan-level differences in the venture capital industry (see Florida and Kenney, 1988d, for a critique). While Leinbach and Amrhein (1987) allude to the regional mismatch of venture capital investment as evidence of regional "capital gaps" or "imperfections" in the market for ventural capital, they offer limited evidence to support this claim.

McNaughton and Green (1986) use Small Business Investment Companies (SBIC) investment data as a proxy for venture capital investment. However, SBICs are a relatively unimportant type of venture capital institution whose investment patterns differ markedly from those of the broader universe of venture capital institutions. While their conclusion that venture capitalists invest locally may be appropriate for SBICs, there is little reason to expect that it will hold for other types of venture capital institutions, such as limited partnerships. It is contradicted by recent research by Florida and Kenney (1988a) that shows an overall flow of venture capital toward major high-tech centers, such as Silicon Valley and Route 128.

Green (1987) uses venture capitalists' investment preferences (as published in Venture Economics' *Guide to Venture Capital*, various years) to derive a set of preference indicators from which he constructs a model of venture capital investment. This is problematic because the preferences reported by venture capitalists are not necessarily followed in practice—a fact the author acknowledges. An analysis of venture capital preferences leads Green (1987) to conclude that venture capitalists have no geographic preference beyond the entire United States. This analysis is directly contradicted by our findings, which show a distinct concentration of venture capital in Silicon Valley and Boston's Route 128.

Venture Capital Supply

Venture capital supply refers to both the geographic distribution of offices of venture capital funds and the dollar volume of resources available in a given place. In addition, venture capital supply refers only to venture capital funds that collect capital from other investors, who in turn invest those funds in firms. This aspect of supply is a key dimension of the venture capital process because it is the venture capital funds themselves that mobilize and distribute this form of finance capital. Previous research has examined the broad regional distribution of venture capital supply (McNaughton and Green, 1986; Leinbach and Amrhein, 1987). However, this work provides insufficient insight into patterns of supply at the state and metropolitan level.

Our research used two measures to examine venture capital supply: the dollar amount of venture capital and the number of venture capital fund offices in a given place. The first provides a measure of resource concentration and the second provides a measure of the number of potential investors. Both measures are adapted from data published in Venture Economics' *Venture Capital Journal* and other sources.

The national maps portrayed in Figure 9.1 show the pattern of venture capital supply as measured in terms of offices and resources. These figures indicate that venture capital supply exhibits a "bicoastal" pattern, with significant concentrations on the East and West coasts and lesser concentrations in the nation's interior. At the regional level, the Northeast and Pacific regions together account for 78 percent of all venture capital resources. While the proportion of resources jointly controlled by the Pacific and Northeast regions has remained fairly stable over the past decade, the Pacific region has increased its share of venture capital resources from 21 to 36 percent while the Northeast's share has fallen from 55 to 46 percent. The same pattern is evident in venture capital offices, with the Pacific increasing its

FIGURE 9.1

Venture Capital Offices, Resources

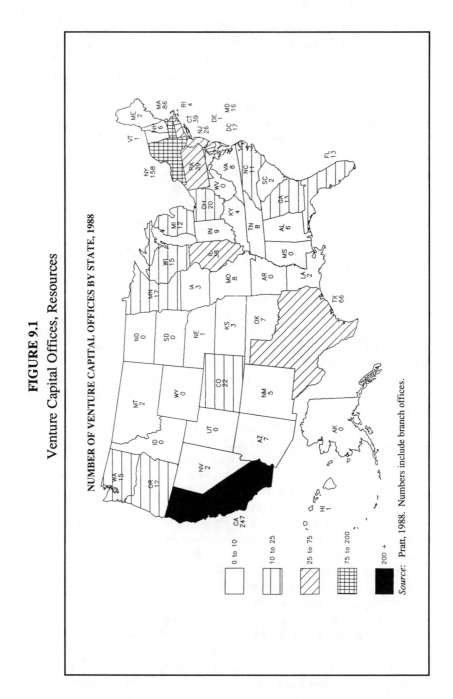

NUMBER OF VENTURE CAPITAL OFFICES BY STATE, 1988

0 to 10
10 to 25
25 to 75
75 to 200
200 +

Source: Pratt, 1988. Numbers include branch offices.

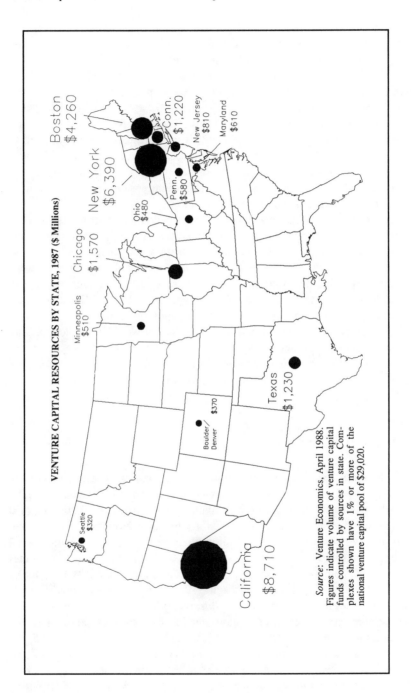

VENTURE CAPITAL RESOURCES BY STATE, 1987 ($ Millions)

Boston
$4,260

Conn.
$1,220

New Jersey
$810

Maryland
$610

New York
$6,390

Penn.
$580

Ohio
$480

Chicago
$1,570

Minneapolis
$510

Texas
$1,230

Boulder/
Denver
$370

Seattle
$320

California
$8,710

Source: Venture Economics, April 1988.
Figures indicate volume of venture capital
funds controlled by sources in state. Complexes shown have 1% or more of the
national venture capital pool of $29,020.

share from 18 to 28 percent and the Northeast dropping from 49 to 37 percent. Much of this relative shift is attributable to the rapid rise of venture capital activity in California coupled with stagnation in New York.

At the state level, just three states, California, New York, and Massachusetts, are home to 70 percent of the nation's venture capital resources. California is the leading state, with 30 percent of total resources, followed by New York and Massachusetts with 22 and 15 percent, respectively. Together, these states control two-thirds of the U.S. venture capital pool, as well as more than half of the venture capital offices. With the addition of Illinois, Texas, and Connecticut, the only other states with more than $1 billion in resources, the top six states accounted for slightly more than 80 percent of the nation's venture capital resources in 1987.

The venture capital industry is concentrated at the metropolitan level as well. Just three metropolitan areas—San Francisco, New York City, and Boston—account for approximately 60 percent of total venture capital resources. For example, two-thirds of all venture capital offices in California are located in the San Francisco/Silicon Valley area, with the remaining one-third located in the Los Angeles/San Diego area. In fact, San Francisco/ Silicon Valley is home to more offices than any other state—more than 16 percent of the U.S. total. More than 95 percent of New York state's venture capital offices are located in the New York City area, while Chicago is home to 90 percent of the Illinois offices. Boston and the surrounding Route 128 suburbs account for the vast majority of Massachusetts's venture capital offices.

VENTURE CAPITAL INVESTMENT

Figure 9.2 shows the distribution of venture capital investment. Venture capital investments are even more concentrated than venture capital supply—primarily flowing to a very limited number of areas. At the regional level, the Pacific and Northeast regions together attracted almost three-fourths (74 percent) of the $2.9 billion funds invested by the venture capital industry in 1986. The Pacific region is led by California, which dominates the rest of the nation in its ability to attract venture capital. The Northeast region places second behind the Pacific. Within the Northeast region, Massachusetts attracts the majority of this region's venture investments. The Midwest region has seen a precipitous decline in venture capital investments. According to one study (Rubel, 1975), during the period 1968 to 1975, the Midwest attracted roughly 20 percent of the total share of venture capital investments. However, by the early 1980s, the Midwest's share had declined to a mere 8 percent of the national total. For the past decade, the distribution of venture capital throughout the United States has remained relatively con-

FIGURE 9.2

Number of Venture Capital Investments by State, 1983–1987

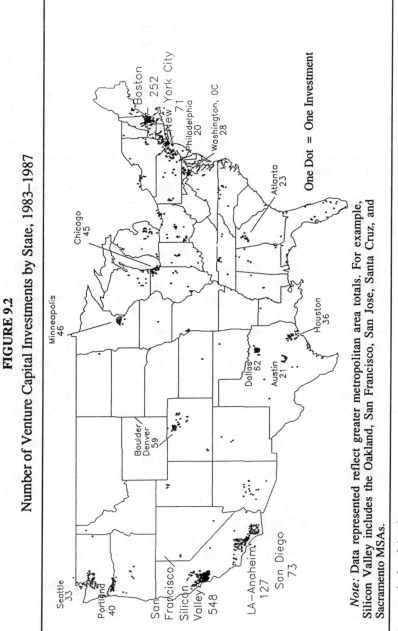

One Dot = One Investment

Note: Data represented reflect greater metropolitan area totals. For example, Silicon Valley includes the Oakland, San Francisco, San Jose, Santa Cruz, and Sacramento MSAs.

Source: Authors' data base.

stant, with the minor exception of the South region, which has shown a steady increase, from 6 percent in the early 1970 period to 9 percent in 1986.

Venture capital investment is quite concentrated at the state level. Just two states, California and Massachusetts, account for more than half of all venture capital investment. California attracted the lion's share of the investment dollars, with $1.1 billion, or 38 percent of the national total in 1986. Massachusetts was second—receiving approximately $400 million, or 14 percent of the total venture capital invested—while New York, Texas, and New Jersey attracted $200 million, $170 million, and $140 million, respectively. No other state drew more than $100 million in venture capital investments. Although in recent years California and Massachusetts have commanded the majority of venture capital investments, this pattern did not always hold. Prior to the late 1970s, the *combined* share of investments for these two states was 35 percent. Since that time, their share has grown while that of New York and Illinois has fallen from a combined 18 percent in 1986–75 to just 6 percent in 1987.

Venture capital is also highly concentrated at the metropolitan level. Silicon Valley was by far the leading recipient of venture capital investments, with 650 investments, more than two-thirds of all venture capital investments made in California. These were tightly clustered in the cities of Sunnyvale, Santa Clara, and San Jose, which together received 30 percent of the California total and 12 percent of total investments. Of the states, only Massachusetts received more venture capital investments than this three-city area. Silicon Valley was followed by Boston's Route 128 area with 295 investments, almost 75 percent of Massachusetts's investments. Just three communities, Newton, Waltham, and Woburn, received 62 percent of the Route 128 investments—almost 3 percent of the *national* total of venture capital investments (Florida, Smith, and Sechoka, 1990).

Interestingly, this pattern of metropolitan-level concentration can also be seen in areas that control relatively small amounts of venture capital. Atlanta, for example, accounts for more than 96 percent of all venture capital investments in the state of Georgia. More than 90 percent of venture capital investments in Colorado are concentrated along the Interstate 25 corridor between Denver and Boulder (Florida et al., 1990b).

Together, these findings lead to the conclusion that venture capital investments flow mainly to areas with established concentrations of high-tech businesses. This contradicts both academic studies and the conventional wisdom that suggests that there is a coincidence between venture capital supply and investments. Our findings indicate that the main centers of venture capital investment are high-tech centers, such as Silicon Valley and Route 128. In contrast, venture capital centers such as New York City and Chicago receive a relatively minor share of venture investments. However, it should be noted that the major centers for venture capital investment also possess significant concentrations of venture capital supply. In this sense, the supply of venture capital is important but only when combined with a significant concentration of high-tech firms.

Investment Flows

In addition to examining the aggregate investments for states, regions, and metropolitan areas, the research also looked at the flows of investment between the major venture capital centers. Figure 9.3 depicts venture capital investment flows for the three largest venture capital centers: California, New York, and Massachusetts. More than 70 percent of the 3,012 investments made by California venture capitalists were located in-state. The next largest concentration was in Massachusetts, with 6 percent. This was still more than ten times fewer investments than in the state of California. New York received less than 2 percent of California investment, finishing behind Texas and Colorado as preferred investment locales. In short, California venture capitalists invest locally, attract a great deal of capital from other centers, and frequently coinvest with venture capitalists from their own and other centers.

In sharp contrast, New York venture capitalists tend to export their venture capital. For example, just 7 percent of the investments made by New York venture capitalists were made in-state. Roughly 43 percent of New York investments were placed in California, followed by Massachusetts (16 percent) and Texas (5 percent). Massachusetts venture capitalists split their investments between local high-tech and capital exports. While venture capitalists in Massachusetts placed more than 40 percent of their investments within the state, roughly 30 percent went to California.

Coinvestment Patterns

Coinvestment provides an important link between various venture capital centers. Coinvestment refers to the process where venture capitalists invest together, syndicating deals to diversify their portfolios and to pool risk among themselves. Venture capitalists seldom invest alone. Coinvestment syndicates are comprised of two or more venture investors. Coinvestment provides access to a much wider range of investment possibilities and enables venture capitalists to spread risk by investing in a larger number of deals (Bygrave and Timmons, 1986; Florida and Kenney, 1988a).

In order to analyze the coinvestment patterns of venture capitalists, the research developed a separate data base for venture capital coinvestments. The data base includes information on all of the coinvestors in the venture

FIGURE 9.3

California, New York, and Massachusetts Venture Capitalists' Investment Locations, 1983–1987

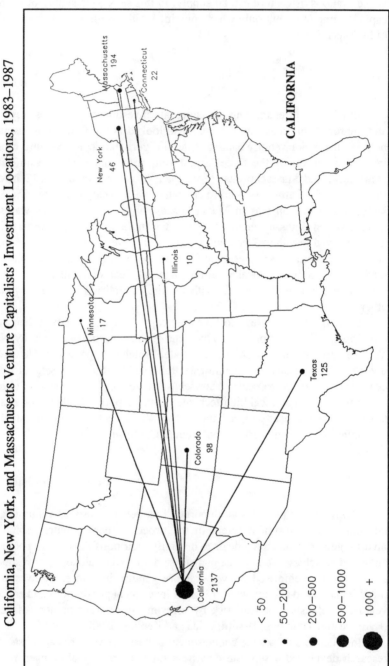

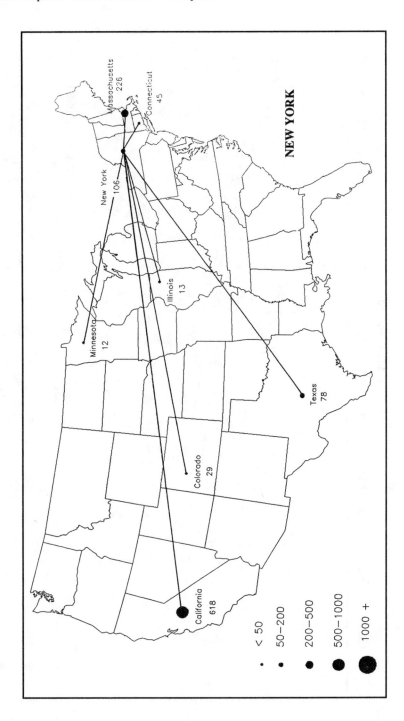

FIGURE 9.3 (Continued)

California, New York, and Massachusetts Venture Capitalists' Investment Locations, 1983–1987

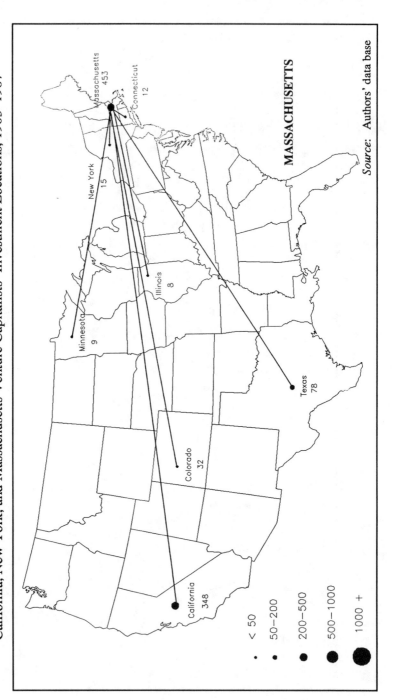

Source: Authors' data base

capital investments. It measures investment decisions rather than the actual dollar amount invested; that is, each time a venture capitalist from a state participates in a deal, it is recorded as one investment decision regardless of the size of the investment. It should be further noted that a deal in which four venture capitalists participate is recorded as one investment decision for each of the venture capitalists.

The coinvestment flows identified in the data are depicted in Figure 9.4, which highlights coinvestment patterns for the three leading venture capital centers: California, Massachusetts, and New York. The main findings from the coinvestment data are as follows. First, venture capitalists coinvest most frequently with their counterparts in established high-tech centers, especially those in California's Silicon Valley. Second, venture capitalists in high-tech centers do more internal coinvesting, indicating an abundance of "good deals." Heavy internal coinvesting also reflects the well-developed internal information- and investment-sharing networks that characterize technology-oriented complexes. This is evidenced by the fact that California venture capitalists placed 44 percent of their coinvestment with other California venture capitalists. Third, venture capitalists in financially oriented venture capital centers such as New York and Chicago coinvest primarily with venture capitalists in high-tech regions. For example, venture capitalists in New York coinvested most frequently with those in California, even more so than with venture capitalists in their own state. New York venture capitalists also coinvested frequently with Massachusetts venture capitalists. In short, coinvestment forms an important vehicle through which export-oriented venture capitalists in New York and Chicago are able to invest in the high-tech firms located in established high-tech centers, thereby enhancing the mobility of venture capital.

Venture Capital and High-technology Development

In order to understand the factors that differentiate the structure of venture capital industry within regions, the research undertook more detailed empirical analyses of eight key venture capital centers: California (San Francisco/Silicon Valley), Massachusetts (Boston), New York, Illinois (Chicago), Texas, Connecticut, Minnesota (Minneapolis), and Colorado. Based on the typology of venture capital complexes suggested by Florida and Kenney (1988a, 1988b), this aspect of the research developed empirical measures of the various characteristics of the eight major complexes. "Technology-oriented" venture capital complexes are defined as those with large concentrations of high-tech firms relative to their overall financial resources (for example, bank capital). "Financial-oriented" complexes are defined as those with large concentrations of financial institutions and/or

FIGURE 9.4

California, New York, and Massachusetts Venture Capitalists' Coinvestment Locations, 1983–1987

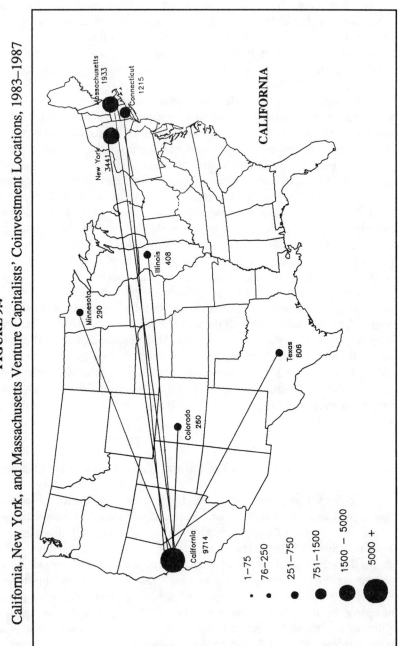

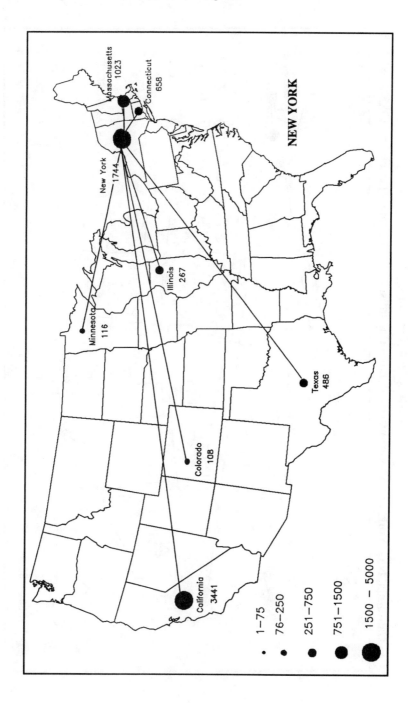

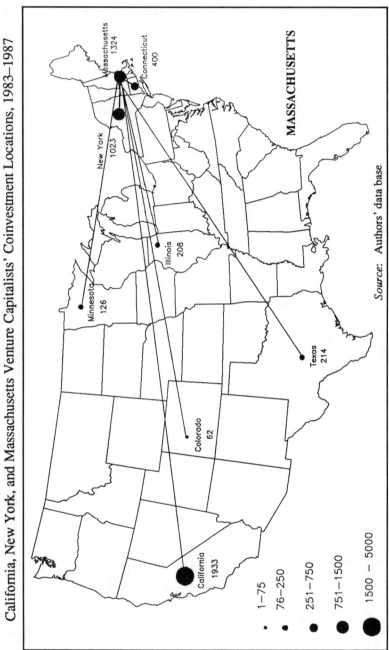

200　　　　　　　　　　　　　　　　R. FLORIDA AND D. SMITH

FIGURE 9.4 (Continued)

California, New York, and Massachusetts Venture Capitalists' Coinvestment Locations, 1983–1987

Massachusetts
1324

Connecticut
400

New York
1023

Illinois
208

Minnesota
126

Texas
214

Colorado
62

California
1933

MASSACHUSETTS

Source: Authors' data base

1–75
76–250
251–750
751–1500
1500 – 5000

financial resources (for example, bank capital) relative to high-tech firms. "Hybrid" complexes are defined as those that possess significant concentrations of both high-tech firms and financial resources.

Table 9.1 summarizes the data on the structure of the eight leading venture capital complexes. The number of high-tech firms is used as a measure of "technology orientedness." The number of high-tech firms represents the strength of a region's technology base and opportunities for technology-oriented investing. The dollar volume of bank assets is used as a measure of "financial orientedness." Commercial bank assets provide the best available proxy measure for the relative size of the financial sector in a complex. Both measures were normalized to control for the significant variation in population size among the eight complexes.

There are two technology-oriented complexes: California and Colorado. California is identified as technology-oriented because it possesses a high level of high-tech firms per 100,000 population relative to bank assets, indicating a technology-intensive economy. Colorado ranks fourth in high-tech firms and eighth in bank assets. There are two financial-oriented complexes:

TABLE 9.1

Typology of Venture Capital Centers

	High-tech Firms[a]		Bank Assets[a]	
Technology-oriented Complexes				
California	14.41	(3)[b]	.91	(7)
Colorado	10.62	(4)	.78	(8)
Hybrid Complexes				
Massachusetts	22.70	(1)	1.32	(2)
Minnesota	9.68	(5)	1.28	(3)
Texas	5.02	(8)	1.20	(5)
Connecticut	14.45	(2)	1.02	(6)
Financial-oriented Complexes				
New York	7.67	(6)	2.37	(1)
Illinois	6.67	(7)	1.28	(3)

Notes: a = per 100,000 population.

b = numbers in parentheses refer to rank.

Sources: Corporate Technology Information Services Directory (Wellesley, Mass., Corporate Technology Information Service, 1988); U.S. Bureau of the Census, *State Metropolitan Area Databook* (Washington, D.C., U.S. Government Printing Office, 1988).

New York and Illinois. New York ranks first in the volume of commercial bank assets per 100,000 population but ranks sixth in high-tech firms. Illinois ranks third in bank assets and next to last in high-tech firms. There are four hybrid complexes: Massachusetts, Minnesota, Texas, and Connecticut. This does not imply that all hybrids are alike, however. The various hybrid complexes are better thought of as points on a continuum, running from predominantly technology-oriented to predominantly financial-based. For example, Massachusetts, a hybrid complex, ranks very high on both measures, being first in high-tech firms per 100,000 population and second in bank assets per 100,000. Texas, on the other hand, ranks low on both counts.

The research used Pearson product moment correlation coefficients to provide rough empirical estimates of the determinants of venture capital supply and investment. For venture capital supply, correlations examined the relationship between two measures of venture capital supply (for example, offices and resources), the number of high-tech firms, and the dollar amount of bank assets. For venture capital investment, correlations examined the relationship between the dollar volume of venture capital investments, high-tech firms, and bank assets.

Venture capital offices are a measure of venture capital supply. Correlations were run between the number of venture capital offices and the number of high-tech firms in the state and between the number of venture capital offices and the dollar amount of bank assets for all fifty states and for our eight major complexes (Table 9.2). For all fifty states, there were relatively strong correlations across both dimensions. There was a correlation of .954 between the number of venture capital offices and the number of high-tech firms and a correlation of .830 between the number of venture capital offices and bank assets. These indicate that venture capital supply tends to concentrate in areas with both large numbers of high-tech firms and high concentrations of bank assets.

We then ran the same correlations for the eight major venture capital complexes. Here the correlation between venture capital offices and high-tech firms was again strongly positive (.943). However, the correlation between the number of venture capital offices and bank assets was weaker (.720). When adjusted for population, the correlation between venture capital offices and high-tech firms remains strong (.874), while the correlation between venture capital offices and bank assets is quite weak (.054) and insignificant.

Separate correlations were run to explore the relationship between the dollar amount of venture capital resources (another measure of supply) for the eight major complexes and the number of high-tech firms and the dollar amount of bank assets. Here again, there were strong positive correlations with both high-tech firms (.903) and bank assets (.708). When we controlled

TABLE 9.2

Correlations Between Venture Capital, High-tech Firms, and Bank Assets

Measure of Venture Capital	High-tech Firms[a]	Bank Assets[a]
Venture Capital Supply		
Number of Venture Capital Offices	.954	.830
(50 States)	(.873)	(.090)[b]
Number of Venture Capital Offices	.943	.720
(8 Leading Complexes)	(.874)	(.054)[b]
Dollar Volume of Resources	.903	.708
(8 Leading Complexes)	(.870)	(.222)[b]
Venture Capital Investment		
Dollars Invested	.982	.348[b]
(8 Leading Complexes)	(.955)	(.259)[b]

Notes: a = figures in parentheses have been normalized by population.

b = insignificant at the .05 level.

Sources: *Venture Capital Journal* (various years); authors' data base; *Corporate Technology Information Services Directory* (Wellesley, Mass., 1988); *State and Metropolitan Area Databook* (Washington, D.C., 1988).

for population, the correlation between venture capital resources and high-tech firms remained strong (.870) while that between venture capital resources and bank assets was rather weak (.222).

Next, correlations were run to examine the determinants of venture capital investment. We were especially interested in seeing if venture capital investment was associated with the same variables that are related to venture capital supply. This generated especially interesting results. The correlation between high-tech firms and venture capital investment was very strong (.982) and remained strong when the data were normalized by population (.955), an overwhelming indication that high-tech firms draw venture investment into an area. The correlation between venture capital investment and the volume of bank assets in a region, though, was weak (.348) and insignificant at the .05 level. When the variables were adjusted for population, the correlation was negative (-.259) and insignificant. This indicates that investment tends to be determined by the high-tech base rather than the volume of bank assets.

This aspect of the research forms a basic conclusion. Venture capital supply is determined by both high-tech firms and bank assets. However, venture capital investment is determined by the former only.

Policy Implications for Public Venture Capital Programs

Between the real contributions of venture capital to high-tech development and the folklore that has grown up around high-tech success stories, such as Apple, Digital Equipment Corporation, Intel, and Genentech, it is not surprising that the public sector has become enamored with venture capital as a mechanism for generating technology-based economic development (Peltz and Weiss, 1984). Boosters of high-tech development have promoted venture capital as a key ingredient in the process of "growing the next Silicon Valley" (Miller and Cote, 1985). Indeed, government now views venture capital investment as an essential ingredient of technology-based development. While Connecticut and Massachusetts were the only states with venture capital programs prior to 1980, the number increased by twenty-eight by 1988 (State of Minnesota, 1988; U.S. Small Business Administration, 1988). Total capitalization of these efforts currently exceeds $1 billion.

State and local governments are actively experimenting with a variety of mechanisms for providing venture capital (Donovan, 1984; Fisher et al., 1986; Watkins, 1985). Two often cited programs, the Massachusetts Technology Development Corporation (MTDC) and the Connecticut Product Development Corporation (CPDC), invest directly in technology-oriented businesses in their respective states. A number of states use public money to underwrite privately managed venture capital partnerships. Public entities generally function as passive limited partners in these arrangements, placing few stipulations on the type or location of investments. The New York Business Venture Partnership is a $40 million limited partnership backed by two public pension funds and managed by Rothschild Ventures. The Primus Fund in Cleveland is a $30 million limited partnership backed in part by public capital that is constrained though not limited to investments in Ohio (personal interview with David DeVore, 1986). Some states—including Ohio, Pennsylvania, Michigan, New York, Utah, Oregon, and Washington—allow public pension funds to commit a small percentage of assets to venture capital partnerships without regard for location. A number of others, most notably Ohio and Michigan, have experimented with direct investment in new enterprises (personal interview with Robert McLaughlin, 1986). Still others use tax incentives to stimulate private venturing. Much of this policy is premised on the notion that "regional gaps" exist in the distribution of venture capital and that by alleviating such gaps, states and localities can stimulate technology and entrepreneurship.

A key aspect in determining the efficacy of public provision of venture capital thus lies in whether or not so-called regional "capital gaps" exist. The research findings suggest that venture capitalists are quite proficient in locating the high-tech firms that offer such good investment opportunities where they exist. This suggests that perceived capital gaps are a function of an inadequate high-tech base—not an absence of financial capital. In the words of Daniel Holland, a leading venture capitalist, "It is not venture capital that is the start of entrepreneurial activity. You can't simply put six venture capitalists in Butte, Montana, and expect that the availability of venture capital will engender a Route 128" (U.S. Congress, 1984a). Simply put: Capital gaps exist because there are few good deals to attract venture capital in the first place.

The most important implication of the research findings for economic development policy is that despite the very important contribution venture capital has made to the making of high-technology regions (for example, Silicon Valley and Route 128), public venture capital should not be considered a panacea for an area's economic woes. Public provision of venture or risk capital is likely to be effective only in a very limited number of areas. The reason for this is simple. Venture capital is just one of a host of necessary inputs to technology-intensive economic development. As the cases of New York and Chicago illustrate, the presence of abundant venture capital does not necessarily translate into high-tech development. The consensus view in the literature on high-tech and regional development is that only a very limited set of areas possess the attributes needed to generate and sustain a high level of high-tech development (Dorfman, 1983; Florida and Kenney, 1988a; Malecki, 1987; Stohr, 1986; U.S. Office of Technology Assessment, 1984). Increasing the volume of venture capital in areas that lack such conditions is likely to have little effect on their technology capabilities and can have perverse effects if this capital simply flows to established centers of high technology. It is quite possible that current models of public equity finance will confer disproportionate benefits to already advantaged regions, enabling them to consolidate their hold on high-tech development.

In fact, public provision of venture capital may be most appropriate in areas that are just developing the technology base or "social structures of innovation" needed for high-tech growth (Florida and Kenney, 1988a, 1988c). Since venture capital is just one of many important inputs into the technology development process, public intervention in venture capital will be most successful in areas which already have a supply of the other inputs but do not have sufficient venture capital. In these few cases (and only in these cases), relief of the venture capital constraint is likely to have a significant impact.

A different set of problems crops up when public funds are managed by private venture capitalists. This may turn out to be a catch-22 situation. Placing tight restrictions on the investment activities of public venture capital pools is problematic because it narrows potential investment opportunities, constrains deal flow, and is likely to negatively influence the fund's rate of return. When no such strings are attached, however, investment will flow to areas where the most attractive investments and highest rates of return are available, resulting in interregional transfers of capital and further depletion of local resources. It will be difficult for many states to balance successfully the goals of high rates of return and local venture investment to spur economic development.

Public venture capital programs must also face the fact that finance is only a small part of the activities of a venture capitalist. The success of new ventures is highly contingent upon the support services supplied by venture capitalists. It is questionable whether the public sector can or should attempt to compete with private venture capitalists to recruit individuals with the skills to provide such service. There may also be barriers prohibiting representatives of public funds from accessing private venture capital networks.

Given this reality, the rapid expansion of public venture capital programs may end up generating yet another round of interlocality competition, pitting jurisdiction against jurisdiction in the scramble for high-tech businesses and jobs (Harrison and Kanter, 1978). The costs of such duplication may well exceed potential benefits. Despite the rhetoric of indigenous job generation that surrounds them, entrepreneurial and venture capital programs are confronted by the same "zero sum" consequences evidenced by more traditional economic development strategies. Beyond this, the benefits of venture investments tend to be quite narrow. While they provide great wealth and profits for entrepreneurs and investors, they tend not to generate large numbers of jobs and other social benefits. In fact, a common pattern is that such jobs are exported to the Third World. Put another way, U.S. high-tech complexes produce technological breakthroughs but are less and less capable of follow-through in the development of high-quality, mass-manufactured products (Florida and Kenney, 1990).

Summary

The main findings of this research can be summarized in terms of five basic conclusions. First, the supply of venture is extremely concentrated geographically. The major centers of venture capital supply in the United States include California's Silicon Valley, New York City, and Route 128 around Boston. Less important, though still significant, concentrations of venture capital are found in Chicago, Texas, Connecticut, Minnesota, and Colorado. Second, venture capital investment flows mainly to established high-technology centers, such as Silicon Valley and Route 128. Other venture capital centers that are not high-tech centers, such as New York and Chicago, serve primarily to collect venture capital, the majority of which is then exported to established high-tech centers. Third, venture capital's impact on economic development is context sensitive. In areas with an established high-tech infrastructure, venture capital fuels the growth of that sector. In areas without such a base, venture capital alone is not likely to stimulate innovation and high-tech development. Fourth, coinvestment or investment syndication forms an important link between the various centers of venture capital activity. It allows venture capital firms located in financial centers to participate in deals originated by venture capitalists in high-tech centers. Coinvesting facilitates long-distance flows of venture capital and reinforces the flow of venture capital toward locations with the most potential investment opportunities or best deal flow.

Fifth, and finally, while venture capital is an important element of high-tech complexes, it is not a panacea for the problems of declining states or metropolitan areas. Public policymakers need to recognize that efforts to stimulate high-tech development by enhancing the supply of venture capital without influencing the other elements of a region's economic infrastructure will not succeed. In light of our findings, public policymakers would do well to avoid "quick-fix" remedies, such as venture capital programs, and get back to the business of building integrated strategies to bolster the underlying economic and technological capacities of states, regions, and metropolitan areas.

Notes

1. *Venture Capital Journal* is published monthly by Venture Economics, Needham, Massachusetts.

References

Bean, A., D. Schiffel, and M. Mogee. "The Venture Capital Market and Technological Innovation." *Research Policy* 4 (1975): 380–408.

Bullock, M. *Academic Enterprise, Industrial Innovation, and the Development of High Technology Financing in the United States.* London: Brand Brothers, 1983.

Bygrave, W., and J. Timmons. "Networking Among Venture Capital Firms." Unpublished paper. Babson College, 1986.

Charles River Associates. *An Analysis of Capital Market Imperfections.* Cambridge: Charles River Associates, 1976.

Donovan, W. "Turning to the States for Venture Capital." *New England Business* (December 3, 1984): 96–99.

Dorfman, N. "Route 128: The Development of a Regional High Technology Economy." *Research Policy* 12 (1983): 299–316.

Fisher, P., M. Seehan, and R. Colton. *Public/Private Enterprise as an Economic Development Strategy for States and Cities.* Report prepared for the U.S. Department of Commerce, Economic Development Administration. Washington, D.C.: 1986.

Florida, R., and M. Kenney. *The Breakthrough Illusion: Corporate America's Failure to Move from Innovation to Mass Production.* New York: Basic Books, 1990.

———. "Venture Capital, High Technology, and Regional Development." *Regional Studies* 22 (1988a): 31–48.

———. "Venture Capital and Technological Entrepreneurship." *Journal of Business Venturing* 3, 4 (Fall 1988b): 301–319.

———. "Venture Capital and Technological Innovation in the U.S." *Research Policy* 17 (1988c): 119–137.

———. "Venture Capital's Geography: A Comment on Leinbach and Amrhein." *Professional Geographer* 40 (May 1988d): 214–217.

Florida, R., M. Kenney, and D. F. Smith, Jr. *Venture Capital, Innovation, and Economic Development.* Washington, D.C.: Report to the U.S. Economic Development Administration, 1990.

Florida, R., D. Smith, Jr., and E. Sechoka. "Regional Patterns of Venture Capital Investment." In *The Venture Capital Industry.* Ed. M. Green. London: Routledge, 1991. pp. 102–133.

Green, M. "Patterns of Preference for Venture Capital in the United States, 1970–1985." Paper presented at the American Association of Geographers, Annual Meeting, Portland, Oregon, 1987.

Harrison, B., and S. Kanter. "The Political Economy of State Job Creation Business Incentives." *Journal of the American Institute of Planners* 44 (1978): 424–435.

Horseley Keogh and Associates. Unpublished data on venture capital fund performance. (Made available to Richard Florida and Martin Kenney by permission.) 1986.

Kozmetsky, G., M. Gill, and R. Smilor. *Financing and Managing Fast Growth Companies: The Venture Capital Process.* Lexington, Mass.: Lexington Books, 1985.

Leinbach, C., and T. Amrhein. "A Geography of Venture Capital in the U.S." *Professional Geographer* 39 (1987): 2, 145–158.

Luger, M. "Does North Carolina's High-Tech Development Program Work?" *Journal of the American Planning Association* 50 (Summer 1984): 280–289.

McNaughton, R., and M. Green. "Patterns of Venture Capital Investment in the United States." Paper presented at the East Lake Division of the American Association of Geographers, 1986.

Malecki, E. "Hope or Hyperbole? High Tech and Economic Development." *Technology Review* 90 (October 1987): 7, 50.

Markusen, A., P. Hall, and A. Glasmeier. *High Tech America.* Boston: Allen & Unwin, 1986.

Miller, R., and M. Cote. "Growing the Next Silicon Valley." *Harvard Business Review* 63 (July–August 1985): 114–123.

Peltz, M., and M. Weiss. "State and Local Government Roles in Industrial Innovation." *Journal of the American Planning Association* 503 (Summer 1984): 270–279.

Personal interview with David DeVore, Primus Fund, Cleveland, Ohio, by Richard Florida and Martin Kenney, July 1986.

Personal interview with Robert McLaughlin, Ohio Public Employees Retirement System, Columbus, Ohio, by Richard Florida and Martin Kenney, March 1986.

Rubel, S. M., and Company. "Analysis of Venture Capital Industry Investing: 1968–1975." Chicago: S. M. Rubel & Co., 1975.

Scott, A., and M. Storper. "High Technology Industry and Regional Development: A Theoretical Critique and Reconstruction." *International Social Science Journal* 112 (1988): 215–232.

State of Minnesota, Office of Science and Technology. *State Technology Programs in the United States*. St. Paul: Department of Trade and Economic Development, 1988.

Stohr, W. "Regional Innovation Complexes." *Papers of the Regional Science Association* 59 (1986): 29–44.

U.S. Congress, Joint Economic Committee. *Climate for Entrepreneurship and Innovation in the United States* (August 27–28, 1984a).

_____. *Venture Capital and Innovation*. Study prepared for the Joint Economic Committee of Congress. Washington, D.C.: U.S. Government Printing Office, 1984b.

U.S. Office of Technology Assessment. *Technology, Innovation and Regional Economic Development*. Washington, D.C.: U.S. Government Printing Office, 1984.

U.S. Small Business Administration, Office of Advocacy. *Capital Formation in the States*. Washington, D.C.: U.S. Government Printing Office, January 1988.

Venture Economics. *Guide to Venture Capital* (various issues). Wellesley Hills, Massachusetts.

_____. *Venture Capital Journal* (various issues). Wellesley Hills, Massachusetts.

_____. "Regional Patterns of Venture Capital Investment." Prepared for U.S. Small Business Administration. Washington, D.C.: Small Business Administration, 1983.

Watkins, C. *Programs for Innovative Technology Research in State Strategies for Economic Development*. Washington, D.C.: National Governors' Association, Center for Policy Research and Analysis, 1985.

Wilson, J. *The New Venturers: Inside the High Stake World of Venture Capital*. Reading, Mass.: Addison-Wesley, 1985.

CLAUDIA BIRD SCHOONHOVEN and KATHLEEN M. EISENHARDT

10 Regions as Industrial Incubators of Technology-based Ventures

Northern California's Silicon Valley is one of the premier technology regions of the world. Annually, thousands of people stream into Silicon Valley to learn its secrets, including economic development officials from China, Japan, Ireland, and elsewhere around the world, as well as from other regions of the United States—all seeking to enhance the innovative and economic capabilities of their home regions. Silicon Valley is perceived to be an incubator region that supplies the resources necessary for the birth of high-technology firms. At present, little is known about why the Silicon Valley has spawned so many successful, innovative firms. Is it the local culture of entrepreneurship that creates so many new firms? Are the creative fires fueled by the nearby presence of two world-class universities, Stanford and the University of California, Berkeley, both known for technical excellence? Is it a contagious *Silicon Valley Fever* (Rogers and Larsen, 1984) that has spread throughout the region to create so many new ventures or the prospect of making *The Big Score* (Malone, 1985) and becoming *Innovation Millionaires* (Bylinsky, 1976)? Books such as these are long on imagery and

Several of our colleagues have commented and provided advice during this research. We appreciate the help and comments of Howard A. Aldrich, John Freeman, James G. March, W. Richard Scott, Andrew H. Van de Ven, Peter Ring, Gerald R. Schoonhoven, and participants in the University of Minnesota New Venture Research Group Seminar, December 1988.

interviews with wealthy innovators, and they serve to capture the popular imagination. However, accounts like these are short on systematic research and statistical analysis to help distinguish causal factors from random, chance events.

Regardless of whether the causal agents are deemed to be the culture or entrepreneurial fires, it is typically believed that new technology-based firms founded in Silicon Valley are advantaged: They are presumed to have a greater likelihood of survival and prosperity when compared to new ventures founded in other regions of the world and the United States. Any Silicon Valley "advantages," though, are actually assumptions about such advantages with virtually no objective research to support the premise. Indeed, the rosy accounts of Silicon Valley successes typically overlook the mercuric failures, such as Atari or Osborne Computers. Because the Silicon Valley has both spectacular successes (Jelinek and Schoonhoven, 1990) as well as funereal failures to its credit, substantially more knowledge is needed about what creates regions of high-tech excellence. To be useful, this knowledge must be based on large-scale, comparative research analyzing many new ventures founded in different geographic regions.

This paper reports on systematic research that addresses the extent to which different geographical regions of the United States function as industrial incubators for the founding and growth of new technology-based ventures. Following passage of the Investment Tax Incentive Act (ITIA) and the Employee Retirement Income Security Act (ERISA) in 1978, expansion of available investment capital released a flood of new high-tech companies. For example, between 1978 and 1985, 102 new semiconductor companies were founded in the continental United States (Schoonhoven and Eisenhardt, 1989). The distribution of the new companies in this industry has a regional basis: Rather than being randomly distributed throughout the United States, new semiconductor firms are concentrated in eighteen regions of the country, with 70 percent of them founded in Northern California's Silicon Valley.

With the nonrandom, regionally based distribution of new semiconductor ventures, three questions arise: (1) Do these regions, especially the Silicon Valley, function as incubators, providing an unusually rich set of resources to enhance the birthrate of new technology-based firms? Is there a relationship between resources in a region and a region's ability to generate entrepreneurs and thereby increase the birthrate of new firms in a specific industry? (2) For new firms founded in regions richer with industry-specific resources, do the resources concentrated in such regions provide a differential advantage compared to new ventures founded in other regions? Do Silicon Valley firms have a higher new venture survival rate? Conversely, does the high density of existing semiconductor firms in some regions, such as the Silicon Valley, overtax resources within the region, resulting in a disproportionately high rate of new firm failures compared to the relative prosperity of firms founded in regions less densely settled with new semiconductor companies? (3) Beyond survival, are Silicon Valley firms advantaged in other ways: Do they capture higher proportions of available venture capital or do they have faster growth rates or greater sales revenues when compared to ventures founded in other regions of the United States?

To understand the role of regions as incubators in the birthrate and survival of new technology-based ventures, a multivariate approach has been taken. The research reported here is derived from a larger study of new venture success in the semiconductor industry (Eisenhardt and Schoonhoven, 1990; Schoonhoven and Eisenhardt, 1987, 1989; Schoonhoven et al., 1990). The overall model guiding the research focuses on multiple levels of analysis and on multiple variables likely to influence the survival and success of new organizations. The four levels of analysis are the macro level, where environmental factors such as market and state of the economy operate; the regional level of analysis, where objective resources of the region reside; the organizational level of analysis, where firm attributes such as the distribution of ownership operate; and the team level of analysis, where characteristics of the founding entrepreneurs are relevant. Figure 10.1 summarizes the variables expected to influence new venture outcomes.

FIGURE 10.1
A Multiple-level Model of New Venture Outcomes

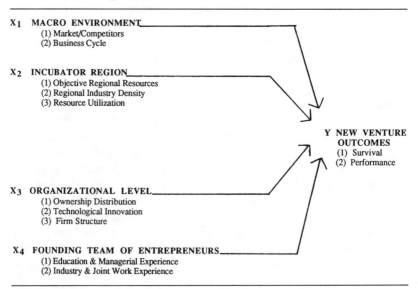

X_1 MACRO ENVIRONMENT
    (1) Market/Competitors
    (2) Business Cycle

X_2 INCUBATOR REGION
    (1) Objective Regional Resources
    (2) Regional Industry Density
    (3) Resource Utilization

Y NEW VENTURE OUTCOMES
    (1) Survival
    (2) Performance

X_3 ORGANIZATIONAL LEVEL
    (1) Ownership Distribution
    (2) Technological Innovation
    (3) Firm Structure

X_4 FOUNDING TEAM OF ENTREPRENEURS
    (1) Education & Managerial Experience
    (2) Industry & Joint Work Experience

Research Design and Methods

We will briefly describe our research methods here.[1] The population studied is all new semiconductor industry companies founded in the United States between 1978 and 1985.[2] These firms are distributed throughout eighteen geographical regions of the United States. Seventy percent of the population was founded in the Northern California region called Silicon Valley.

These firms were founded to produce six broad classes of semiconductor devices: memories (32.3 percent), application-specific integrated circuits (26.4 percent), logic devices (12.7 percent), gallium arsenide devices (11.8 percent), linear components (7.8 percent), and discrete devices (8.8 percent). The company participation rate is 96 percent of the 102 firms founded during the period. This participation rate is unusually high when compared to other studies of the U.S. semiconductor industry. For example, Scott and Angel (1987) received a 10.2 percent return rate.

Original within-firm data were gathered on-site and by telephone and were augmented by existing data on industry-specific resources indigenous to the region of birth. Data sources are interviews with new venture entrepreneurs and major officers of the firms, supplemented by data provided by the heads of finance and personnel. Our study extends Freeman and colleagues' (1983) work by taking the research and development (R&D) period into account. Earlier studies of semiconductor firms relied on existing information where date of market entry was used in lieu of actual founding date. Earlier methods underestimate the company's age at death and other age-related dynamics by failing to take into account the initial R&D period. Because the data for the research reported here are based on original, proprietary information gathered from the new semiconductor ventures themselves, the analysis yields a reliable set of estimates of age of death and other variables.

Data on regional resources were collected from a variety of sources, including government documents, the semiconductor industry, the service industry, and venture capital industry directories. Data are quantitative, and the models we analyze are investigated using correlation, multiple regression, logistic regression, analysis of variance, and survival analysis. The research design is longitudinal; firms were followed forward in time from their date of founding through 1988 for this analysis.

Research Findings: Birthrate Analysis

Figure 10.2 places the population of semiconductor firms in historical perspective. The graph shows that the birth of new semiconductor firms has not been a linear progression over time. Rather, it has been characterized by

FIGURE   10.2

New Semiconductor Firms in Historical Perspective, 1955–1987

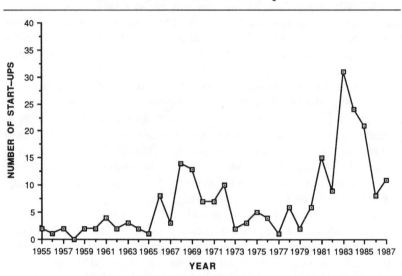

Sources: Dataquest and New Venture Research Project.

three waves. The first wave occurred between 1955 and 1965, following discovery of the transistor at Bell Labs in 1948 by Walter Brattain, John Bardeen, and William Shockley. One of the first firms to commercialize semiconductor products was Shockley Semiconductor Laboratories, founded by an inventor of the transistor. As one of the first "spin-offs," Fairchild Semiconductor was also founded during this period by a group of eight scientists and engineers originally employed by Shockley Semiconductor. Fairchild Semiconductor is the documented parent company of more than twenty firms that followed it over the next decade, all founded by former employees of Fairchild.

The graph shows a second wave of foundings between 1966 and 1973. At its peak, fourteen new firms were founded between 1968 and 1969. Figure 10.2 shows a steep drop in new firm foundings after 1972, with only one new semiconductor firm founded in 1977. With passage of the ITIA and the ERISA in 1978, the third wave of new semiconductor ventures was launched. These laws reduced the corporate and individual tax rates while simultaneously relaxing investment restrictions on institutional investors. Shortly after 1978, the number of new semiconductor firm foundings grew dramatically. The peak year in the third wave was 1983. The figure shows that thirty-six new firms were founded in 1983 in the United States. While the rate of new firm foundings has decreased since 1983, it has nonetheless remained reasonably high through 1987, with twelve new semiconductor ventures founded in 1987.

The distribution of this third wave of new semiconductor firms has a regional basis. Figure 10.3 shows that new semiconductor firms were founded in eighteen regions of the United States between 1978 and 1986. The distribution of new firm births is skewed because eleven regions contain only one new firm birth, or .9 percent of all new semiconductor industry ventures, per region. Six regions have two to five new firm births, and these range from 2.8 to 4.6 percent of the total new firm foundings in this industry. The distribution then jumps from 4.6 percent of the firms (founded in the San Diego region) to 69.5 percent in the Silicon Valley region. Northern California's Silicon Valley region has produced more than fifteen times more new semiconductor ventures than any other region of the United States during the period covered by our research.

These findings regarding the skewed regional clustering of new semiconductor ventures are consistent with other recent research. Ó hUallacháin and Satterthwaite (1988) reported that fast-growing U.S. industries are concentrating in larger metropolitan areas. This was attributed to intraindustry "externalities," associated with established industrial clusters, which are assumed to reduce the costs of searching for talented labor, suppliers, distrib-

FIGURE 10.3

Number of Births by Region, 1978–1986

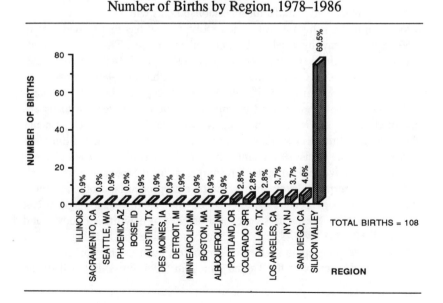

utors, and services. The costs of key personnel are minimized if the firm locates in a major center of industry-related labor supply (Ó hUallacháin and Satterthwaite, 1988). While an important contribution, Ó hUallacháin and Satterthwaite (1988) stop short of measuring industry-specific externalities, which are presumed rather than quantified, nor is the relationship between specific regional attributes and the number of *new firm births* in a region part of the inquiry. Measures of the Standard Metropolitan Statistical Area (SMSA) infrastructure that are quantified are generic and applicable to a wide variety of industries. For example, airport access and the presence of an enterprise zone (EZ) are resources widely applicable across industries and not specific to any. Therefore, the infrastructure is not tailored to the needs of any particular industry within the region. While their data are suggestive, cross-sectional studies limit causal conclusions because data are not gathered over time.

While existing research studies such as Ó hUallacháin and Satterthwaite (1988) are important springboards, this research moves beyond by asking: "What accounts for the regional distribution of new semiconductor firm births across regions of the United States?" To investigate this question, the concept "incubator region" becomes relevant; we will examine its effects on new firm births.

DEFINING THE INCUBATOR REGION CONCEPT

The incubator hypothesis was articulated by Hoover and Vernon (1962), who argued that small manufacturing establishments will find it advantageous to locate initially at high-density, metropolitan locations that provide ready access to space, raw materials, labor, and other services. The incubator concept has been defined several ways in previous research (Allen and Levine, 1986; Beesley, 1955; Cooper and Bruno, 1977; Johnson, 1986; Johnson and Cathcart, 1979; Smilor and Gill, 1986). The concept has been operationalized as (1) a single, established organization where new venture ideas are incubated and where industry training is provided for future entrepreneurs who spin off to form a new venture (Cooper, 1979); (2) a single building that houses several new business tenants under a single roof and provides common administrative and laboratory resources at an inexpensive price, variously called enterprise development centers, entrepreneurial centers, or business and technology centers (Allen and Levine, 1986); (3) a single urban area, such as New York City's core, as a breeder of new firms (Hoover and Vernon, 1962); (4) SMSAs, called urban communities by Pennings (1982); and (5) larger geographic sectors of a country, such as the Yorkshire and West Midlands sectors of the United Kingdom (Johnson, 1986). All of the implicit definitions and actual operationalizations of the term incubator imply a confluence of resources for nurturing a fledgling new venture.

We define an *incubator region* as a confluence of industry-specific resources contained within a circumscribed geographic area that may be mobilized to create and sustain new ventures in a given industry. The level of analysis is that of a circumscribed geographic region and thus may be seen as an ecological-environmental concept. There are multiple resources whose richness may vary across regions, so the incubator region concept is a multivariate construct. The definition is focused on industry-specific resources, excluding a wide range of regional attributes used in prior research, such as availability of transportation, number of foreign immigrants, and the energy rate, which are not specific to a given industry. For example, when Pennings (1982) studied the plastic products, telecommunications equipment, and electrical components industries, he included a wide range of metropolitan characteristics, such as urban centrality, unemployment rate, and energy rate, among resources of the SMSA.

Our interest is to identify and quantify industry-specific resources that might make a difference in the birthrate of new semiconductor firms in a given region. We have identified a number of *objective resources* specific to the semiconductor industry. They include: (1) number of existing semiconductor firms, (2) number of venture capital firms, (3) available venture capital resources for disbursement, (4) electrical engineers, (5) semiconductor production workers, and (6) the number of service companies that specialize in supporting semiconductor companies, such as design analysts, failure analysts, and photomask services.

We found that regions do vary in the extent to which they contain objective resources of importance to the semiconductor industry. For example, Figure 10.4 displays the number of semiconductor establishments by region. It reveals that in the 1985–86 period, the number of semiconductor firms in each of the eighteen regions varied from one in the Des Moines, Iowa, region to ninety-three in the Silicon Valley region. Existing semiconductor firms are important because they contain a pool of trained employees for the new venture, and these include experienced engineers, managers, and production workers. They also contain manufacturing capacity, some of which may be underutilized and thus available for use by a new venture when it reaches the manufacturing stage.

Figure 10.5 graphs the average number of semiconductor service firms, by region, from 1977 to 1987. Recall that specialized services are businesses that support the semiconductor industry, such as mask makers, silicon crystal growers, and the like. It shows that some regions, such as the Sacramento, California, region, contain no services of specific importance to the semiconductor industry. Other regions, such as the greater Boston and Los Angeles

FIGURE 10.4

Number of Semiconductor Establishments by Region

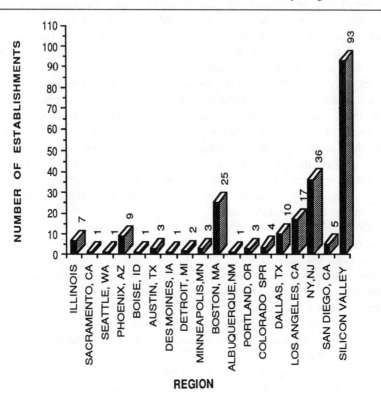

regions, contain an average of thirty-seven and forty-six businesses, respectively, that support the semiconductor industry. The greatest number of service firms that specialize in the semiconductor industry are located in the Silicon Valley region of Northern California: 158 firms over the ten-year period.

Figure 10.6 shows the distribution of a crucial resource to new technology-based ventures: the number of venture capital firms in the region. For the period studied, the mean number of venture capital firms varied from .1 in the Boise, Idaho, region to eighty-eight in the Silicon Valley region to ninety-five in the New York City–New Jersey region. Although the new ventures are physically located in New Jersey, the close proximity of New York City renders the greater New York–New Jersey region well off in terms of available venture capital.

The last regional resource graph is the number of electrical engineers (EEs) in each region. Because these numbers are derived from the U.S.

FIGURE 10.5

Mean Number of Specialized Service Companies by Region
1978–1986

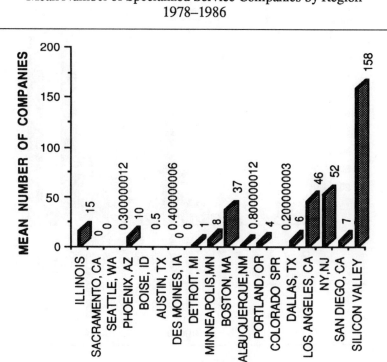

Census, data were only available for 1980. Figure 10.7 indicates that several regions had relatively few EEs: the fewest were found in Boise, Idaho, and Des Moines. The regions richest in EEs were Silicon Valley and the Los Angeles region, with 19,000 and more than 27,000 engineers, respectively.

Taken together, these industry-specific resources represent the regional *infrastructure* for a given industry. A rich regional infrastructure provides the underpinnings for the creation of new firms and for the efficient functioning of an industry.

EFFECT OF INCUBATOR REGION RESOURCES ON NEW VENTURE BIRTHS

Pearson correlations were run between (1) regional resources and the cumulative number of new semiconductor venture births in each region between 1978 to 1986 and (2) between the indicators of objective regional

FIGURE 10.6
Venture Capital Firms by Region

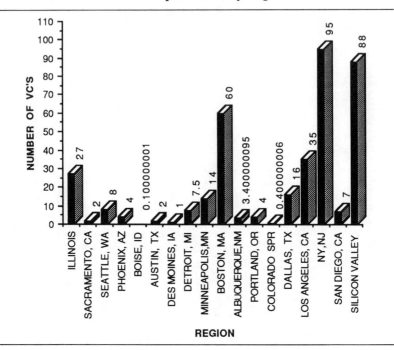

resources themselves. Although zero-order correlations cannot establish causality, they do indicate whether a significant relationship exists as well as the direction of the relationship. We found that regional resources that are specific to the industry are highly and significantly correlated with new semiconductor venture births. Specifically, the number of existing semiconductor firms in the region is highly, significantly correlated with the number of new firm births ($r = .87$, $p \geq .0001$). The greater the number of existing semiconductor firms in a region, the greater the number of new semiconductor firm births in the region. The existing members of an industry provide technical and industry business training for future entrepreneurs in a region, an experienced top management team, and a pool of experienced engineers and production workers, all essential human and technical capital for the start-up of a new venture in the semiconductor industry.

In addition to experienced and technically trained organizational members, new companies need capital to finance the venture. Semiconductor firms are especially capital-intensive, and they require millions of dollars in

FIGURE 10.7

Number of Electrical Engineers in 1980

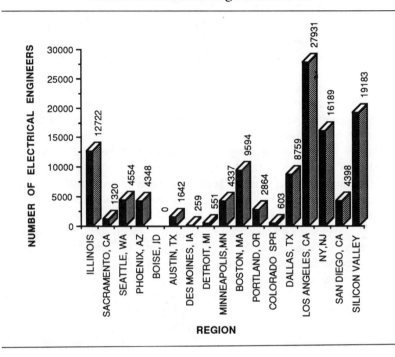

REGION

start-up capital and in subsequent rounds of financing. The correlation between the average number of venture capital firms in a region during the period of the study and the number of new semiconductor start-ups in the region is substantial and statistically significant ($r = .57, p \geqslant .01$).

Beyond capital and experienced members of an industry, new firms also require suppliers who help create the industry support structure. The correlation between number of new semiconductor start-ups in a region and the average number of supporting service firms in a region is very high and significant ($r = .93, p \geqslant .0001$). Similarly, the correlation between the number of supporting service firms and the number of existing semiconductor producers in the region is also very high ($r = .96, p \geqslant .0001$).

Beyond these simple zero-order correlations, regression analyses were conducted. This analysis showed that objective regional resources, such as the number of existing semiconductor firms, available venture capital, EEs, and firms that service the semiconductor industry, are incubator characteristics with significant, positive effects on new firm births. These variables had significant and substantial effects on new venture births. The greater the number of objective regional resources specific to an industry, the greater the number of new venture births in the region.[3]

These data support the conclusion that regions do act as incubators in the process of creating new technology-based ventures. Seventy percent of the new semiconductor ventures were founded in the Silicon Valley region of Northern California, and the data show that this region also has the richest array of industry-specific resources.

We conclude that the likelihood of a new firm being founded in a specific region is substantially enhanced if the region contains a well-developed industry infrastructure. Under these circumstances, entrepreneurs find that investors within the region understand the industry. There is a pool of potential employees, already trained within existing companies, from which the new firm can draw. A body of knowledge about running a semiconductor company exists within the collective memories of the region's managers and executives, some of which will be recruited to join the new venture. So, too, does knowledge about the business, its markets, and the semiconductor industry reside within the region; this information can be acquired by entrepreneurs through modeling and direct experience within existing companies.

In contrast to the vast semiconductor industry knowledge base that resides in the Silicon Valley, a different story emerged from the entrepreneurs of a new semiconductor company founded in a region remote from the Silicon Valley. They reported that substantial investment capital existed in their region. However, the local investors were not familiar with the semiconductor industry, its large capital requirements, nor with the technicalities of semiconductor circuit design and production. As a consequence, these entrepreneurs experienced great difficulty in raising the initial capital to found their firm in a region without substantial semiconductor industry experience. Indeed, that it was successfully founded at all in such a region, remote from the center of the industry, is a tribute to the skills and tenacity of its entrepreneurs.

Research Findings: Interregional Comparison of New Venture Outcomes

To this point, we have reported the relationship between objective resources of an incubator region and the new venture birthrate within the region. The data reveal that regional attributes play a significant part in the creation of new ventures. In this section, we move from statistical analyses to a more descriptive approach to the data. We ask, What are the similarities and differences among the new ventures when region of birth is taken into account? Since 70 percent of the new semiconductor ventures were founded in Northern California during the period from 1978 to 1986, we will examine the data for any qualitative differences that region of birth might make. We will examine how new ventures within a given region differ with respect to (1) composition of ownership in years 1 to 5 after founding, (2) the amount of R&D spending by the new ventures, (3) how innovative the firms are, (4) the number of months it takes the firms to produce their first working prototypes, (5) the number of months it takes to ship their first product for revenues, (6) the number of jobs created, and (7) the sales revenues in the first several years.

OWNERSHIP

The distribution of ownership in a new venture is very important for a number of reasons. First, any discussion of ownership distribution with entrepreneurs invariably leads to a discussion of "the Golden Rule." This was described to us as, "He who has the gold rules." The ownership distribution affects the relative leverage that various participants in the firm enjoy, whether they are founders, venture capital investors, individual investors, corporate investors, or other key employees. In Figure 10.8, all new U.S. semiconductor ventures are divided into two categories: those founded in the Silicon Valley and those founded in all other U.S. regions. The figure contains five years of data, with each graph describing the mean ownership distribution for firms founded in each of the regional categories. Each figure contains data for the proportion of ownership held by seven categories of potential owners: (1) the founding entrepreneurs themselves, (2) individual private investors, (3) other corporations who invest in the firm, (4) R&D partnership form of investors, (5) venture capital investors, (6) employees of the firm other than the founders, and (7) public ownership.

Founders as Owners. A substantial difference between Silicon Valley firms and those founded in other regions of the United States is the percentage of ownership held by the original entrepreneurs. In the first year, Silicon Valley entrepreneurs hold 46.28 percent of their firms, and entrepreneurs in all other regions hold a somewhat smaller 39 percent of the ownership at founding: a difference of about 7 percent. However, by the fifth year after founding, the relative percent held by entrepreneurs is dramatically different. Whereas entrepreneurs in other regions of the United States have relinquished only 1.4 percent control over their firms (from 39.51 to 38.12 percent by year 5), Silicon Valley entrepreneurs have relinquished 28 percent of the ownership in their firms (from 46 to 18 percent). This is indeed a strikingly different pattern when the regions are compared.

What is the relationship between percent of the new venture owned by

FIGURE   10.8
Percentage of Ownership by Year

SILICON VALLEY   ALL OTHER REGIONS

YEAR 1

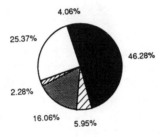

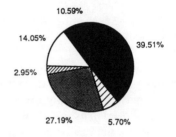

YEAR 2

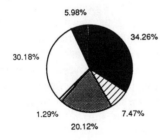

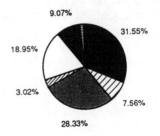

YEAR 3

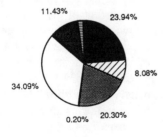

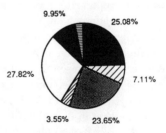

FIGURE 10.8 (Continued)
Percentage of Ownership by Year

SILICON VALLEY   **ALL OTHER REGIONS**

YEAR 4

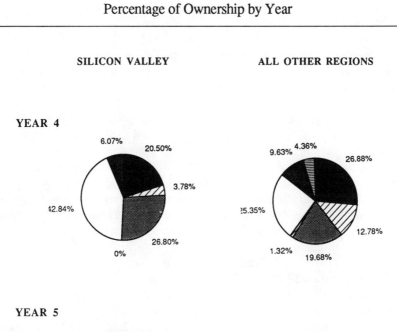

YEAR 5

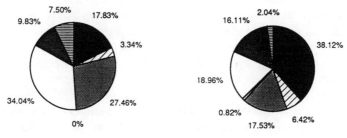

- ■ FOUNDERS
- ☑ INDIVIDUALS
- ▨ OTHER FIRMS
- ▨ R&D PARTNERSHIP
- ☐ VENTURE CAPITAL
- ■ EMPLOYEE

the founders and subsequent sales performance of the firm? A bivariate analysis of the relationship between percentage of founding team ownership and sales revenues for various years after founding shows that higher sales in later years are associated with entrepreneurs who hold a smaller percentage of ownership. That is, the greater the proportion of ownership held by the founders as a group, the lower the sales in the fourth and fifth years of life for the new venture.[4]

Venture Capital Owners. Venture capitalists have long played an important role in supplying much of the enormous capital required by high-technology ventures, including newly founded firms in the semiconductor industry. By venture capitalists, we mean traditional venture capital firms and funds that provide risk capital. Our data indicate that approximately 63 percent of the firms in the study received some form of venture capital in their first year of funding. The percentage held by venture capitalists ranges from 20 to 89 percent. This suggests that venture capital funds do not become involved in companies in the semiconductor industry unless they can have a substantial stake (at least 20 percent) in the firm—whether this is individually or in syndication with a group of venture investors.

Figure 10.8 reveals that when the Silicon Valley firms are compared to firms founded in the other seventeen regions of the United States, there is a substantial difference in the initial ownership distribution in the first year. Other than the founders, "other corporate investors" have the greatest proportion of ownership of new ventures in the group of seventeen other regions (26.19 percent). However, in Silicon Valley, venture capital firms hold the greatest percentage of ownership in the first year, 25.37 percent, on average. In their first year of existence, Silicon Valley firms' venture capital investors have nearly twice the ownership in these new ventures when compared to venture capital ownership in the firms in the group of all other regions. Twenty-five percent of the average firm in Silicon Valley is held by venture capitalists, as compared to only 14 percent venture capital ownership in the other regions.

Figure 10.8 also reveals the evolution of the ownership distribution over time. As the Silicon Valley firms age, from years 1 through 5, venture capital investors own a greater and greater percentage of these firms, on average. By the fourth year after founding, venture capitalists own 42.84 percent of the average new semiconductor firm in the Silicon Valley. This drops back somewhat in the fifth year to 34.04 percent retained by venture capital investors, with much of the difference due to the firms' going public so that public and employee ownership percentages increase. In contrast, venture capital investors retain only 18.96 percent of the ownership of firms founded in other regions of the United States in their fifth year after founding. This is a statistically significant difference in venture capital ownership by year 5.

Silicon Valley firms allocate more and more ownership control to the venture capital community over time. After the initial public offering, venture capital still plays a prominent part in the ownership structure of Silicon Valley ventures. As we saw earlier in the statistical analysis, the Silicon Valley region is rich in venture capital resources. These are utilized extensively by the Silicon Valley's entrepreneurs throughout the first five years of their firms' existence.

What is the relationship between venture capital ownership in a new venture and its subsequent sales performance? We found that venture capital ownership is associated with stronger sales performance in years 4 and 5, that is, the correlation between percentage of venture capital ownership and sales is positive and becomes stronger over time ($r = +.27$ and $+.36$, significant at .05 for years 4 and 5, respectively). It appears that venture capital provides an important boost to young companies.

Individual Investors, Public Ownership, and R&D Partnership Investors. Private individuals hold a relatively constant percent of the ownership in non–Silicon Valley firms. Figure 10.8 reveals that in the founding year, they hold 5.7 percent of the firm and in year 5, they hold 6.4 percent. In the Silicon Valley, private individuals begin with approximately the same share, 6 percent of the ownership. However, by the fifth year after founding, the percentage has dropped to only 3.3 percent for individual investors in Silicon Valley firms.

There is a substantially different pattern in public ownership when the two regional groups are compared. Both begin with no public ownership, as would be expected for newly founded firms. However, by the fifth year, the average public ownership in a Silicon Valley firm is 7.5 percent, whereas in the other regions, only 2 percent of the average firm is publicly owned.

R&D partnerships have played a minor role in the development of new firms in the semiconductor industry over the past ten years. In the Silicon Valley, the average ownership was 2.3 percent in the first year; this dropped to zero by years 4 and 5. In the other regions, the first-year ownership is 2.9 percent; this drops to .8 percent by year 5.

INNOVATION AS RESEARCH INTENSITY AND KNOWLEDGE SYNTHESIS

Research intensiveness is one indicator of the innovativeness of a given firm. It is generally measured for public corporations as expenditures for R&D as a percent of annual sales revenues. Since these firms have little income in their first several years, their R&D/sales ratios are quite high. We can compare the relative research intensiveness of semiconductor firms across birth region. In Figure 10.9, the new ventures are divided into three

FIGURE   10.9

R&D As a Fraction of Sales

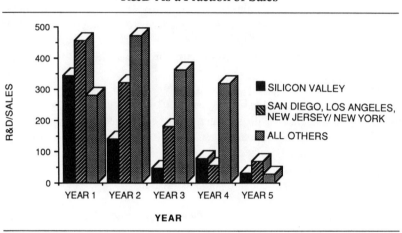

regional clusters: (1) Silicon Valley region firms, (2) San Diego plus Los Angeles plus New Jersey–New York region firms, and (3) firms founded in all other regions.

Since all firms in our study are technology-based, one might assume that they are equally research intensive. Figure 10.9 suggests otherwise. The graph shows that the most research-intensive regions are in the cluster of regions with several new semiconductor firms: San Diego, Los Angeles, and New Jersey–New York. In their first year, firms in this cluster spent 454.7 percent on research as a percent of sales, on average. The Silicon Valley is second most research-intensive (344.1 percent) by this measure. The firms in the one-birth regions (other regions) are the least research-intensive of the three, though still high by any comparison, spending 281.3 percent of sales on R&D.

In year 2, the relative rankings have shifted substantially. In their second year of life, firms founded in regions where they are the only semi-conductor start-up spend 471.7 percent of sales on R&D; this is the highest of the three clusters. The Silicon Valley expenditures for R&D have dropped, on average, by more than a factor of two, to 141.7 percent. In their second year, the Silicon Valley firms are only 30 percent as research-intensive as firms founded in regions by themselves.

During years 2 through 4, the regions with only a single new semicon-ductor firm far outstrip the other regions in research intensiveness. In contrast, firms in the Silicon Valley and in the San Diego, Los Angeles, and New Jersey–New York groupings bring their research expenditures dramatically lower as a percent of sales in these years. By year 5, all three clusters are substantially above the mean for this industry as a whole, yet they are all spending less than 100 percent of sales on research, at .30, .69, and .29 for the Silicon Valley, the intermediate region firms, and the one-birth region firms, respectively.

Figure 10.10 compares the Silicon Valley region with firms founded in all of the remaining seventeen regions of the United States. The graph reveals that there is no significant difference in research intensiveness during the first year when firms in the remaining seventeen regions are averaged: 344.1 versus 344.4 percent, respectively. However, as the previous graph has shown, although the figures for the Silicon Valley firms drop dramatically in the second year, the average R&D ratio remains extremely high and even increases to 411.9 percent in the other regions during the second year. The Silicon Valley ratio of expenditures for R&D drops below 100 percent in years 3, 4, and 5, but it is not until year 5 that the other regions have their research expenditures under relative control, at 55 percent of sales revenues. Of course, research intensiveness is calculated as a percentage of sales here. As a consequence, as sales go up, the relative research intensiveness drops.

Another way to measure technological innovativeness is to examine what we call "knowledge synthesis." Knowledge synthesis is the extent to which entrepreneurs have combined existing knowledge in unique ways to create their new technology-based products. (Knowledge synthesis is

FIGURE 10.10

R&D As a Fraction of Sales

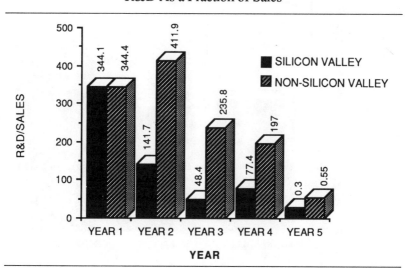

differentiated from knowledge creation, which relies on the creation of new knowledge rather than the synthesis of existing knowledge.) Figure 10.11 graphs the relative knowledge synthesis of the three regional clusters. On a scale of zero to ten, where zero represents no knowledge synthesis and a ten represents exceptionally high combinations of existing knowledge in unique ways, the Silicon Valley firms and the intermediate-birth regions are nearly the same. Firms in both groups exhibit moderate degrees of knowledge synthesis while the firms in the one-birth regions exhibit substantially higher degrees of unique combinations of knowledge, at 7.1 on average (on a ten-point scale). On the one hand, these differences may reflect the fact that the firms founded in regions with no other new semiconductor firms have little data for social comparison. On the other, these differences may indeed be real. As we saw in the previous graphs, the one-birth firms spend substantially larger percentages of their annual revenues on R&D for several years longer than the other two regional groups.

FIRST WORKING PROTOTYPES AND FIRST SHIPMENTS FOR REVENUES

The speed with which an organization develops and then ships its first product for revenues is a significant entrepreneurial indicator. Fast products

FIGURE   10.11

Knowledge Synthesis

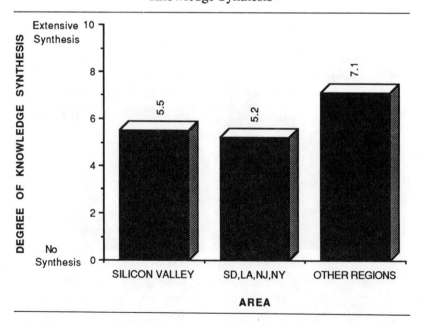

are important (1) to gain early cash flow for greater financial independence, (2) to gain external visibility and legitimacy as soon as possible, (3) to gain early market share, and (4) to increase the likelihood of survival. In general, the more quickly a new venture develops its first product and ships it to the first customer, the more quickly it will embark upon the path to greater financial independence (Schoonhoven et al., 1990).

Figure 10.12 graphs the mean waiting time to first working prototype in months after founding, comparing the three regional clusters. Consistent with their initial year's high research intensiveness (344.1 percent), the Silicon Valley firms take 12.4 months, on average, to produce their first working prototypes. Firms founded in all other regions of the United States take nearly twice as long as Silicon Valley firms to produce their first working prototype: 23.1 months for firms founded in the combined San Diego, Los Angeles, and New Jersey–New York regions and 20.3 months for firms founded in any other region of the United States. This is a major difference when the R&D productivity of Silicon Valley firms is compared to that of semiconductor firms founded elsewhere in the continental United States.

The length of time it takes a new venture to ship its first product (beyond the prototype) to market is a very important milestone because shipment of

FIGURE 10.12

Mean Waiting Time to Prototype

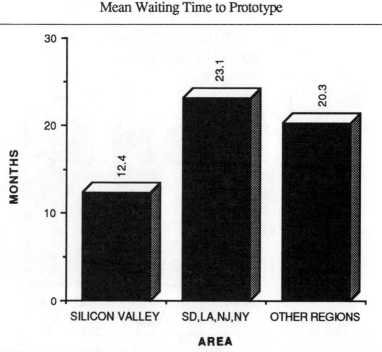

the first product generates a firm's first significant revenues. Figure 10.13 graphs the number of months to first shipment after founding. Silicon Valley firms take only 17.5 months after founding, on average, to ship their first products. In less than eighteen months, Silicon Valley firms have created a revenue stream based on the product they were founded to develop. Firms founded in all other regions of the United States take substantially longer to ship their first product for revenues, about seven months longer than the Silicon Valley firms, on average. Firms founded in any of the seventeen non–Silicon Valley regions ship their first product for revenues in about their twenty-fifth month after founding, on average.

OUTCOMES: NEW JOBS CREATED AND SALES REVENUES

The size of a new venture, measured by the number of employees per year and by sales revenues, is important for several reasons. First, complex projects, such as the development of an integrated circuit or a microprocessor, take years of labor hours to produce, even with sophisticated computer-aided design machines to facilitate the work. Labor hours translate into more people when new firms are time-pressed to get their first products developed. More employees are expensive, however, and so more labor hours drive up

FIGURE   10.13
Months to First Shipment

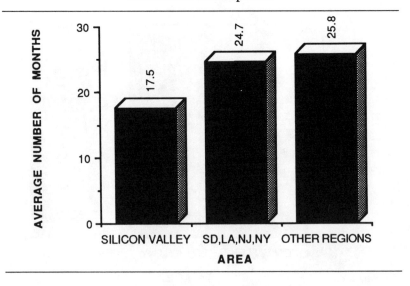

the relative costs of payroll to a new venture and thus the capital requirements for a new firm. From an economic development perspective, though,
new ventures create new jobs and so are an important contributor to
economic development in the regions in which they are founded.

Figure 10.14 graphs the jobs created in the first three years of the firms'
operations. Although the creation of new jobs is a laudable goal, new firms
without a stable stream of revenue must support all employees they hire on
the current revenue base.

Reflecting a relatively conservative expenditure of funds for salaries and
wages, all three regional clusters have firms whose average size at the end of
the first year is quite modest, with 8.6 employees on average in the seventeen
other regions of the United States beyond the Silicon Valley. Firms in the Silicon Valley were slightly larger, with 12.1 employees on average at the end
of their first year of operations. In their second year, all firms are about three
times larger than in their first year of operations.

However, by the third year, the number of new jobs created is
significantly different across the regions. The Silicon Valley firms have
grown nearly six times larger when compared to their first year, with 72.1
employees, on average, at the end of their third year of operations. Firms in
the one-birth regions (other regions) have grown about five times larger than
their first year, with 41.9 employees, on average, in their third year. The San
Diego, Los Angeles, and New Jersey–New York firms lag, with only 28.8
employees in their third year, still only about three times larger than their
first year of operations. Therefore, the Silicon Valley firms do show the

FIGURE 10.14

Jobs Created in First Three Years of Firms' Operations

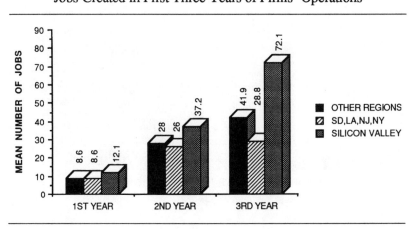

fastest and largest growth in number of new jobs created in the first three years of existence.

Sales revenues are another important indicator of firm performance, in addition to indicating new firm size. Figure 10.15 graphs the average sales in the first three years, again comparing the three regional groupings. In their first years, all three groups generated negligible sales revenues, as would be expected during the development period. In year 2, the San Diego, Los Angeles, and New Jersey–New York regional group lagged behind the Silicon Valley and the other regions where only a single semiconductor firm was founded. Firms in these latter regions generated about $1.5 million in sales, on average, in their second year of operations. By year 3, the Silicon Valley firms had generated $6 million in sales, on average, outstripping the firms in all other regions of the United States by approximately three times greater sales revenues. The relatively high Silicon Valley revenues help to explain why their R&D expenditures as a proportion of sales drop so quickly in the third year. Whereas absolute research expenditures may not decrease significantly, sales revenues have increased substantially. However, given that Silicon Valley firms ship their first products for revenues in less than eighteen months, on average, this suggests that R&D costs also drop substantially in the second and third years, along with the increase in sales. The enhanced sales revenues also support a much larger organization, on average, in the third year in the Silicon Valley; thus, more jobs are created.

Overall, the picture emerges of Silicon Valley firms being supported by

FIGURE   10.15

Mean Sales in the First Three Years of Operation

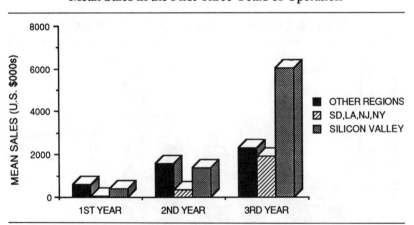

the venture capital industry to a relatively larger extent than their counterparts in other regions of the United States. Silicon Valley ventures quickly produce their first working prototypes in only twelve months, on average. They ship their first products for revenues substantially faster than new ventures in other regions, only eighteen months after founding, creating a seven-month lead on the new ventures founded in the remaining seventeen regions of the United States. Therefore, before their second birthdays, the Silicon Valley firms are producing revenues from their new products. Marketplace participation quickly enhances their sales revenues, so that by the third year after founding, these are firms of substantial size, having generated seventy-two new jobs, on average. With sales revenues three times greater than those of new semiconductor firms founded in the other seventeen regions of the United States, the Silicon Valley firms do appear to be on a faster track to growth and development than the rest of the newer firms in the industry.

Research Findings: Survival Analysis

We have seen that objective regional characteristics enhance the birthrate of new, technology-based ventures in a region. Now we explore the impact of the incubator region's resources on subsequent outcomes, such as new venture survival over time. Like all new firms, semiconductor ventures must overcome a number of liabilities imposed by their newness as organizations. This phenomenon is referred to as the "liability of newness," in which new organizations are argued to be particularly prone to failure (Stinchcombe, 1965). New firms such as these face a perilous childhood. Newness liabilities pose conditions that, if not successfully dealt with, threaten the survival of the new firm. For example, death rates of up to 46 percent within the first eighteen months after founding have been reported for new U.S. firms (Van de Ven and Walker, 1984).

Given the high density of existing semiconductor companies in the Silicon Valley, we investigated whether birth in this region was advantageous to a new venture or whether the high birthrate might overtax resources of the region and create a disproportionately high death rate. We have conducted several analyses. First, we examine the overall death rates, comparing the three regional clusters: (1) Silicon Valley, (2) Los Angeles plus San Diego plus New York–New Jersey, and (3) the one-birth regions, then we report on statistical analyses of the overall death rates. Next, we analyze deaths over time, taking region of birth into account. This is a longitudinal analysis referred to as survival analysis.

COMPARING SURVIVAL RATES IN SILICON VALLEY AND OTHER U.S. REGIONS

Recall that the distribution of new semiconductor firm foundings is highly skewed. Eleven regions of the United States have had only one new firm birth. A few have had two to five births, and the Silicon Valley region has had sixty-nine new semiconductor firms founded in the period of our study. Figure 10.16 graphs the survival rate for all regions in the United States with at least one new semiconductor founding in the period 1978 to 1986. There is wide variation across U.S. regions, from a low of no survivors to a high of all new firms survived. The figure reveals that two regions had a survival rate of zero, one region had a .67 survival rate, three other regions had survival rates between .75 and .81, and twelve regions had survival rates of 1.00, where no firms died in the observation period.[5]

Figure 10.16 reveals that survival rates, like birthrates, are skewed when regions of the United States are compared. Because eleven of the

FIGURE 10.16
Survival Rate by Region

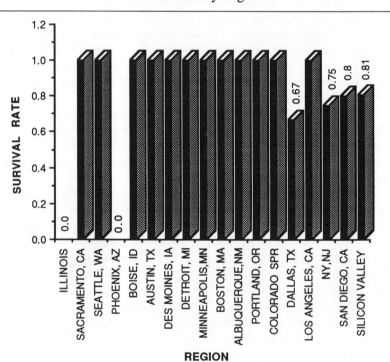

regions had only one birth, these had survival rates of either 0 or 100 percent. Of these one-birth regions, 18 percent of the regions had their single
new firm dissolve—a total extermination of new firms in the semiconductor
industry in these two regions. While this is an exceptionally heavy loss for
these two regions, the remainder of the eleven regions with only one new
birth fared very well from a survival perspective. The mean survival rate for
all eighteen regions is .835: Eighty-three percent of the firms founded in a
given region of the United States survived through 1988.

Because the new venture birthrates are neither equally nor randomly
distributed throughout the regions of the United States, we grouped the eighteen regions by number of new firm births in a region. Three clusters are
obtained, and they reveal a slightly different perspective on the data. The
three clusters are (1) the high-birth region (Silicon Valley), (2) the
moderate-birth regions (San Diego, Los Angeles, New York–New Jersey),
and (3) the low-birth regions (the eleven remaining regions). Mean survival
rates were calculated for each of these three regional groups and graphed.

Figure 10.17 reflects the survival rate for small-, medium-, and large-
birth areas. Visual inspection of the graph indicates that there is no
significant difference between the three regional groupings' mean survival

FIGURE 10.17

Survival Rates for Small-, Medium-, and Large-Birth Areas

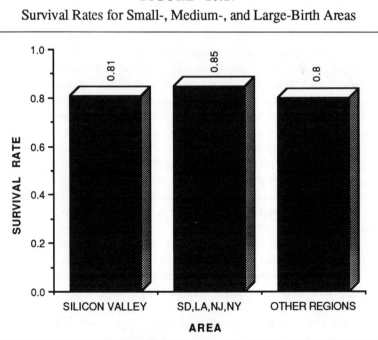

rates. The survival rate for the Silicon Valley is .81; for the moderate-birth areas, .85; and for the one-birth regions, .80. This graph suggests that firms founded in regions with no other semiconductor firms in their geographic area are not necessarily disadvantaged with respect to survival. Analysis of variance results also indicates no statistically significant differences in survival rates across the three regional clusters.

REGRESSION RESULTS: PREDICTING FIRM SURVIVAL

Beyond comparing overall survival rates by regional categories, we also ran regression analyses predicting survival. Logistic regression results that examined the effect of total number of semiconductor companies in a region on the overall survival rate of new ventures in a region showed no significant effect of regional industry density on death or survival of new ventures in a region. Thus, there was no significant effect of the number of existing semiconductor companies in a region on the survival of a new venture founded in the region. Similarly, an index of regional resources showed no significant causal effect on new venture survival. We conclude that survival of a new venture is neither guaranteed nor enhanced by being founded within a region rich with objective resources of importance to the industry.

These are unexpected findings. Since industry-specific regional resources play a significant role in the births of new semiconductor firms, it is somewhat surprising that these analyses reveal no significant difference in the overall survival rates across regional clusters.

Taken together, these results shed light on one of the primary questions addressed in this research: Does the high density of new semiconductor ventures in the Silicon Valley overtax resources within the geographical region, resulting in a disproportionately high rate of new firm failures compared to firms founded in less densely settled regions? On average, firms founded in the Silicon Valley have equally as high a survival rate as those founded in other U.S. regions. There are no significant differences in survival. Therefore, even with its high density of new semiconductor firm foundings as well as existing semiconductor firms, the Silicon Valley has been able to successfully nurture a very large number of new ventures through their early years of existence.

These findings are consistent with more recent research on the effects of industry population density on firm failures (Delacroix et al., 1989). Delacroix and colleagues have argued that environments are not rigidly fixed in their capacity to absorb new organizations of a given type. Rather, they argue that firms may respond to the pressure of high numbers: (1) by altering slightly the nature of their activities, thereby collectively enlarging the initial organizational niche (Hawley, 1986), or (2) by migrating laterally to neighboring niches (Swaminathan and Delacroix, 1988). They observe that in modern societies, environments are sufficiently flexible that these alternative responses to rising numbers in a population are at least as likely as elimination or death of members of the population (Delacroix et al., 1989).

The high survival rate of the population of new semiconductor firms in Silicon Valley appears to demonstrate the flexibility of environments. These firms have pioneered entirely new approaches to the manufacture of semiconductor components; they have developed Application Specific Integrated Circuits (ASICs) and new ways of efficiently designing customized circuits through computer-aided silicon compiler technologies and the like. Twenty-five percent of new Silicon Valley firms were founded to provide ASIC products, a market that did not exist until California Devices, a firm founded in 1978 in the Silicon Valley, began to develop the techniques for creating them.

By the same token, the Silicon Valley region does not appear to provide a differential survival advantage to new ventures founded in the region. Recall that the number of new firm births is substantially higher and significantly related to resources of the region, as we saw earlier. However, survival rates after founding are not significantly different when the regions are compared. The Silicon Valley does not appear to provide a set of regional circumstances that make a significant difference in the new firm survival rate. Because the markets for semiconductor components are worldwide and because there is wide variation in organizational and entrepreneurial circumstances across firms, survival after founding may relate to variables beyond the region as well as to internal variables within the firms.

The Timing of Firm Deaths: A Dynamic Analysis

While the overall death rates do not vary across regions, the timing of deaths may. Companies may die more quickly in some regions or live longer without dying but then die in clusters later in time. To understand the influence of regional characteristics in the development of these new firms at various points over time, survival analyses were conducted. This type of analysis allows us to understand the likelihood of a firm dying (hazard rate) at each month after its birth. The data are longitudinal, and thus we can track the survival of these firms over time. Some companies were founded as early as 1978 and were nearly eleven years of age when data collection was completed. Since the bulk of the new firm births were in the 1983–84 time frame, the largest group of new ventures was between thirty-six and forty-eight months old.

Regions were assigned a value to indicate the degree of resource richness present in the region, using the objective industry-specific resources described earlier. Regions were then grouped according to resource richness and survival analyses were conducted, comparing new ventures founded in high-resource regions versus those in low-resource regions. Figure 10.18 plots the hazard rates for company failure in low- and high-resource regions.

As the figure shows, high-resource regions show more death activity than low-resource regions. This is likely due to the greater number of cases available in the high-resource regions. The hazard of death in the high-resource regions fluctuates between 0 and less than 3 percent for the first three and a half years. It then begins to increase (when it is not zero) in the periods between four and seven years (thirty-six-plus months to eighty-four months). However, there are no deaths beyond seven years of age in firms founded in the high-resource regions (through the end of the observation period of the study).

The figure shows that there are no deaths in the low-resource regions in months 1 through 35. However, the greatest likelihood of death for firms founded in low-resource regions is at thirty-six months, where it jumps to a 13 percent hazard. In contrast, firms founded in high-resource regions had only a 1 percent hazard of death at thirty-six months.

This suggests that surviving infancy to become an older company is associated with regional resources: 92 percent of the firms founded in high-

FIGURE   10.18

Hazard Rates for Company Failure in
Low- and High-Resource Regions

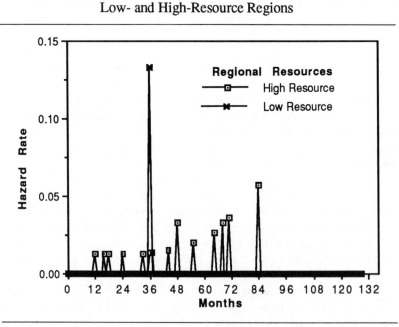

resource regions survived the thirty-sixth month. Still, after the third-year shakeout, firms founded in low-resource regions had relatively high survival rates (.87) through 123 months of life. Therefore, it appears that surviving the third year of life is an important event for these firms; it predicts subsequent survival well. The survival rate for firms founded in high-resource regions was somewhat lower at month 123, although still quite high at .73.

When all the new semiconductor firms are examined as a population, one can chart the overall death rate. Figure 10.19 shows the hazard rate for all companies in all regions. It reveals that there have been two particularly vulnerable periods in the lives of these new companies. The highest rates of death for the entire population of semiconductor firms founded in the United States between 1978 and 1986 were at three and seven years (thirty-six and eighty-four months, respectively). There were no deaths in the first twelve months. There were also no deaths in companies older than seven years up to the point of this analysis (observations through December 1988). The hazard rate fluctuates between 0 and .01 for the first three years, relatively small risks of death for new ventures pursuing a high-technology strategy. However, between the third and seventh years (months 36 to 84), the hazard rates peak at much higher levels. In this period, they fluctuate between 11 percent in the forty-fifth month of life and 46 percent in the eighty-fourth month of life. Keep in mind, though, that there were substantially fewer companies

FIGURE 10.19

Hazard Rates for All Companies in All Regions

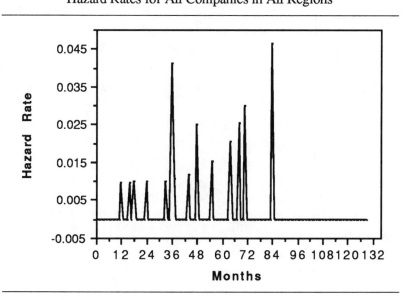

that even qualified to reach eighty-four months of age because the bulk of the new births in the semiconductor industry was in 1983 and 1984. As the number of cases for analysis diminishes, the effect of even a single death produces a much higher hazard rate. Therefore, the exceptionally high hazard rate in the eighty-fourth month is somewhat attributable to the much smaller number of firms that were born earlier in the period of our research; very few companies were founded between 1978 and 1981.

Figure 10.20 reveals that, overall, there is a high rate of survival for all semiconductor firms founded in the United States between 1978 and 1986. Less than 25 percent have died. The steepest decline, which reflects the greatest proportions dying, is between thirty-six and seventy-two months, especially around thirty-six months, and then again in the sixty-to-seventy-two-month range. There are no deaths in the first twelve months. At the end of the observation period, for firms 130 months old, .76 of the companies still survived. This indicates that new ventures in the semiconductor industry are resilient. There is a high firm survival for the population as a whole.

FIGURE   10.20

Survival Rates for All Companies in All Regions

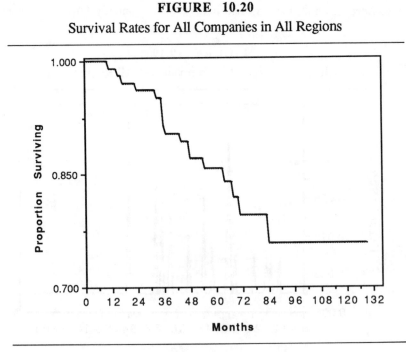

Implications of the Research

The research reported here has implications for regional governments seeking to create regions of high-tech excellence, as well as for national policy and for entrepreneurs and their investors. Until this research, little was known about whether differences in industry-specific regional resources have a measurable impact on the birth and survival of new, technology-based ventures. Understanding how geographic regions function as incubators may contribute to economic development.

REGIONAL ECONOMIC DEVELOPMENT

If a region wishes to promote the creation of new, technology-based ventures, replication of environmental conditions that exist in high-birth regions is a strategy to consider. The first implication of our research for regional economic development is to recognize that the creation of new-technology-based ventures is an organizational process concentrated within specific industries. To build jobs and the regional economy, our research suggests a strategy of focused industrial development within the region—that specific industries be targeted to build critical mass. Rather than funding or awarding tax advantages to stand-alone projects, ask how potential projects contribute to building a critical industrial concentration within a region. Economic development, as indicated by the number of new firms in a specific industry founded within a region, is better served by targeting industries than by a shotgun approach to firms randomly spread across several industries. This is supported by the finding that new firm births were greatest in regions with the larger industry-specific infrastructures.

Established plants are an important aspect of the regional industry infrastructure. Established plants are important because entrepreneurship is largely a local phenomenon. Entrepreneurs are typically individuals who found their new ventures in regions where they already reside (Cooper and Bruno, 1977). Established plants are also important because potential entrepreneurs in high-tech industries receive their business and industry training in existing firms. These companies play an important role in educating employees, some of whom become the region's entrepreneurs. Existing organizations provide the managerial, manufacturing, engineering, development, and marketing experiences necessary for successful conduct of high-tech businesses. This appears to apply even in relatively new industries, such as biotechnology. Initial biotechnology commercialization experiments took place in university laboratories, and thus the very first new ventures were dependent upon university faculty expertise. However, the knowledge of how to manufacture products in high volume, how to navigate the drug approval process, and how to market new products is gained in the business world, not in a university laboratory. Industry-specific business knowledge is absorbed by subsequent waves of employees, some of whom leave to form new ventures within the region.

In some industries, novices without experience in the industry may successfully found a new firm. However, in industries with a sophisticated science base, such as the semiconductor industry, existing firms provide the business experience for survival in the industry. Firms founded by novice entrepreneurs without industry experience do not have sufficient time to learn the necessary skills to compete in high-tech industries. Since products and processes change very quickly, development times in new firms must be short. On average, the firms founded in the Silicon Valley region of our study produced their first working prototypes within twelve months of founding. Manufacturing and marketing of the new product must be equally as rapid because revenues are required to offset the heavy operating expenses of capital-intensive industries. Silicon Valley firms sold their first products within eighteen months of founding. Firms founded in other, less munificent regions had significantly longer development times before first products were sold, twenty-five months, on average. The longer it takes to develop the first product, the slower the growth in firm revenues and in new jobs created.

Regions should also target service firms to build the industry infrastructure. Beyond the firms in the targeted industry itself, other objective regional resources important in the birthrate of new ventures are manufacturing service organizations and venture capital firms. In our research, industry-specific regional resources include mask makers, crystal growers, failure analysts, and semiconductor equipment manufacturers. All of these provide essential inputs to the semiconductor firms. In our data base, the correlation between the number of existing semiconductor firms in a region and the number of specialized-industry service firms was quite high ($r = + .96***$). This suggests that regional governments not overlook the significance of firms in related service industries as they seek to replicate regions of high-tech excellence.

Another objective regional variable is the availability of venture capital. Some argue that venture capital is not a regional resource but rather a national one. Transportation costs via air travel are minimal; thus, raising sufficient capital to found a new firm should not depend on local capital availability but rather on the simple cost of an airplane ticket. Theoretically, entrepreneurs should have easy access to venture capital firms in the United States regardless of the region in which they are located. This argument overlooks the social network aspects of new venture formation and the behavior of venture capital investors. Our data have shown that the local availability of venture capital has a significant impact on the birthrate of new ventures in a region. Regions with minimal venture capital resources have produced the minimum number of new semiconductor ventures, one new firm. The correlation between number of new firm births in a region and the number of venture capital firms in the region is high and statistically significant. The more venture capital firms in the region, the greater the number of new venture foundings.

These quantitative findings are supported by qualitative interviews with entrepreneurs who founded ventures in regions with minimal local venture capital. Entrepreneurs revealed that venture capitalists from other regions (Silicon Valley and New York, for example) were reluctant to fund companies to which they could not have easy access (for example, within driving distance or within the same time zone). While some venture firms undoubtedly fund entrepreneurs outside of their immediate region, the preference for within-region funding was clearly communicated to entrepreneurs. Other data support the entrepreneurs' reports. New ventures founded in regions outside of the Silicon Valley have significantly less venture capital participation in their ownership structures, on average, than do the firms founded within the Silicon Valley: 25.2 percent venture capital ownership in Silicon Valley firms versus only 13.8 percent venture capital ownership in non–Silicon Valley firms.

The implication for regional economic development is that state and local governments should not overlook the venture capital industry as they seek to replicate regional infrastructure conditions. Many venture capital firms headquartered in New York, Chicago, and even Cleveland have opened Silicon Valley branch offices. A casual analysis of the *Guide to Venture Capital Resources* (Pratt and Morris, 1970–86) and the number of major firms with branch offices confirm this with data. Strategically located branch offices increase what venture capitalists call their "deal flow." This is the number of technology-based business plans that cross their desks that, in turn, provide the opportunities to invest. Venture capital investors report anecdotally that their technology deals increase when they have offices located in regions already populated with technology-based firms.

It is important to recognize that regional economic development via the creation of new technology-based ventures is dependent upon existing organizations within a targeted industry and upon the firms that service the target industry, whether they be technical service providers or investment capital providers. Organizations within this cluster of industries (all with specialized knowledge about a specific industry) should be created to increase the probability of new technology-based ventures being founded in a given geographic region.

IMPLICATIONS FOR NATIONAL POLICY

It has been documented that industries naturally tend to develop around centers and to be concentrated geographically (Porter, 1990). For example, the robotics and computer-aided design industries have developed around Detroit. The minicomputer industry has developed in the vicinity of Boston. Pharmaceuticals and chemicals are concentrated in the New Jersey and Delaware regions, and the U.S. semiconductor industry has developed in Northern California (Schoonhaven and Eisenhardt, 1989). Because of this natural industrial concentration effect, there is some opportunity at the federal level to facilitate regional economic development.

We have found that economic development in the form of new firm foundings is related to a region's industry-specific infrastructure and that a critical industry mass is important to subsequent new firm start-ups. Were the federal government to promote industrial development, then targeting a few centers or locales for industry-specific development would be more appropriate than supporting solitary start-up efforts in each of twenty different regions or locales. Basically, the same implication applies at the federal level as has been developed for the regional level above. Economic diversification can be created nationally by choosing centers throughout the country for targeted development. This, of course, is the approach that appears to characterize Japan's industrial policy efforts: targeting specific industries for development within specific regions, time frames, and resource commitments (Kojima, 1990; Rogers and Chen, 1990; Williams, 1990).

IMPLICATIONS FOR ENTREPRENEURS AND THEIR INVESTORS

This research also has implications for entrepreneurs who found firms beyond regions where the existing industry is concentrated and for investors in such firms. Our study demonstrates that each party to the new firm needs to anticipate that it will take longer for the new firm to become established than firms that are founded near the industry center. Although survival rates are the same, it takes longer to build a high-tech company in the more remote regions. By their third year, the Silicon Valley firms had sales that were three times greater than new firms founded in other regions less endowed with industry-specific resources. Firms founded in more remote regions need to plan accordingly.

We also found that the greatest hazard of death for new semiconductor firms is in their third year of existence, but that third-year deaths were primarily concentrated in the other, non–Silicon Valley region companies. Founders and investors in more remote regions need to recognize that survival through the third year is not guaranteed and that high death liabilities exist in that time period. The need for investment capital continues into the third year for firms founded in the more remote regions: Their sales growth is slower and the alternative to additional capital infusion is death for the firm.

These findings also demonstrate why investors with knowledge about specific industries are crucial for new venture survival. Industry-naive investors might assume that most new ventures should be well established by their third year of life. However, additional infusions of capital are necessary for a new high-tech company to make its presence known in the semiconductor marketplace—especially if it is founded in a region remote from the industry's center.

The data have shown that whereas industry-specific objective resources of the incubator region play a significant role in the formation of new ventures, objective regional resources have little direct impact on new venture outcomes after founding. In contrast, it is how the entrepreneur utilizes resources of the region that has an impact on financial performance of the new venture.

For example, we found significant differences across the regions in contact frequency between entrepreneurs and members of their boards of directors, their current investors, and other executives in the industry who also reside in the local region (Schoonhoven and Eisenhardt, 1989). Silicon Valley entrepreneurs made substantially higher use of resources located within their region.

Entrepreneurs should consider diversifying the ownership structure of their new ventures. While it is true that the founders give up a percent of the firm's ownership when outsiders invest in the firm, the better-performing firms in our study have founders with smaller percentages of ownership. Outsiders, such as venture capital investors, other corporations, and individual investors, bring an even greater diversity of experience to the firm. Their influence is typically expressed through the positions they gain on the board of directors and the decisions thereby made by the board. Perhaps even more important is that firms with greater percentages of venture capital ownership did significantly better financially in the fifth year of life when compared to those with no venture capital ownership. Therefore, potential entrepreneurs should take a longer term perspective on the development of their new ventures. Our data suggest that entrepreneurs should consider that greater wealth is created when founders retain less personal control over the ownership structure.

Summary and Conclusion

This study has investigated whether regions of the United States function differentially as incubators for the successful founding and development of new technology-based ventures. Original, within-firm data were gathered on the population of new semiconductor industry ventures founded in the United States between 1978 and 1985. Firms were founded in eighteen regions of the United States, and the new venture participation rate in this study is 96 percent. As a consequence, these data describe the functioning of virtually the entire population of new firms in this industry during the period studied rather than just a sample.

The first question we asked was whether there is a relationship between characteristics of a geographic region and the birthrate of new, high-tech companies. We found that geographic regions do function differentially as incubators in the birth of new technology-based ventures. We defined the concept of an *incubator region* as a confluence of industry-specific resources contained within a circumscribed geographic area, which may be mobilized to create and sustain new ventures in a given industry. We found that objective regional resources specific to the semiconductor industry are significantly correlated with the number of new firm births in a given region. The greater the number of regional semiconductor-relevant resources, the greater the number of new semiconductor firm foundings.

Second, for new firms founded in regions rich with industry-specific resources, we asked whether the resources concentrated in such regions provide a differential advantage compared to new ventures founded in other regions. Specifically, do Silicon Valley firms have a higher new venture survival rate? Conversely, might the high density of existing semiconductor firms in some regions, such as the Silicon Valley, overtax resources within the region, resulting in a disproportionately high rate of new firm failures compared to firms founded in regions less densely settled with semiconductor companies?

A dynamic survival analysis revealed that firms founded in the Silicon Valley region faced very low probabilities of death at "any age" after founding: The survival rate ranged from 100 percent in the first twelve months to 73.1 percent for firms that entered the seventh year of life. "Any age" was measured to 130 months of age, the age of the oldest firms at the end of the observation period.

Firms founded in any other region of the United States had more variable survival rates. This is especially true because eleven of the non–Silicon Valley regions had only one new venture birth apiece. Eighteen percent of these regions had survival rates of zero, whereas in the remaining one-birth regions, the sole firm survived, thereby producing a survival rate of 100 percent.

A more telling survival comparison juxtaposes the Silicon Valley firms with those founded elsewhere in the United States. When the Silicon Valley firms were compared to ventures founded in all other regions of the United States as a group, there were no significant differences in overall survival rates. Overall, the Silicon Valley mean survival rate was 81 percent for the period of our research, compared to 83 percent for the other regions combined. These results shed light on a central question in this study: Does the high density of new semiconductor ventures in the Silicon Valley overtax resources within the region, resulting in a disproportionately high rate of new firm failures? On average, Silicon Valley firms have equally as high a survival rate as those firms founded in other regions of the United States. Therefore, the Silicon Valley has been able to successfully support a large number of new ventures in the semiconductor industry in their early years of existence. This suggests that regional concentration of firms within a specific industry is not a disadvantage *at the level of the firm*. These new firms were no less likely to survive than firms born into a less crowded regional environment, nor does regional disbursement of new firms in a specific industry increase the likelihood of death of the firm after founding.

Beyond survival, the third question we asked was whether Silicon Valley firms are advantaged in other ways: Do they capture higher proportions of available venture capital or do they have faster growth rates or greater sales revenues when compared to ventures founded in other regions of the United States? We found that firms founded in the Silicon Valley are advantaged in several ways. First, they produce their first products for revenues significantly faster than firms founded in other regions. Therefore, the innovation-to-product development cycle is shorter and economic benefits are reaped faster by new firms in the Silicon Valley. Second, the new Silicon Valley firms have higher sales growth rates than firms founded in other regions of the United States, with revenues three times higher than those of other firms in their third year of life. Third, the Silicon Valley firms produce *more* new jobs *faster* than semiconductor firms founded in other regions of the United States. While there are no survival advantages to being founded in either the Silicon Valley or in another region of the United States, new firm performance differences are substantial and the Silicon Valley firms bring greater economic benefits to their region sooner than do the other new firms. Thus, regional concentration of new high-tech firms appears to have a greater economic impact than does disbursement of new firms over many different regions.

Notes

1. For greater detail, the interested reader is referred to Schoonhoven and Eisenhardt, 1989, pp. 149–176.

2. A new venture in the semiconductor industry is defined as a new organization founded for the purpose of developing, producing, and selling semiconductor devices on the merchant market. Excluded, by definition, are captive, in-house producers that manufacture only for their own corporations; new divisions of existing

corporations, which cannot be considered newly founded organizations; in-house divisions spun off from parent corporations that did not compete in the merchant market at the time of their creation; electronic distributors that only sell devices made by the semiconductor producers themselves; and electronic design houses that only design circuits for others and neither produce nor market semiconductor devices.

3.   Greater detail on this analysis can be found in Schoonhoven and Eisenhardt, 1989, pp. 15–29.

4.   Interested readers are referred to Schoonhoven and Eisenhardt, 1989, pp. 124–132, for greater detail on this analysis.

5.   We define organizational death as the dissolution of the organization, when the company ceases to be identifiable as a separate organizational form. The definition is consistent with leading research on organizational mortality and survival (Freeman et al., 1983). Closing the organization's doors for business, a dissolution of the organization, is an indicator of death in this research. We distinguish organizational death from mergers and acquisitions, which indicate a change in the ownership status of an organization. An acquired organization was coded as surviving if it continued to operate as a relatively independent subsidiary and was coded as a dissolution if the new firm was disbanded and its assets and people absorbed into the acquiring company's operations at any time before the end of our observation period. Two new firms in our population were acquired and subsequently disbanded through absorption into the acquiring corporation. These were coded as dissolutions.

References

Allen, D. N., and V. Levine. *Nurturing Advanced Technology Enterprises: Emerging Issues in State and Local Economic Development Policy.* New York: Praeger, 1986.

Beesley, M. "The Birth and Death of Industrial Establishments: Experience in the West Midlands Conurbation." *Journal of Industrial Economics* 4 (1955): 45–61.

Bylinsky, G. *The Innovation Millionaires: How They Succeed.* New York: Charles Scribners Sons, 1976.

Cooper, A. C. "Strategic Management: New Ventures and Small Business." In *Strategic Management.* Eds. D. Schendel and C. W. Hofer. Boston: Little, Brown, 1979.

Cooper, A. C., and A. Bruno. "Success Among High-Technology Firms." *Business Horizons* 20 (April 1977): 16–22.

Delacroix, J., A. Swaminathan, and M. E. Solt. *American Sociological Review* 54 (April 1989): 245–262.

Eisenhardt, K. M., and C. B. Schoonhoven. "Organizational Growth: Linking Founding Team, Strategy, Environment, and Growth Among U.S. Semiconductor Ventures (1978–1988)." *Administrative Science Quarterly* 35 (September 1990): 504–529.

Freeman, J., G. Carroll, and M. T. Hannan. "Age Dependence and Organizational Death Rates." *American Sociological Review* 48 (October 1983): 692.

Hawley, A. H. *Human Ecology: A Theoretical Essay.* Chicago: University of Chicago Press, 1986.

Hoover, E. M., and R. Vernon. *Anatomy of a Metropolis*. New York: Anchor Books, 1962.

Jelinek, M., and C. B. Schoonhoven. *The Innovation Marathon: Lessons from High Technology Corporations*. Oxford, England: Basil Blackwell, 1990.

Johnson, P. S. *New Firms: An Economic Perspective*. London: Allen & Unwin, 1986.

Johnson, P. S., and D. G. Cathcart. "The Founders of New Manufacturing Firms: A Note on the Size of Their Incubator Plants." *Journal of Industrial Economics* 28 (1979): 219–224.

Kojima, T. "Informationization in Local Areas." Paper presented at Western Academy of Management–Shizuoka International Management Conference, Shizuoka, Japan, June 1990.

Malone, M. S. *The Big Score: The Billion Dollar Story of Silicon Valley*. Garden City, N.Y.: Doubleday, 1985.

Ó hUalláchain, B., and M. A. Satterthwaite. *Sectoral Growth Patterns at the Metropolitan Level: An Evaluation of Economic Development Incentives*. Report to the U.S. Department of Commerce, Economic Development Administration. Evanston, Ill.: NCI Research, 1988.

Pennings, J. M. "Organizational Birth Frequencies: An Empirical Investigation." *Administrative Science Quarterly* 27 (March 1982): 120–144.

Porter, M. E. *The Competitive Advantage of Nations*. New York: The Free Press, 1990.

Pratt, S. E., and J. K. Morris, eds. *Pratt's Guide to Venture Capital Sources*. Editions 1–10. Wellesley Hills, Mass.: Capital Publishing, 1970–86.

Rogers, E. M., and Y.-C. A. Chen. "Technology Transfer and the Technopolis." In *Managing Complexity in High Technology Industries: Systems and People*. Eds. M. Von Glinow and S. Mohrman. Oxford, England: Oxford University Press, 1990.

Rogers, E. M., and J. K. Larsen. *Silicon Valley Fever: Growth of High-Technology Culture*. New York: Basic Books, 1984.

Schoonhoven, C. B., and K. M. Eisenhardt. *The Impact of Incubator Region on the Creation and Survival of New Semiconductor Ventures in the U.S. 1978–1986*. Final Report prepared for the U.S. Department of Commerce, Economic Development Administration, EDA Project No. RED–870–G–86–15 (99–7–13675), August 1989.

———. *A Study of the Influence of Organizational, Entrepreneurial, and Environmental Factors on the Growth and Development of Technology-Based Start Up Firms*. Final Report submitted to the Economic Development Administration, U.S. Department of Commerce. Washington, D.C.: National Technical Information Service, 1987.

Schoonhoven, C. B., K. M. Eisenhardt, and K. Lyman. "Speeding Products to Market: The Impact of Organizational and Environmental Conditions on Waiting Time to First Product Introduction in New Firms." *Administrative Science Quarterly* 35 (March 1990): 177–207.

Scott, A. J., and D. Angel. "The U.S. Semiconductor Industry: A Locational Analysis." *Environment and Planning A* 19 (1987): 875–912.

Smilor, R. W., and M. D. Gill, Jr. *The New Business Incubator*. Lexington, Mass.: Lexington Books, 1986.

Stinchcombe, A. "Social Structure and Organizations." In *Handbook of Organizations*. Ed. J. March. Chicago: Rand McNally, 1965.

Swaminathan, A., and J. Delacroix. *Selection and Differentiation in an Organizational Population: The Case of the Wine Industry*. Paper presented at the Academy of Management Annual Meeting, Anaheim, Calif., August 1988.

Van de Ven, A. H., and G. Walker. "The Dynamics of Interorganizational Coordination." *Administrative Science Quarterly* 35 (December 1984): 598–621.

Williams, F. "Information Technologies in Technopolis." Paper presented at International Technopolis Conference, San Francisco, May 1990.

PART V

Economic Change and Urban Social Problems

STEPHEN NORD and ROBERT G. SHEETS

11 Service Industries and the Working Poor in Major Metropolitan Areas in the United States

Over the last forty years, the U.S. economy experienced a major structural transformation, with the largest share of employment shifting from manufacturing to service industries. This transformation was predominantly a metropolitan phenomenon; most of the largest one hundred metropolitan areas survived the 1970s largely on the strength of their service industry growth. However, this transformation was felt differently across metropolitan areas.

The degree and nature of service industry growth varied tremendously, depending on regional population growth and the size and economic function of metropolitan areas within the U.S. metropolitan system. Some metropolitan areas expanded their share of administrative headquarters and advanced corporate service industries, such as finance and business and professional services. Service growth in other areas was fueled by government and nonprofit service industries. In still others, it was driven by growth in wholesale and retail trade along with personal services.

Previous research has raised the issue of the quality of the employment and earnings opportunities afforded by service industries in major metropolitan areas compared to the manufacturing jobs that have been lost over the last forty years. Early readings on service growth in the national economy emphasized a generalized upgrading of work, as manifested in the growth of managerial, professional, and technical occupations (Bell, 1973). More pessimistic researchers have argued that service industries are producing a bifurcated employment and earnings structure, as the concentration of high-wage managerial and professional jobs increases along with growth in low-wage,

255

unstable sales, clerical, and service occupations (Singlemann, 1978; Stanback and Noyelle, 1982; Stanback et al., 1981). Research has tended to confirm that some types of service industries create higher concentrations of managerial and professional jobs (Nelson and Lorence, 1985). The impact of service industries on the lower tiers of the labor market, though, remains open to considerable debate.

One pivotal issue in addressing the quality of employment and earnings opportunities generated by service industries is how researchers define and measure labor market hardship at the lower tiers of the labor market. In general, labor market hardship refers to the inability of labor force participants to earn above-poverty-level earnings through their labor market activity. This concept addresses the working poor and the marginal labor force participants who are most sensitive to the changing quality and availability of entry-level jobs in metropolitan labor markets. A major research question is what impact service industry growth has had on this type of structural underemployment, especially among women and minorities.

To explore this question, we focus on service industries and labor market hardship in the largest one hundred metropolitan areas. We first define different types of service industries and their basic employment and earnings characteristics. We then define a Poverty-level Earnings (PLE) index as a measure of labor market hardship and compare it to more conventional concepts of unemployment and poverty. In addition, we summarize its distribution across service industries and metropolitan areas. Next, we present our findings on the impact of service growth on labor market hardship, with special attention to women and minorities. We conclude with a discussion of research and policy issues related to (1) future trends in the employment and earnings structures of service industries and (2) expanding the PLE index to include noncash benefits and government transfer income.

Labor Market Characteristics of Service Industries

The central debate over the impact of service growth on labor market hardship revolves around the labor market characteristics of different types of service industries relative to manufacturing industries and the growth and development of these types of service industries in metropolitan economies.

SERVICE INDUSTRIES IN METROPOLITAN ECONOMIES

Drawing upon the earlier work of Singlemann (1978) and Stanback and Noyelle (1982), we divide service industries into six major classifications (Table 11.1). The most basic distinction is between intermediate- and final-

TABLE 11.1

Service Industry Classification Framework

Producer Services (Intermediate Demand)	
Distributive services	Transportation (400–432)
	Communications (330–342)
	Wholesale trade (500–571)
Advanced corporate services	Finance, insurance, and real estate (700–712)
	Business services (721–742)
	Legal services (841)
	Membership organizations and professional services (881–892)
Social Services (Mixed Demand)	
Nonprofit services	Health services (812–840)
	Education services (842–861)
	Social services (862–865, 867–871)
	Museums, art galleries, and zoos (872)
	Religious organizations (866)
Government services	Public administration (900–932)
Consumer Services (Final Demand)	
Personal services	Repair services (750–760)
	Personal services (761–791)
	Entertainment and recreation services (800–802)
Retail trade	Retail trade (580–691)

Note: Numbers in parentheses are Census Standard Industrial Classification (SIC) codes.

Source: U.S. Department of Commerce, Bureau of the Census, *Census of Population and Housing, 1980: Public-Use Microdata Sample File, Appendix H,* 1983.

Reprinted by permission of the publisher, from *The Impact of Service Industries on Underemployment in Metropolitan Economies* by Robert G. Sheets, Stephen Nord, and John J. Phelps. (Lexington Books, D. C. Heath and Company, Copyright 1987, D. C. Heath and Company.)

demand services. Intermediate services are those industries that provide services mainly to other businesses engaged in the production and distribution of goods and services to the final consumer. Intermediate services include both distributive and advanced corporate services, generally referred to as "producer services." Final-demand services include both retail trade and personal services. The market for social services—nonprofit and government—is mixed, with most industries providing services to consumers.

The growth of the service sector has transformed major metropolitan economies and redefined the structure of the metropolitan system in the national economy. A driving force behind the growth of service industries in the largest metropolitan areas has been the restructuring of major corporations and their increasing requirements for outside producer services, such as accounting, advertising, banking, insurance, personnel, and legal services. Between 1970 and 1980, these "advanced corporate services" created the largest number of jobs in national and regional nodal centers (for example, New York, Los Angeles, Chicago, and Boston). Nonprofit and retail trade industries showed strong employment growth throughout the metropolitan system. Growth of personal and distributive services was also strong. Growth of retail and personal services was most heavily concentrated in special residential centers, such as Las Vegas, Tampa, and Orlando. Although manufacturing industries were growing in most major metropolitan areas between 1970 and 1980, this growth was being overwhelmed by the growth in service industries. Manufacturing actually dropped as a share of total employment in all of the largest one hundred metropolitan areas (Sheets et al., 1987).

The impacts of different service industry growth patterns on metropolitan labor markets can best be understood by examining the employment and earnings characteristics of each type of service industry.

EMPLOYMENT AND EARNINGS CHARACTERISTICS

Service industries have quite different employment and earnings characteristics. As shown in Table 11.2, distributive services and government have mean wages and earnings comparable to manufacturing industries. In contrast, consumer service industries—personal services and retail trade—have wages and earnings less than half that of manufacturing industries. Advanced corporate services and nonprofit services fall in the midrange of service industries.

These wage and earnings differences can be attributed to differences in product market characteristics, occupational structure, and demographic composition of the entry-level labor force employed in service industries. "Product market characteristics" refers to the typical organizational and market characteristics of an industry group that determine the capacity of firms within an industry to establish higher wage rates and more stable employment relations. Surprisingly, the degree of market concentration is roughly similar for manufacturing and service industries (see the figures for "Share of Employment" and "Sales" of the top eight firms, Table 11.3). However,

TABLE 11.2

Average Annual Earnings and Employment Concentrations for Occupational Groups
in Manufacturing and Service Industries, 1980[a]

	Manufacturing	Distributive Services	Advanced Corporate Services	Nonprofit Services	Government Services	Personal Services	Retail Services
Executive, administrative, and managerial staff	$24,968 (7.7%)	$23,211 (11.1%)	$17,962 (19.6%)	$15,522 (5.9%)	$17,978 (17.8%)	$12,035 (8.6%)	$13,287 (9.0%)
Professional technician and related support staff	18,636 (8.6)	21,062 (5.0)	13,683 (15.3)	12,223 (48.0)	17,006 (17.8)	6,875 (8.6)	10,364 (9.0)
Sales staff	16,243 (3.1)	15,591 (12.0)	14,168 (14.0)	6,391 (0.70)	11,903 (0.60)	6,874 (4.8)	6,295 (36.9)
Administrative support, including clerical staff	10,536 (12.4)	11,960 (27.2)	7,728 (37.6)	6,384 (16.7)	9,848 (31.0)	6,210 (7.7)	6,692 (9.2)
Service staff	10,562 (2.3)	10,304 (3.0)	5,822 (8.3)	5,488 (23.9)	14,011 (22.0)	3,879 (43.7)	3,617 (24.3)
All other occupations	11,983 (65.3)	13,539 (41.7)	9,858 (5.1)	7,775 (4.2)	12,043 (9.6)	7,425 (26.8)	7,981 (18.2)
All occupations	13,473 (100%)	14,710 (100%)	11,491 (100%)	9,588 (100%)	13,754 (100%)	6,093 (100%)	6,710 (100%)

[a]Employment concentrations appear in parentheses. These should be read as the percent of industry employment in the occupational group.

Source: U.S. Department of Commerce, Bureau of the Census, 1/100 Census of Population and Housing, 1980: Public-Use Microdata Sample File, 1983.

Reprinted by permission of the publisher, from The Impact of Service Industries on Underemployment in Metropolitan Economies by Robert G. Sheets, Stephen Nord, and John J. Phelps. (Lexington Books, D. C. Heath and Company, Copyright 1987, D. C. Heath and Company.)

TABLE 11.3

Product Market Characteristics of Service Industry Groups, 1982

	Average Employment per Firm	Average Sales per Firm ($ Thousands)	Share of Total Employment for Firms with 1–50 Employees	Share of Total Sales for Firms with 1–50 Employees	Top Eight Firms' Share of Total Employment	Top Eight Firms' Share of Total Sales
Manufacturing	73.9	6,372.8	11.5%	8.2%	17.7%	23.3%
Distributive Services	17.9	2,792.5	37.3	40.5	24.1	14.1
Advanced Corporate Services	19.0	3,115.2	31.8	34.6	11.3	14.2
Nonprofit Services	82.6	2,256.7	9.2	9.5	3.2	3.1
Retail Trade	12.8	801.1	45.6	42.6	10.3	11.6
Personal Services	8.8	291.7	53.3	57.0	12.3	14.2

Source: U.S. Department of Commerce, Office of Advocacy of the U.S. Small Business Administration, *U.S. Establishment and Enterprise Microdata File*, 1982.

Reprinted by permission of the publisher, from *The Impact of Service Industries on Underemployment in Metropolitan Economies* by Robert G. Sheets, Stephen Nord, and John J. Phelps. (Lexington Books, D. C. Heath and Company, Copyright 1987, D. C. Heath and Company.)

there are important differences in the average firm size. In 1983, the average firm size for manufacturing was about seventy-five employees. In contrast, the average firm size for producer services (that is, distributive and advanced corporate services) was about eighteen employees; for consumer services, it was even less—about ten employees (Sheets et al., 1987). Nonprofit services closely approximated the average size of manufacturing industries because of the presence of large health care facilities and educational institutions.

The most distinctive feature of service industries is the high concentration of low-wage service, clerical, and sales occupations (see Table 11.2). In manufacturing industries, less than 20 percent of employment is in these occupations. In service industries, the concentration ranges from 65 percent in consumer service industries to about 50 percent in producer and social service industries. As Table 11.2 shows, these occupations tend to pay substantially less than the craft and production jobs that predominate among nonmanagerial and nonprofessional occupations in manufacturing industries.

The wage and earnings differences between manufacturing and service industries can be explained to some degree by the predominance of service, clerical, and sales occupations within these industries, but the demographic composition of the work force of many service industries may also play a part. Demographic segmentation processes within labor markets can serve to crowd women and minorities into a narrow range of industries and occupations that pay low wages. These industries and occupations are able to maintain a strong supply of labor because of entry barriers to other occupations. In general, service industries employ twice the concentration of women and minorities compared to manufacturing industries. Service industries also have twice the concentration of women, minorities, and youth in management positions. These demographic differences together with differences in product market characteristics may explain the substantial earnings differences between managers in manufacturing and service industries. Although manufacturing and service industries have roughly similar concentrations of women in administrative support and clerical positions, service industries have twice the concentration of women in sales and service occupations. They also employ twice the concentration of blacks in clerical positions (Sheets et al., 1987). Thus, discrimination may explain a large share of the significant differences in earnings in clerical, sales, and service occupations between manufacturing and service industries.

Labor Market Hardship in Metropolitan Economies

Since the mid-1960s, traditional measures of unemployment and poverty have come under heavy criticism for failing to address the economic hardship caused when workers are unable to earn adequate incomes through their labor market participation (Levitan and Taggart, 1974; Taggart, 1982). Researchers have proposed a number of alternative approaches to the definition and measurement of labor market hardship, ranging from "subemployment" indices (Miller, 1973; Vietorisz et al., 1975; Wirtz, 1967) to "employment and earnings inadequacy" indices (Levitan and Taggart, 1974).

POVERTY-LEVEL EARNINGS (PLE) INDEX

In our research on service industries, we used the concept of poverty-level earnings to refer to the inability of labor force participants to earn poverty-level wages and salaries through their labor market activity over the previous year. We defined poverty-level wages and salaries as 125 percent of poverty-level income as determined by the U.S. Census Bureau. In so doing, we hoped to capture that segment known as the "working poor." We defined a labor force participant as an individual between the ages of eighteen and sixty-four who had been employed or seeking employment for at least fifteen weeks during the previous year. Institutionalized individuals, noncivilians, and students were not included.

The major problem in measuring poverty-level earnings is distinguishing between primary and secondary workers (Sheets et al., 1987). This distinction is critical in studying impacts on service workers because of the high proportion of women and youth who may be secondary earners. Primary workers include (1) householders and spouses with the highest earned income within a family household and (2) all members of a nonfamily household. Secondary workers are all other labor force participants. Based on this distinction, PLE status was assigned if an individual's labor force participation was inadequate to raise earnings above 125 percent of poverty in 1979. The poverty threshold for primary workers was $9,265 and for secondary workers $4,608. As in previous research (Levitan and Taggart, 1974), it was assumed that primary workers should be able to earn sufficient income to support a family of four at the poverty level. It was assumed that secondary workers should be able to support themselves at the poverty level. No matter what their earned income, secondary workers were not considered below PLE if they were in households with income above the median. In these cases, low earnings may be in part a voluntary decision (Levitan and Taggart, 1974).

The PLE index is measured through three poverty-level earnings indicators distinguished by patterns of work time (Table 11.4). Each indicator is taken as a percentage of the labor force. "Low-wage PLE" refers to workers who worked full-time, full-year over the previous year. "Part-time PLE" refers to workers who were employed part-time, full-year. "Intermittent PLE" captures workers who earned below poverty-level earnings because of

TABLE 11.4

Poverty-level Earnings in the One Hundred
Largest Metropolitan Areas, 1980

Poverty-level Earnings (PLE) Indicator[a]	Family Status		Total
	Primary	Secondary	
Low-wage PLE	5.37	0.70	6.07
Part-time PLE	1.01	0.50	1.51
Intermittent PLE	6.86	4.04	10.90
Total PLE	13.24	5.24	18.48

[a]Each indicator is taken as a percentage of the labor force.

Source: U.S. Department of Commerce, Bureau of the Census, *1/100 Census of Population and Housing, 1980: Public-Use Microdata Sample File*, 1983.

Reprinted by permission of the publisher, from *The Impact of Service Industries on Underemployment in Metropolitan Economies* by Robert G. Sheets, Stephen Nord, and John J. Phelps. (Lexington Books, D. C. Heath and Company, Copyright 1987, D. C. Heath and Company.)

part-year employment, whether they were part-time or full-time workers. Part-year employment may be due to seasonal or temporary employment or to job loss. Unlike the traditional concept of unemployment, which refers to joblessness in a particular survey week, intermittent PLE refers to joblessness that leads to poverty-level earnings over a total year. This indicator includes the most extreme case of no employment over the previous year as long as an individual was actively seeking employment for a combined period of fifteen weeks over the previous year. "Total PLE" is the sum of the three poverty earnings indicators.

INCIDENCE OF POVERTY-LEVEL EARNINGS

Tables 11.4 and 11.5 reveal that poverty-level earnings are a basic feature of the one hundred largest metropolitan areas in the United States. As Table 11.4 shows, intermittent PLE accounted for the largest share of total PLE for both primary and secondary workers. The next largest concentration was of low-wage PLE among primary workers. Surprisingly, the incidence of part-time, full-year PLE was an insignificant portion of total PLE. In 1980, 18.5 percent of the total labor force of the one hundred largest metro-

TABLE 11.5

Poverty-level Earnings Index for the
One Hundred Largest Metropolitan Areas[a]

Metropolitan Areas	Total
New York, N.Y.–N.J.	20.6%
Los Angeles–Long Beach, Calif.	21.8
Chicago, Ill.	15.0
Philadelphia, Pa.–N.J.	18.0
Detroit, Mich.	14.5
San Francisco–Oakland, Calif.	17.9
Washington, D.C.–Md.–Va.	15.0
Dallas–Fort Worth, Tex.	18.6
Houston, Tex.	17.4
Boston, Mass.	16.5
Nassau–Suffolk, N.Y.	13.6
St. Louis, Mo.–Ill.	17.5
Pittsburgh, Pa.	15.3
Baltimore, Md.	17.9
Minneapolis–St. Paul, Minn.–Wis.	15.9
Atlanta, Ga.	19.6
Newark, N.J.	15.4
Anaheim–Santa Ana–Garden Grove, Calif.	16.2
Cleveland, Ohio	15.8
San Diego, Calif.	24.6
Miami, Fla.	24.3
Denver–Boulder, Colo.	18.0
Seattle–Everett, Wash.	16.3
Tampa–St. Petersburg, Fla.	26.5
Riverside–San Bernardino–Ontario, Calif.	20.9
Phoenix, Ariz.	19.9
Cincinnati, Ohio–Ky.–Ind.	16.9
Milwaukee, Wis.	14.3
Kansas City, Mo.–Kans.	16.9
San Jose, Calif.	14.6
Buffalo, N.Y.	18.3
Portland, Ore.–Wash.	21.0
New Orleans, La.	22.2
Indianapolis, Ind.	17.9
Columbus, Ohio	18.8
San Antonio, Tex.	27.0
Fort Lauderdale–Hollywood, Fla.	19.6
Sacramento, Calif.	22.0
Rochester, N.Y.	14.7
Salt Lake City–Ogden, Utah	17.5
Providence–Warwick–Pawtucket, R.I.	17.2

TABLE 11.5 (continued)

Poverty-level Earnings Index for the
One Hundred Largest Metropolitan Areas[a]

Metropolitan Areas	Total
Memphis, Tenn.–Ark.–Miss.	25.1%
Louisville, Ky.–Ind.	19.5
Nashville–Davidson, Tenn.	20.4
Birmingham, Ala.	18.8
Oklahoma City, Okla.	20.2
Dayton, Ohio	18.7
Greensboro–Winston–Salem–High Point, N.C.	23.2
Norfolk–Virginia Beach–Portsmouth, Va.	23.1
Little Rock–North Little Rock, Ark.	22.8
Albany–Schenectady–Troy, N.Y.	16.2
Toledo, Ohio–Mich.	14.9
Honolulu, Hawaii	20.1
Jacksonville, Fla.	24.7
Hartford, Conn.	13.5
Orlando, Fla.	24.0
Tulsa, Okla.	18.5
Akron, Ohio	16.1
Syracuse, N.Y.	20.2
Gary–Hammond–East Chicago, Ind.	14.6
Northeast Pennsylvania	22.3
Charlotte–Gastonia, N.C.	22.1
Allentown–Bethlehem–Easton, Pa.	17.1
Richmond, Va.	16.0
Grand Rapids, Mich.	16.4
New Brunswick–Perth Amboy–Sayreville, N.J.	12.4
West Palm Beach–Boca Raton, Fla.	21.1
Omaha, Nebr.–Iowa	20.5
Greenville–Spartanburg, S.C.	23.6
Jersey City, N.J.	20.4
Austin, Tex.	23.9
Tucson, Ariz.	21.9
Youngstown–Warren, Ohio	15.1
Raleigh–Durham, N.C.	18.9
Springfield–Chicopee–Holyoke, Mass.	18.5
Oxnard–Simi Valley–Ventura, Calif.	17.2
Wilmington, Del.–N.J.–Md.	18.8
Flint, Mich.	15.6
Fresno, Calif.	21.8
Long Branch–Asbury Park, N.J.	14.1
Baton Rouge, La.	16.6
Tacoma, Wash.	20.3

TABLE 11.5 (continued)

Poverty-level Earnings Index for the
One Hundred Largest Metropolitan Areas[a]

Metropolitan Areas	Total
El Paso, Tex.	30.4%
Knoxville, Tenn.	19.3
Lansing–East Lansing, Mich.	14.7
Las Vegas, Nev.	23.7
Albuquerque, N. Mex.	24.7
Paterson–Clifton–Passaic, N.J.	8.4
Harrisburg, Pa.	18.1
Mobile, Ala.	23.9
Johnson City–Kingsport–Bristol, Tenn.–Va.	23.4
Charleston–North Charleston, S.C.	22.0
Chattanooga, Tenn.–Ga.	21.8
New Haven–West Haven, Conn.	17.7
Wichita, Kans.	15.5
Columbia, S.C.	19.9
Canton, Ohio	15.3
Bakersfield, Calif.	23.1
Bridgeport, Conn.	16.8
Davenport, Iowa–Rock Island–Moline, Ill.	16.5

[a]Ranked by 1980 population

Source: U.S. Department of Commerce, Bureau of the Census, *1/100 Census of Population and Housing, 1980: Public-Use Microdata Sample File*, 1983.

Adapted from tables previously published in *The Impact of Service Industries on Underemployment in Metropolitan Economies* by Robert G. Sheets, Stephen Nord, and John J. Phelps. (Lexington Books, D. C. Heath and Company, Copyright 1987, D. C. Heath and Company.)

politan areas had poverty-level earnings. However, there was wide variation among areas (see Table 11.5). The total PLE rate in major metropolitan areas ranged from 30 percent in cities such as El Paso and San Antonio to as low as 12 to 15 percent in cities in the Northeast.

Table 11.6 shows that workers with poverty-level earnings are heavily concentrated among women and minorities. Although white males between the ages of twenty-five and sixty-four had total PLE rates of around 10 percent, their female counterparts had rates exceeding 20 percent. Rates were even higher among minority males and females, ranging from 23 percent among older black males to extremely high rates of 31 to 42 percent among black and Hispanic females.

TABLE 11.6

Poverty-level Earnings by Age, Race, and Gender
in the One Hundred Largest Metropolitan Areas, 1980

	Low-wage	*Part-time*	*Intermittent*	*Total*
WHITE				
Male				
18–24	4.7%	0.6%	10.7%	16.0%
25–44	4.1	0.5	6.7	11.3
45–64	4.0	0.6	5.0	9.6
Female				
18–24	6.3	1.5	16.2	24.0
25–44	6.0	2.5	13.4	21.9
45–64	8.7	3.9	12.1	24.7
BLACK				
Male				
18–24	7.7	1.2	21.8	30.7
25–44	9.1	1.0	15.8	25.9
45–64	10.3	1.6	11.3	23.2
Female				
18–24	7.7	2.0	26.1	35.8
25–44	11.9	2.6	20.7	35.2
45–64	15.2	7.5	19.4	42.1
HISPANIC				
Male				
18–24	10.4	1.0	18.0	29.4
25–44	11.9	1.0	14.8	27.7
45–64	12.1	1.1	12.2	25.4
Female				
18–24	8.4	1.1	22.0	31.5
25–44	11.5	2.4	23.2	37.1
45–64	15.9	4.4	21.4	41.7

Reprinted by permission of the publisher, from *The Impact of Service Industries on Underemployment in Metropolitan Economies* by Robert G. Sheets, Stephen Nord, and John J. Phelps. (Lexington Books, D. C. Heath and Company, Copyright 1987, D. C. Heath and Company.)

Impact of Service Industries on Labor Market Hardship

Service industry employment can be expected to have both direct and indirect effects on the concentration of workers with earnings below the poverty level. The direct effects are from service industries having a bifurcated employment and earnings structure. This bifurcated structure is reflected in high concentrations of unskilled jobs that are in unsheltered occupations (that is, those with low levels of professionalism, unionization, and other institutional protection) and that pay low wages (Stanback and Noyelle, 1982; Stanback et al., 1981). As discussed above, these employment and earnings patterns result from product market characteristics as well as demographic and occupational compositions. As a result of these differences, summarized in Table 11.2, the effect of service industry employment on the concentration of workers with earnings below the poverty level will vary depending on the mix of service industries in a particular metropolitan area.

The indirect effects of service industry employment on the earnings of working poor will be felt in those industries that compete with service industries for low-skilled labor. Dominant industries exert wage rollout effects on local labor markets by establishing wage expectations and prevailing wage rates that affect other industries competing for labor in the same occupational labor markets (Parcel, 1981; Thompson, 1969). If low-paying service industries become a dominant part of an economic base, they may depress wages of other industries and thus lead indirectly to higher levels of labor market hardship.

Based on these direct and indirect effects, larger concentrations of employment in producer, social, and consumer service industries should contribute to higher concentrations of those with poverty-level earnings among full-time, full-year workers. The effect should largely be the result of high concentrations of low-wage clerical, sales, and service occupations. Small firm size and unstable product markets of consumer services should cause these industries to have the added effect of increasing the concentration of part-time and intermittent working poor.

IMPACTS BY METROPOLITAN AREA

In a study using microdata from the U.S. Census Bureau's 1980 Census of Population and Housing, we found service industries to have mixed and offsetting effects on the PLE index in the one hundred largest metropolitan areas after adjusting for other possible contributing factors (Nord et al., 1988).[1] In general, higher concentrations of service employment were shown to have significant effects on poverty-level earnings in some cases, in particular for workers in the full-time, full-year PLE category. This effect was driven largely by producer service industries, especially advanced corporate service industries. In this study, it was estimated that a 1 percent increase in advanced corporate service employment as a share of total employment would result in a corresponding 0.37 percentage increase in the low-wage PLE measure.[2] The expected contribution of consumer service industries to the part-time PLE measure was clearly evident, especially in retail service industries. A 1 percent increase in the concentration of retail trade employment was associated with a 0.88 percentage increase in the low-wage PLE measure.

To summarize our 1988 study, service growth can be expected to increase the share of both low-wage and part-time workers with earnings below the poverty level. Distributive services and advanced corporate services are primarily responsible for increases in the low-wage PLE measure while retail trade and nonprofit services tend to increase the part-time PLE measure. However, these effects are partly offset because producer and social services industries are linked to decreases in the level of the intermittent PLE measure. This suggests that producer and social services reduce the intermittent PLE measure by providing jobs with more stable labor force attachment. Still, further research is needed to clarify the impact of service growth on intermittent labor force attachment among the poor. What the findings do make clear is that the overall impact of service industry growth on the concentration of working poor depends on the service industry mix in a metropolitan area.

IMPACTS ON WOMEN AND MINORITIES

As discussed earlier, women and minorities experienced the highest rates of poverty-level earnings in major metropolitan areas. One major issue is understanding the higher PLE rates for minority males. Tables 11.7 and 11.8 show that within the service sector, black and Hispanic males have substantially different employment and wage patterns from white males. The largest share of urban youth aged eighteen to twenty-four are employed in retail services, with concentrations of 35 percent, 42 percent, and 45 percent for blacks, Hispanics, and whites, respectively. The lower concentration of black youth in retail trade is largely offset by their higher concentrations in nonprofit services and government. Employment of mature adults aged twenty-four to sixty-five is distributed more evenly across the service industries, except for advanced corporate services, where about 21 percent of whites find employment compared to only 14 percent of blacks and 16 percent of Hispanics.

Tables 11.7 and 11.8 also reveal significant racial differences in wages. For male youth, some inequality in wages is evident in distributive, govern-

TABLE 11.7

Black and White Male Employment Distributions and Wage Differentials in Service Industries Within the One Hundred Largest Metropolitan Areas

Industry	Black Youth Employment	White Youth Employment	Black Youth Wage	White Youth Wage	White/Black Youth Wage Ratio	Black Adult Employment	White Adult Employment	Black Adult Wage	White Adult Wage	White/Black Adult Wage Ratio
Distributive Services	13.05	15.56	4.81	5.33	1.11	28.89	26.71	7.92	9.72	1.23
Advanced Corporation Services	14.04	12.52	4.37	4.87	1.11	13.93	20.76	6.85	10.33	1.51
Nonprofit Services	18.04	10.99	4.19	4.22	1.01	20.37	16.57	7.20	9.23	1.28
Government Services	9.82	3.82	4.10	4.77	1.16	14.10	11.94	7.98	9.86	1.24
Personal Services	10.79	11.95	4.03	4.14	1.03	8.02	6.30	5.60	7.49	1.34
Retail Services	34.26	45.16	3.92	4.10	1.05	16.69	17.72	6.07	7.75	1.28
Total Services	100.0	100.0	4.18	4.43	1.06	100.0	100.0	7.18	9.29	1.29

Source: U.S. Department of Commerce, Bureau of the Census, *1/100 Census of Population and Housing, 1980: Public Use Microdata Samples,* 1983.

Reprinted by permission of the publisher, from *The Impact of Service Industries on Underemployment in Metropolitan Economies* by Robert G. Sheets, Stephen Nord, and John J. Phelps. (Lexington Books, D. C. Heath and Company, Copyright 1987, D. C. Heath and Company.)

TABLE 11.8

Hispanic and White Male Employment Distributions and Wage Differentials in Service Industries Within the One Hundred Largest Metropolitan Areas

Industry	Hispanic Youth Employ-ment	White Youth Employ-ment	Hispanic Youth Wage	White Youth Wage	White/ Hispanic Youth Wage Ratio	Hispanic Adult Employ-ment	White Adult Employ-ment	Hispanic Adult Wage	White Adult Wage	White/ Hispanic Adult Wage Ratio
Distributive Services	17.79	15.56	4.90	5.33	1.09	25.02	26.71	8.01	9.72	1.21
Advanced Corporation Services	11.73	12.52	4.36	4.87	1.12	15.60	20.76	7.47	10.33	1.38
Nonprofit Services	11.49	10.99	4.31	4.22	0.98	14.92	16.57	7.11	9.23	1.30
Government Services	4.97	3.82	4.87	4.77	0.98	10.11	11.94	8.15	9.86	1.21
Personal Services	12.40	11.95	3.85	4.14	1.08	12.36	6.30	6.02	7.49	1.24
Retail Services	41.62	45.16	4.06	4.10	1.01	21.99	17.72	5.99	7.75	1.29
Total Services	100.0	100.0	4.29	4.43	1.03	100.0	100.0	7.12	9.29	1.30

Source: U.S. Department of Commerce, Bureau of the Census, *1/100 Census of Population and Housing, 1980: Public-Use Microdata Samples,* 1983.

Reprinted by permission of the publisher, from *The Impact of Service Industries on Underemployment in Metropolitan Economies* by Robert G. Sheets, Stephen Nord, and John J. Phelps. (Lexington Books, D. C. Heath and Company, Copyright 1987, D. C. Heath and Company.)

ment, and advanced corporate services. Wage inequality is more apparent among adults, particularly in advanced corporate services where whites averaged 51 percent higher wages than blacks and 38 percent higher wages than Hispanics.

In Table 11.7, we observe that the average wage rate in 1980 for white youth employed in service industries was $4.43. This was $0.25 higher than the $4.18 average wage for black youth. A standard wage decomposition model revealed that very little of this difference could be explained by differences in white and black representation in the service industry categories (Sheets et al., 1987). Virtually all of the wage difference was explained by the higher pay received by white youth within the service categories, with 39 percent of the wage difference attributable to higher white wages in retail trade and another 13 percent attributable to the higher wages that white youth received in advanced corporate services. Among older males, whites earned $2.11 more in average hourly wages than blacks. Approximately 13.5 percent of this difference was due to relatively lower representation and wages of blacks in advanced corporate services. Most of the wage difference was attributable to the generally lower levels of schooling and work experience of blacks, in conjunction with lower returns to their schooling and work experience.

Table 11.8 shows that for Hispanics, the overall youth wage in service industries was only $0.14 lower than that of white youth. About 31 percent of this difference was due to the higher pay that whites received in retail trade (Sheets et al., 1987). Another 18.5 percent was from the higher wages that whites received in advanced corporate services. Very little of the wage difference could be explained by the variations in white and Hispanic representation in the different service industries. Table 11.8 also shows that older whites earned $2.17 more in average hourly wages than older Hispanics. Our wage decomposition model showed that virtually all of this wage differential was attributable to lower amounts of schooling and work experience for Hispanics, in combination with the lower rates of returns they received on schooling and work experience.

Service industry growth has been a double-edged sword for women. It has created unprecedented employment and earnings opportunities in managerial and professional positions, but it has also created a large concentration of low-wage, unstable "female-typed" jobs that account for more than two-thirds of female employment. Table 11.6 shows that within racial groups, females suffer the highest rates of poverty-level earnings. A further breakdown (not shown) revealed an especially striking PLE rate of 53 percent for single mothers, which is four times that of males and twice that of other females (Sheets et al., 1987). We also found that advanced corporate services and retail trade had major impacts on the PLE rates of women in metropolitan areas, with retail trade having a substantial effect on poverty-level earnings among single mothers. For every 1 percent increase in employment concentration in retail trade, total PLE for females and for single mothers was estimated to increase by .30 and .41 percent, respectively. A similar increase in advanced corporate services employment was found to boost female total PLE by .08 percent. Government and distributive services were found to have significant offsetting effects on the concentration of females with earnings below the poverty level.

In estimating the effects of service industries on poverty-level earnings among single mothers, the work disincentive effects of welfare payments, especially Aid to Families with Dependent Children (AFDC), must be taken into consideration (Kodras, 1986). Service industries are expected to increase the concentration of females with earnings below the poverty level by increasing the likelihood of female labor force participation, low earnings, and unstable employment patterns. However, welfare payments that are sufficiently high to compete with earnings opportunities in low-wage secondary markets will have strong disincentive effects on labor force participation, with single mothers choosing to maximize income through nonmarket sources. Nord and Sheets (1990) found that the average AFDC payment level in major metropolitan areas had a strong impact on the concentration of single mothers with earnings below the poverty level. Although service industry growth increased jobs with low earnings, high AFDC payment levels offset this effect by reducing labor force participation. This choice between work and welfare had the combined effect of lowering the concentration of single mothers with poverty-level earnings in metropolitan areas with high AFDC payments.

Conclusion and Implications

The service sector has been a driving force in the growth and development of large metropolitan economies in the United States. This strong service growth, especially in advanced corporate service industries, led to strong overall employment and population growth in the one hundred largest metropolitan areas between 1970 and 1980. However, this strong employment growth did not substantially improve the employment and earnings opportunities of the working poor and the economically disadvantaged. Although service industries as a whole had mixed and offsetting effects on earnings levels in metropolitan areas, advanced corporate services and retail trade were associated with an increase in the concentration of working poor, especially among women. These same industries also had a negative impact on black youth. The effects of service growth on poverty-level earnings are likely to be greatest in major central cities and specialized residential centers where there are high concentrations of advanced corporate and consumer service industries.

LONG-TERM EFFECTS OF SERVICE GROWTH ON LABOR MARKET HARDSHIP

The growth and development of service industries pose a fundamental policy dilemma for government programs designed to increase employment and earnings opportunities for residents in large metropolitan economies. Between 1970 and 1980, most major metropolitan areas survived largely on the strength of their service industry growth. It is likely that their future health will depend on how successful they are in capturing additional service industry growth. Still, based on the findings from our research, strong employment growth, especially in advanced corporate and consumer service industries, will not alleviate the problems of labor market hardship and poverty. They will not address the most fundamental problem posed by these service industries—the crowding of large numbers of youth, women, and minorities into low-wage, unstable service, clerical, and sales occupations that keep them in the ranks of the working poor.

Despite these findings on the impact of service growth during the 1970s, there are some indications that the effects of service industry growth on labor market hardship may moderate over the next twenty years. One can speculate that these changes will come from three major sources: (1) increasing industry concentration, (2) technological advances and productivity growth, and (3) labor shortages.

Some researchers have speculated that the employment and earnings structures of service industries will improve over time as these industries mature (Ginzburg, 1981). In this view, service industries, like their manufacturing counterparts, will become more concentrated, allowing for larger firm sizes and greater market stability. Industry concentration had already started in retail trade and nonprofit services and is likely to occur in health and business services as well.

Major technological changes are likely to vastly improve productivity, which, in turn, may have effects on wages and earnings. Technological advances in office automation will likely have a major effect on the service sector as a whole. The rapid advancement and merging of computer and communications technology would have the greatest impact on advanced corporate and distributive services. In addition, new point-of-sale computer systems that help businesses manage inventory and schedule labor time may well improve productivity in consumer services, especially retail trade.

These technological changes will likely be accompanied by changes in job design and raising skill requirements, particularly for nonmanagerial and nonprofessional employees. Labor-saving technology in traditionally labor-intensive service industries may lead to job upgrading and advanced training requirements. These changes could reduce low-wage jobs and increase the demand for higher skills leading to higher wage rates and more stable employment relations. Such technological and organizational changes may be accompanied by the growth of unions and professional organizations, which could further stabilize earnings gains and promote greater employment security.

Other researchers point to the potential impacts of labor shortages in moderating the effects of service industries on labor market hardship. Service industries may be forced to raise wages and improve employment relations in unskilled, entry-level occupations as the number of youth entering the labor force declines and female labor force participation begins to level off (Supple, 1986). As argued by Lawrence (1984), the U.S. economy showed great strength and flexibility in providing employment for women, minorities, and youth as their ranks swelled during a period of unprecedented growth in the U.S. labor force during the 1970s and early 1980s. The rapid growth of service industries in major metropolitan areas absorbed most of these new entrants. The employment and earnings structures of service industries in part reflect the oversupply of labor and the limited education and work experience that most carried with them into service industries during this period. Service sector employment and earnings for minorities, youth, and women may begin to improve as the new entrants of the 1970s and 1980s mature and service industry firms begin to compete with other industries for quality workers in tight metropolitan labor markets.

Metropolitan governments may be able to strengthen and increase the effects of technological changes and labor shortages with two major economic development strategies. The first strategy would be to redirect infrastructure development in ways that would provide metropolitan areas with comparative advantages in the processing and transmitting of information. Since the early days of urban renewal, metropolitan governments have used federal, state, and local resources to subsidize land-use changes and infrastucture improvements that were necessary to promote industry growth (Mollenkopf, 1983; Sheets et al., 1987). Some researchers argue that the successful cities of the future will take advantage of their economies of scale and develop computer-age infrastructures that will promote service industry growth by permitting businesses to quickly and efficiently receive, process, store, and transmit immense amounts of data and information (Kasarda, 1987).

The second strategy would be to build public-private partnerships to improve the availability of skilled labor in metropolitan areas. Although labor shortages may drive up comparative wage rates in the short run, they will also hurt the competitiveness of key service industries unless employee skills and productivity increase along with wage rates. Metropolitan governments should target increasing amounts of federal, state, and local resources on employment and training and work-related social welfare programs for women, minorities, and the economically disadvantaged. These programs should promote skill upgrading and retaining for employed workers in low-wage, entry-level jobs, as well as preemployment skill training for disadvantaged workers who have yet to find employment despite tight labor markets.

These programs should also develop new approaches for providing low-wage workers with work-related social services normally purchased by middle- and upper-income workers or provided through private employee benefit systems. Metropolitan governments should assist service industries in developing a social service infrastructure for workers with moderate incomes so as to stabilize the supply of skilled labor and improve the quality of work life in service industries. These services could include subsidized child care, health care, and employee assistance programs. This social service infrastructure would provide needed support to single working mothers—the group experiencing the highest degree of labor market hardship in service industries.

DIRECTIONS FOR FUTURE RESEARCH

Recent speculation on the future development of service industries should provide a fertile ground for researchers to address the impact of industry concentration, technology changes, and labor force dynamics on the employment and earnings structures of service industries in major metropolitan areas. Major emphasis should be placed on measuring and explaining service industry productivity differences between metropolitan areas and the impact of these differences on labor market hardship.

Second, future research should address the growth and development of social service infrastructures in metropolitan areas and their impact on labor force participation and labor market hardship. The PLE index used in this study is a useful measure for exploring the impact of service industry growth on labor market hardship. However, one major problem in measuring hardship is the treatment of private noncash benefits and government transfer income, in-kind benefits, and services. Researchers are now beginning to use noncash benefits and government transfers in their estimates of income inequality and poverty (Levy, 1988). Recent research suggests that employer-provided fringe benefits have quadrupled as a percentage of earned income in the United States over the last forty years (Peterson, 1985). Most of the working poor do not have these benefits, especially health benefits (Berk and Wilensky, 1987). Since service industries employ most of the working poor, one can speculate that service industries are lagging behind other industries in providing fringe benefits, such as medical care and child care. The inclusion of noncash benefits and government transfers in estimating labor market hardship may provide a much fuller understanding of the impact of service growth on labor market hardship in major U.S. metropolitan areas. It may also provide the basis for studying metropolitan differences in social service infrastructures and the impact of these differences on labor force participation and labor market hardship.

Notes

1. U.S. Department of Commerce, 1983.
2. The exact formula used to compute this elasticity is $(PLE/S_i) \times (S_i/PLE_i)$, where S_i represents the service employment category and PLE_i is the measure of poverty-level earnings.

References

Bell, D. *The Coming of Post Industrial Society*. New York: Basic Books, 1973.

Berk, M., and G. Wilensky. "Health Insurance Coverage of the Working Poor." *Social Science and Medicine* 25 (1987): 1183–1187.

Ginzburg, E. "Introduction." In *Services: The New Economy*. Ed. T. Stanback et al. Totowa, N.J.: Rowman & Allanheld, 1981.

Kasarda, J. D. "Economic Restructuring and America's Urban Dilemma." Mimeo. University of North Carolina, 1987.

Kodras, J. O. "Labor Market and Policy Constraints on the Work Disincentive Effect of Welfare." *Annals of the Association of American Geographers* 76 (1986): 228–246.

Lawrence, R. "Sectoral Shifts and the Size of the Middle Class." *Brookings Review* 3 (Fall 1984): 11.

Levitan, S., and R. B. Taggart. *Employment and Earnings Inadequacy: A New Social Indicator*. Baltimore: Johns Hopkins University Press, 1974.

Levy, F. *Dollars and Dreams: The Changing American Income Distribution*. New York: Russell Sage Foundation, 1988.

Miller, H. P. "Subemployment in Poverty Areas of Large U.S. Cities." *Monthly Labor Review* (October 1973): 10–17.

Mollenkopf, J. *The Contested City*. Princeton: Princeton University Press, 1983.

Nelson, J. I., and J. Lorence. "Employment in Service Activities and Inequality in Metropolitan Areas." *Urban Affairs Quarterly* 21 (1985): 106–125.

Nord, S., and R. G. Sheets. "The Relationships of AFDC Payments and Employment Structure on the Labor Force Participation and Underemployment Rates of Single Mothers." *Applied Economics* 22: (1990): 187–201.

Nord, S., J. J. Phelps, and R. G. Sheets. "An Analysis of the Economic Impact of the Service Sector on Underemployment in Major Metropolitan Areas in the United States." *Urban Studies* 25 (October 1988): 418–432.

Parcel, T. L. "The Development and Functioning of the American Urban Export Sector, 1947–1972." In *Sociological Perspectives on Labor Markets*. Ed. I. Berg. New York: Academic Press, 1981.

Peterson, W. "The U.S. 'Welfare State' and the Conservative Counter Revolution." *Journal of Economic Issues* 19 (September 1985): 601–641.

Sheets, R. G., S. Nord, and J. J. Phelps. *The Impact of Service Industries on Underemployment in Metropolitan Economics*. Lexington, Mass.: Lexington Books, D. C. Heath & Co., 1987.

Singlemann, J. *From Agriculture to Service*. Beverly Hills: Sage Publications, 1978.

Stanback, T., and T. Noyelle. *Cities in Transition*. Totowa, N.J.: Allanheld, Osmun & Co., 1982.

Stanback, T. M., P. Bearse, T. J. Noyelle, and R. Karasek. *Services: The New Economy*. Totowa, N.J.: Allanheld, Osmun & Co., 1981.

Supple, T. "The Coming Labor Shortage." *American Demographics* 8 (1986): 32–37.

Taggart, R. B. *Hardship: The Welfare Consequences of Labor Market Problems*. Kalamazoo, Mich.: W. E. Upjohn Institute, 1982.

Thompson, W. R. "The Economic Base of Urban Problems." In *Contemporary Economic Issues*. Ed. N. W. Chamberlain. Homewood, Ill.: Richard D. Irwin, 1969.

U.S. Department of Commerce, Bureau of Census. *1/100 Census of Population and Housing, 1980: Public-Use Microdata Sample File*. Washington, D.C.: U.S. Government Printing Office, 1983.

U.S. Department of Commerce, Office of Advocacy of the U.S. Small Business Administration. *U.S. Establishment and Enterprise Microdata File*. Washington, D.C.: U.S. Small Business Administration, 1982.

Vietorisz, T., R. Mier, and J. E. Giblin. "Subemployment: Exclusion and Inadequacy Indexes." *Monthly Labor Review* 98 (1975): 3–12.

Wirtz, W. *The 1967 Manpower Report of the President*. Washington, D.C.: U.S. Government Printing Office, 1967.

THOMAS R. HAMMER

12 Economic Determinants of Underclass Behavior

The problem of the urban underclass has received a great deal of attention in recent years without commensurate gains in understanding or agreement. The general syndrome is familiar: welfare dependency, teenage pregnancy, family headship by never-married females, drug use and trafficking, career criminality, and nonparticipation in the mainstream labor force—all supported by an underclass subculture that espouses values directly opposed to mainstream values. Our understanding dwindles rapidly beyond this basic description. Observers disagree sharply as to why this syndrome developed, why it persists, and how it can be affected constructively by public policy.

Most differences of opinion revolve around the relative weights assigned to the following four general explanations for the origin and persistence of underclass behavior:

1. Race-specific factors, including past and present job discrimination and residential segregation, plus aspects of recent black history, such as migration into and out of central cities;
2. Lack of jobs accessible to inner-city residents, particularly the loss of factory jobs in central cities since 1970;
3. Available alternatives to mainstream employment, referring primarily to participation in the underground economy for males and dependence upon public assistance programs for females; and
4. Use of illegal drugs, not usually proposed as an original cause of underclass behavior but now perhaps a leading factor since inner-city drug use has reached epidemic proportions.

The relative importance of these factors may have varied over time. For example, one might hypothesize that race-specific factors and/or lack of jobs were primarily responsible for the growth of underclass behavior prior to 1980 but that illegal drugs now dominate through both the human resource impact of drug use and the availability of drug trafficking as an alternative to mainstream employment.

Investigating Underclass Origins

There have been extremely few attempts to establish statistically the relative importance of these competing explanations. One reason is the lack of any standard definition of underclass behavior or underclass membership. Investigators remain somewhat preoccupied with establishing the size of the underclass (estimated variously at 1 to 10 million people) and its demographic composition. Other constraints upon statistical analysis are the lack of data on the underground economy, the difficulty of quantifying discrimination, and the measurement problems encountered in any attempt to examine the underclass as a discrete population group.

Much of what we know about the underclass and the outcome of efforts to assist this group has come from longitudinal studies of individuals. Such studies have achieved modest success in evaluating programs of direct assistance to persons (for example, the Job Corps and CETA, the Comprehensive Employment and Training Act). However, they are fundamentally unsuitable for assessing the broad economic incentives likely to have the greatest impact on the underclass, such as changes in job availability or the attractiveness of the underground economy.

On the other hand, most studies that deal with the underclass problem in aggregate terms merely present tabular data showing that certain events have been co-occurrent across broad categories of time and space. Connections between these events are simply asserted on the basis of logical plausibility and perhaps theoretical considerations.

The best of these studies include analyses by Kasarda (1988), attributing growth of the underclass to inner-city job losses and economic restructuring, and by Wilson (1987), emphasizing segregation-enforced exposure to deficient public services and linking welfare dependency to a shortage of marriageable males among low-income blacks. These works have been critically important in defining the agenda for debate on the underclass issue. Nevertheless, descriptions of co-occurrence are not enough to support policy evaluation because they do not establish the magnitude or statistical significance of relationships, do not offer direct comparisons among competing hypotheses, and do not provide any formal control for extraneous influences.

TESTING THE "LACK OF JOBS" HYPOTHESIS

This paper offers a brief statistical analysis of the lack-of-jobs explanation for the growth of the underclass during 1970 to 1980. The work is preliminary in that it represents a first step toward development of a detailed economic model of underclass behavior. The analysis has been conducted at a metropolitan scale for reasons of data availability and has simply attempted to show the existence and detectibility of certain relationships.

The strategy is to examine the reflection of underclass behavior patterns in the aggregate behavior of black versus nonblack populations. While the responsibility of race-specific factors for the urban underclass remains an open question, there is general agreement that the underclass syndrome affects a much larger proportion of blacks than nonblacks. Estimates of the size and composition of the underclass suggest that the proportion of blacks classifiable as underclass is five to twenty-five times as great as the corresponding proportion of nonblacks. This circumstance provides a basis for attributing behavioral differences between blacks and nonblacks to the greater underclass presence among blacks, if such differences are consistent with reasonable hypotheses about underclass behavior. This is not to imply any identification of underclass behavior with the black population as a whole.

Conceptual Model

The present analysis draws upon an earlier investigation by Beam (1989), which analyzed most of the same variables but in a different model structure. The study employs 1970 and 1980 U.S. Census data and is restricted primarily to variables published by age, sex, and race at the metropolitan level. It focuses upon persons aged fifteen to thirty-four because the emergence of an identifiable urban underclass between 1970 and 1980 largely involved a failure of these young persons to enter and remain in the mainstream economy.

This analysis addresses job opportunities, labor force participation, and several family-related variables that form linkages between male and female labor force behavior. The general themes are that black males who are at risk of underclass behavior are affected by limited job opportunities in the mainstream economy and substantial opportunities elsewhere; at-risk females are affected by the poor economic prospects of males, by low earnings if they choose to work, by the availability of public assistance as an alternative source of economic support, and by both the attractions and burdens of child-bearing.

The chain of causality is presumed to extend from male decisions and prospects to female decisions. Child-rearing responsibilities have traditionally placed female labor force participation in a following role relative to male employment (as confirmed by literature studies through 1980).

Figure 12.1 depicts the overall model. Given the assumed flow from male to female behavior with no recursive relationships, the model includes most of the possible linkages among the variables under consideration. The relationship between females heading families and females married with spouse present is omitted as an obvious consequence of arithmetic. The direct linkage from male to female labor force participation is omitted in order to focus upon the intervening variables presumed responsible. This leaves a total of ten relationships, as indicated by the numbered arrows in Figure 12.1.

The study design involved looking for significant racial differences in regression coefficients for the variables appearing at the heads of the arrows.

HYPOTHESIZED RACIAL DIFFERENCES

Table 12.1 summarizes the racial differences expected due to the greater representation among blacks of persons describable as underclass. The expected differences are discussed below by individual relationship as numbered in Figure 12.1.

(1) *Job Opportunities and Male Labor Force Participation.* Loss of inner-city factory employment is often credited with relegating low-skilled

FIGURE 12.1

Conceptual Model of Labor Force and Family-Related Behavior

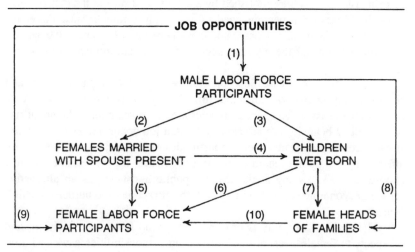

TABLE 12.1

Hypothesized Racial Differences in Labor Force
and Family Relationships

Relationship (by number in Figure 12.1)	Expected Direction and Magnitude of Effect		Expected Difference: Black Minus Nonblack
	Black	Nonblack	
(1)	Large positive	Small positive	Positive
(2)	Positive	Positive	Indeterminate
(3)	Small positive	Positive	Negative
(4)	Small positive	Large positive	Negative
(5)	Positive	Small negative or negligible	Positive
(6)	Small negative	Large negative	Positive
(7)	Large positive	Small positive or negligible	Positive
(8)	Large negative	Small negative	Negative
(9)	Large positive	Small positive	Positive
(10)	Negative	Positive	Negative

blacks to the underclass between 1970 and 1980. The present hypothesis is that blacks have been less able on average than nonblacks to recover from such job losses by changing their skills, occupations, and/or residential locations. (The differences in adjustment may involve segregation and job discrimination along with factors such as education and networking.)

A stronger positive relationship between employment opportunity and male labor force participation is therefore expected for blacks than for nonblacks. This relationship receives special attention in the analysis because it largely drives the rest of the model.

(2) *Male Labor Force Participation and Intact Marriages.* Society traditionally has viewed male participation in the labor force as a precondition for marriage. Male unemployment or departure from the labor force after marriage presumably increases the risk of marital breakup among young adults. Thus, a strong positive relationship should exist between male labor force participation and the share of females who are married with spouse present.

It is not clear that underclass behavior among a subgroup should affect the strength of this relationship because male underclass status involves a simultaneous avoidance of both marriage and the labor force. The expected racial difference is therefore indeterminate.

(3) *Male Labor Force Participation and Fertility Rates.* Presumably, most people have children when the family has financial means to support them. This would create a positive association between the male labor force participation rate and the number of children ever born per female (the fertility rate). A weaker association of this nature is expected for blacks than non-blacks due to the absence of traditional constraints upon childbearing among the underclass, as discussed in the next paragraph.

(4) *Intact Marriage and Fertility.* Mainstream society has always viewed marriage as a precondition for children. The share of women who are married with spouse present should thus have a strong positive influence on the fertility rate. A key aspect of the underclass syndrome, however, is a breakdown of the marriage/children connection. The females at risk of underclass behavior place a relatively low value on marriage due to the poor economic prospects of the at-risk males with whom they associate. These females nevertheless tend to bear children for a variety of reasons.

Fertility tends to have an especially high price for these at-risk females because the disinclination to wait for marriage leads to childbearing at a young age, which inhibits employment preparation and labor force entry. In any case, this underclass behavior should weaken the positive link of fertility to marriage for blacks relative to nonblacks.

(5) *Intact Marriage and Female Labor Force Participation.* Traditional American society generally discouraged women from working outside the home after marriage (at least while children were present). This pattern has been changing very rapidly. For nonblacks in 1970 to 1980, though, we might still expect a small negative relationship between female labor force participation and marriage with spouse present.

A positive, or weaker negative, relationship has been hypothesized for blacks due to two factors. First, the lower average earnings of black husbands compared to nonblack husbands gave black wives less opportunity to stay home. Second, being married with spouse present essentially ruled out public assistance as an alternative to employment for females. Prior to recent changes in welfare laws, low-skilled females were motivated to live in households with either two wage earners or none. This would tend to create a positive linkage between employment and marriage.

(6) *Fertility and Female Labor Force Participation.* Fertility is expected to have a strong negative influence on labor force participation by nonblack females, even though more and more mothers now work. Investigators who view welfare abuse as the primary underclass indicator might hypothesize an even stronger negative relationship for blacks on the presumption that black underclass females have babies by design to draw

larger assistance payments. A weaker negative relationship is expected here for blacks, however, due to the earnings effect noted above. Low male earnings have always made it difficult for black females, whose labor force participation rates are traditionally high, to stay home with their children. Any welfare-related inducement to have babies as a means of avoiding the labor force should be controlled by inclusion of the married-with-spouse-present variable, a general indicator of social stability, in the female labor force regression.

(7) *Fertility and Female Headship of Families.* There is a general expectation that fertility is positively related to female headship of families because the birth of a woman's first baby automatically creates a female-headed family whenever the baby's father is not a household member. The rise in divorce rates over the past quarter century would reinforce this expectation because each additional child increases the probability that a female-headed family will be formed when divorce occurs.

In this case, the hypothesized difference between blacks and whites involves the countervailing influence of cultural support for the nuclear family. "Family-oriented" cultures may feature both high fertility and low female family headship. The absence of this cultural orientation among underclass members would yield a stronger positive relationship between fertility and female family headship for blacks than for nonblacks.

(8) *Male Labor Force Participation and Female Headship.* The expectations for this relationship are based upon two common-sense assumptions. The first is that male inability to earn at least a subsistence-level income is negatively associated with marriage and positively associated with marital dissolution. The second is that male reliance upon the underclass economy for financial support is inimical to married life, given the risks and life-style implications of career criminality (particularly drug trafficking).

These considerations suggest a strong negative relationship for blacks between male labor force participation and female headship of families. For nonblacks, the association should be less strong because labor force nonparticipation is less likely to involve criminality and because higher female earnings provide a greater buffer against adversity.

(9) *Job Opportunities and Female Labor Force Participation.* A stronger positive linkage between job availability and labor force participation has been expected for black females than for nonblack females due to the same circumstances cited for males in relationship 1 above. The racial difference might reasonably be less pronounced for females than males because low-skill females have had generally greater success than their male counterparts in adjusting to structural economic changes.

(10) *Female Headship and Female Labor Force Participation.* Bearing the primary financial responsibility for a family can affect female labor force participation in two general ways. For females with average earning power, family headship can create a strong incentive toward employment. For low-skilled females whose earnings cannot provide a higher net living standard than offered by public assistance, headship of a family can be an inducement not to work. The former consideration has been expected to overrrule the latter for nonblacks, yielding a positive relationship between female family headship and female labor force participation. A negligible or even negative association has been expected for nonblacks due to the statistical influence of underclass behavior. This relationship and relationship 5, both involving female labor force participation, were intended as the primary tests of welfare influence in the model.

The differential influence of underclass behavior has thus been expected to yield divergent regression coefficients for nine of the ten specified relationships.

CALIBRATION PROCEDURES

Sample observations included seventy-six Standard Metropolitan Statistical Areas (SMSAs) for which the 1970 and 1980 Census published the necessary labor force and family-related statistics by age, sex, and race. (Two eligible areas were eliminated due to definitional problems.) Focusing upon central cities rather than entire metropolitan areas would have highlighted the expected racial differences but was infeasible in terms of data availability. The seventy-six areas in the sample included twenty-four of the twenty-five largest metropolitan areas and covered about half of the U.S. population.

The model calibration was conducted entirely on an incremental basis. Changes in population characteristics over the 1970–80 interval were related to changes in explanatory factors over the same period (plus a regional dummy variable). Most dependent and independent variables in the core model consisted of changes in rates per person. For example, the fertility variable equaled the number of children ever born to females of a given race and age in 1980, divided by the 1980 female population in that race and age group, all minus a corresponding measure for 1970. (The 1970 measure could pertain to either the same age group or the same population cohort; see below.)

The only important variables not computed as increments in per person rates were the measures of change in job opportunities. These were simply ratios of 1980 employment to 1970 employment in various occupational categories. The employment-change variables were race-specific but not sex-specific.

Data were assembled for two separate groups of young males and females: persons aged twenty-five through thirty-four and persons aged fifteen (or sixteen) through twenty-four. Two different versions of all the labor force and family-related variables were then prepared. The "cohort" version involved 1980 rates for persons aged twenty-five to thirty-four minus 1970 rates for persons aged fifteen to twenty-four. The purpose was to examine the model relationships as they applied to a given set of individuals moving through youth and early adulthood. (The composition of each age-sex-race cohort was of course subject to change from migration and mortality.)

The other version was a "combined" form of each variable computed as a 1980 rate for persons aged fifteen (or sixteen) to thirty-four and a 1970 rate for persons of the same age. The labor force participation variables pertained to ages sixteen to thirty-four and the family-related variables covered ages fifteen to thirty-four. (This discrepancy arose because the 1980 Census did not publish labor force statistics for fifteen-year-olds.) The regression results obtained for the two versions were quite similar in terms of the existence and significance of relationships. The combined version yielded more stable and presumably more reliable regression results, however, because of the larger populations covered.

ALTERNATIVE FORMS OF VARIABLES

The posited behavioral model was known to be incomplete because it failed to address any of the general explanations for the underclass syndrome other than the lack-of-jobs hypothesis. There were also other reasons to expect large amounts of unexplainable variation. The study therefore examined multiple forms of both dependent and independent variables to assist in distinguishing meaningful associations from statistical anomalies. The separate analyses of cohort and combined variables were designed partly for this purpose. Two other divisions involving variables for male labor force participation and employment change were also introduced to perturb the calibration process.[1]

In the case of male labor force participation, the less obvious form of the variable was eventually chosen as best for conceptual as well as statistical reasons. One little recognized aspect of the underclass syndrome is that the at-risk males who drop out of the labor force also tend to drop out of metropolitan Census counts altogether. It is not entirely clear what happens to these young men. Some die; some go to prisons located outside metropolitan areas; and a large number may simply avoid enumeration by the Census, intentionally or not. At least 10 percent fewer black males appear in metropolitan Census statistics by age thirty than would be expected on the basis of black female populations and the gender ratios for nonblacks.[2]

This circumstance was acknowledged in the present study by constructing an alternative male labor force variable in which the male labor force participants of a given age are divided by the female population in that age-race group. Increments are then computed as elsewhere. For nonblacks, this female-denominated form is nearly the same in terms of variation as the labor force participation measure with male population as the denominator. For blacks, the male- and female-denominated forms are substantially different, particularly for the combined (as opposed to cohort) version.

The female-denominated male labor force variable would convey approximately true labor force participation rates for black males if the shortfalls of black males were due entirely to Census undercounting and if none of the uncounted males were members of the mainstream labor force. The female-denominated variable remains appropriate for the present model, whether or not these conditions hold, because it expresses the number of marriageable males per female of a given age. This is the behavioral determinant stressed by Wilson (1987). Such a measure is more directly relevant to female decisions than the proportion of Census-enumerated males working or seeking work.

The other alternative variables used were employment variables in which the ratio of 1980 employment to 1970 employment in a given occupational group was divided by the ratio of 1980 to 1970 population. The logic was that this form might reflect the intensity of competition for jobs better than the growth of occupational employment per se because population would serve as a general index of employment demand. These alternative variables were used for testing but were not brought into the core model.

TESTING PROCEDURES

Each regression addressed one to four of the ten individual relationships shown in Figure 12.1. Most regressions were run in four different forms for each racial group, namely, in cohort and combined versions with two forms of either the male labor force participation variable or the employment change variable. The male labor force regressions were run in eight different forms because all of the different alternatives were involved.

Conventional t-tests were used as the basis for including variables in the core model. An independent variable found significant at the 5 percent level in a majority of regressions for a given racial group was included in the core model for that group and entered in all subsequent regressions. Otherwise, it was used only to test differences from the other racial group (if retained for that group). An exception was the regional dummy variable, which was included or excluded in regressions on the basis of its case-by-case significance. This policy resulted in few regression equations with nonsignificant variables and few deletions of variables that were significant in individual cases.

Differences between the estimated coefficients for blacks and nonblacks were the final object of analysis.[3]

SUMMARY OF VARIABLES

Table 12.2 provides a list of variables entering the analysis. The footnotes to the table indicate which variables are specific to race, sex, and/or age.

TABLE 12.2

Variables Analyzed

Variables Tested for Inclusion in the Core Model
BCE:	Ratio of change in blue-collar employment[a]
WCE:	Ratio of change in white-collar employment[a]
WCLSE:	Ratio of change in white-collar, low-skill employment[a]
MLF/M:	Change in male labor force participation (male-denominated rate)[c]
MLF/F:	Change in male labor force participation (female-denominated rate)[c]
FMSP:	Change in share of females married with spouse present[c]
FERT:	Change in fertility rate (children born per female)[c]
FHF:	Change in share of females who are heads of families[c]
FLF:	Change in female labor force participation rate[c]
FEM:	Change in share of females ever married[c]

Supplementary Variables
DUMMY:	Old South regional dummy variable
BCE/P:	Blue-collar employment change divided by population change (same for white-collar employment and so on)[a]
EARN:	Ratio of 1980 median earnings to 1970 median earnings[b]
EM/EF:	Change in ratio of male median earnings to female median earnings[b]
E/AFD:	Change in ratio of female median earnings to income-equivalent value of AFDC payments[a]
SEG:	Index of residential segregation in 1970

Notes: a = race-specific.
b = race- and sex-specific.
c = specific to race, sex, and age (with age referring to cohort and combined versions of variables).

The analysis considered several employment-change variables pertaining to different occupational groupings. Blue-collar employment covered operatives, laborers, and precision occupations. A division of blue-collar employment into low-skill and high-skill categories was tested in the initial analysis but set aside. The high-skill component (precision occupations) was too minor numerically to assist the regressions; moreover, its separation from blue-collar, low-skill employment weakened rather than strengthened the explanatory power of the latter. Two categories of white-collar employment change were tested: total white-collar employment and white-collar, low-skill jobs (service and clerical occupations). However, blue-collar employment dominated the regressions and was the only employment-change variable retained in the core model.

The female family headship variable was constructed according to the 1970 Census definitions, which always considered the husband to be the head of a married-couple household. This involved eliminating married-spouse-present females from the enumeration of female family heads in 1980.

The regional dummy variable is referenced as an Old South dummy because it isolates the portion of the United States where blacks traditionally lived before the great postwar migrations to industrial cities. The Old South dummy assumes unity values for all metropolitan areas located from 30 to 38 degrees north latitude and from the Atlantic Ocean to 94 degrees west longitude. These latitudes embrace urban areas from Jacksonville and New Orleans to Richmond and Nashville (but not peninsular Florida). The 94-degree west meridian corresponds to the western extremity of Louisiana.

This variable was originally introduced for limited purposes, but it turned out to be statistically significant in more than half of all regressions for both blacks and nonblacks. With one exception for nonblacks, the regression coefficients for this variable describe greater adherence to traditional mainstream behavior in the Old South than elsewhere.

The segregation variable was a racial dissimilarity index developed by Van Valey and colleagues (1977). It was available only for 1970 and thus was tested as a level variable rather than an incremental variable. The value of the segregation index for a metropolitan area could vary from zero to unity, expressing the share of all blacks who would have to relocate in order for the area to have a uniform racial mix at the tract level.

Results of the Regression Analysis

Figure 12.2 summarizes the statistical findings of the analysis, depicting the existence and direction of significant relationships for blacks and nonblacks. Fitted regression equations appear beneath the diagram for each racial group. The cited results pertain to regressions with combined rather

FIGURE 12.2

Calibrated Model for Black and Nonblack Populations Aged 15 to 34

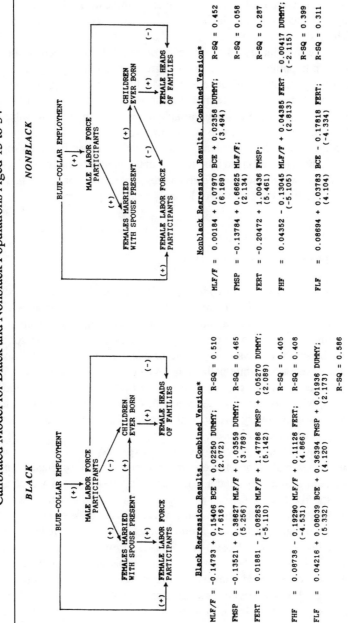

BLACK

NONBLACK

Black Regression Results, Combined Version*

MLF/F = -0.14793 + 0.15406 BCE + 0.02250 DUMMY;   R-SQ = 0.510
                      (7.616)   (2.072)

FMSP = -0.13521 + 0.38627 MLF/F + 0.03559 DUMMY;   R-SQ = 0.465
                      (5.256)   (3.789)

FERT = 0.01881 - 1.08263 MLF/F + 1.47786 FMSP + 0.05270 DUMMY;   R-SQ = 0.405
                    (-5.110)   (5.142)   (2.089)

FHF = 0.08738 - 0.19290 MLF/F + 0.11128 FERT;   R-SQ = 0.408
                    (-4.531)   (4.866)

FLF = 0.04216 + 0.08039 BCE + 0.36394 FMSP + 0.01936 DUMMY;   R-SQ = 0.586
                    (5.332)   (4.120)   (2.173)

Nonblack Regression Results, Combined Version*

MLF/F = 0.00184 + 0.07970 BCE + 0.02358 DUMMY;   R-SQ = 0.452
                    (6.169)   (3.494)

FMSP = -0.13784 + 0.66625 MLF/F;   R-SQ = 0.058
                    (2.134)

FERT = -0.20472 + 1.00436 FMSP;   R-SQ = 0.287
                    (5.461)

FHF = 0.04352 - 0.13045 MLF/F + 0.04385 FERT - 0.00417 DUMMY;   R-SQ = 0.399
                    (-5.105)   (2.813)   (-2.115)

FLF = 0.08694 + 0.03783 BCE - 0.17818 FERT;   R-SQ = 0.311
                    (4.104)   (-4.334)

Note: See Table 12.2 for definitions of variables.

than cohort variables, with female-denominated male labor force participation rates, and with unadjusted employment-change measures. This combination has provided generally the best statistical explanation of model variables.

The t-statistics for regression coefficients appear in parentheses below the coefficient estimates. The critical values of t for rejecting the zero-relationship hypothesis with 72 to 74 degrees of freedom are approximately 1.992 for 5 percent significance and 2.643 for 1 percent significance (two-tailed tests). In the black regression equations shown, all of the t-statistics for variables other than the dummy variable exceed 4.1 in absolute value (0.01 percent significance). The same is true for five of the seven nondummy variables in the nonblack regressions. R-square values range from 0.4 to 0.6 in the black equations and from 0.06 to 0.45 in the nonblack equations.[4]

The following discussion summarizes the results for individual equations then presents the outcome of formal racial comparisons.

RESULTS FOR INDIVIDUAL EQUATIONS

Male Labor Force Participation.   Change in blue-collar employment dominated all other employment measures as a predictor of change in male labor force participation. White-collar, low-skill employment approached positive significance in only one of the nonblack equations. The coefficient for this variable was always negligible or negative in the black regressions. After the deletion of white-collar employment variables, the t-statistics for blue-collar employment change in the eight black regressions ranged from 2.0 to 8.0, with only two t values below 5.6. The relationship for nonblacks ranged from zero to very strong, with nonsignificance at the 5 percent level occurring in a minority of cases.

Median earnings per worker were expected to have a substantial influence upon male labor force participation and were originally intended for inclusion in the core model. The earnings variable consisted of a race- and sex-specific ratio of median earnings in 1980 to median earnings in 1970. The regression results obtained for this variable were quite erratic.

The earnings variable was ultimately deleted from all male labor force equations due to a lack of consistent explanatory power. This outcome may have resulted from the fact that the earnings measure was not occupation-specific and hence lacked relevance to the persons most at risk of leaving the labor force. Another possible explanation is that the positive influence of high earnings on male desire to work is statistically offset by a tendency of high-wage areas (for example, southeast Michigan) to attract and retain redundant labor.

The segregation variable was entered as an explanatory factor for male labor force participation to test for negative influences on blacks involving limited employment access and/or inferior public education (following Wilson, 1987). The segregation coefficients obtained in initial regressions without the dummy variable were consistently negative and often moderately significant. The Old South dummy variable was entered on the suspicion that the segregation variable was capturing regional influences. The segregation variable then lapsed into nonsignificance and was set aside. The regional dummy variable was found to be a highly significant predictor of male labor force behavior in all cases except the black equations explaining female-denominated participation rates.

Females Married with Spouse Present. Change in the proportion of females married with spouse present was linked in the analysis only to change in male labor force participation and the dummy variable. The male labor force variable was highly significant in the black regressions, with t-statistics ranging from 3.0 to 5.3. Male labor force participation had less statistical significance in explaining married-spouse-present females for non-blacks, with t equaling only 1.0 to 3.1. However, the coefficients were generally larger for nonblacks than blacks. The coefficients for both racial groups were positive, as expected.

Fertility. The number of children ever born per female was expected to bear positive incremental relationships with the married-spouse-present variable and with male labor force participation. The first expectation was met, with t-statistics for the marriage variable ranging from 2.2 to 5.1 in the black equations and from 3.1 to 5.5 in the nonblack equations.

Other aspects of the fertility analysis did not turn out as expected. Male labor force participation did not approach statistical significance in the nonblack regressions; more surprisingly, it had a negative relationship to fertility for blacks. This negative relationship existed in only three of the four black regressions but was significant at the 5 percent level in two of those cases and involved a t-statistic of 5.1 in the third.

The negative linkage between fertility and male labor force participation for blacks might be interpreted as a reflection of welfare-motivated child-bearing among the underclass. This interpretation cannot be confirmed or denied with present data, although an analysis of children supported by public assistance might show whether welfare babies numerically account for the full effect at issue. However, a dominance of welfare-related motivations conflicts with the strong observed dependence of fertility upon marriage.

One alternative explanation would involve upward economic mobility. Low-income black families have traditionally been large, but middle-class blacks are among the lowest groups in terms of birthrates. Areas with strong economies and favorable trends in male labor force participation would have the highest rates of household transition from low-income to middle-class status and thus would be expected to exhibit the greatest declines in fertility.

Female Headship of Families.   The proportion of females heading families was expected to relate positively to fertility and negatively to male labor
force participation, with larger absolute effects for blacks than nonblacks in
both cases. These expectations were generally fulfilled. All regression
coefficients for the two variables in the black equations were significant at 1
percent or slightly more than 1 percent. The nonblack equations included one
nonsignificant coefficient (for male-denominated labor force participation)
and one that was significant at only 5 percent. Maximum t-statistics were
generally near 5.

Female Labor Force Participation.   Change in female labor force participation was tested for relationships with the other three female behavior
variables and the employment-change measures. Two of these independent
variables plus the dummy were found significant for each racial group. This
equation yielded the highest overall levels of statistical explanation in the
model, with R-square values ranging up to 0.7 for blacks.

Blue-collar employment dominated the other employment-change variables in explaining female as well as male labor force participation, which
was somewhat unexpected. In the nonblack regressions, consistently positive
coefficients were obtained for both white-collar, low-skill employment and
total white-collar employment when entered along with blue-collar employment. The t-statistics for these variables ranged only from 0.7 to 1.5, however, and were always lower than the t-statistics for blue-collar employment.
In the black regressions, the white-collar employment variables had little
effect on female labor force participation except in one isolated case. Blue-
collar employment was uniformly significant at 1 percent for both racial
groups once the other employment variables had been deleted. Although
low-skill females differ from males in terms of white-collar/blue-collar
employment mix, these findings suggest that the special difficulties of adjusting to blue-collar job losses are the predominant source of worker dislocation
for both sexes.

Black females exhibited a strong positive relationship between labor
force participation and marriage with spouse present, involving t-statistics
above 4 in all regressions. For nonblacks, there was a mix of positive and
negative coefficients with none significant at 5 percent. Both of these findings
were as expected.

For nonblacks, fertility was uniformly significant at 1 percent in a negative relationship with female labor force participation. The corresponding
regression coefficients for blacks were always negative but never significant.
This outcome also basically conformed with expectations.

Regarding the influence of female family headship on female labor force
participation, we had expected a negative relationship for blacks and a positive relationship for nonblacks. Neither of these relationships turned out to be

significant at 5 percent in any of the black or nonblack regressions. All of the female family headship coefficients for blacks were negative, but only one approached statistical significance. The cohort regressions for nonblacks yielded positive coefficients, with t-statistics exceeding 1.5. The differences between these and the respective black coefficients were nearly significant at 5 percent. On the other hand, the combined regressions yielded negative coefficients for nonblacks that were larger in absolute value than their counterparts for blacks. Female family headship was therefore deleted from the model as an influence upon female labor force participation for either racial group.

The analysis failed to establish relationships between female labor force participation and median female earnings, as was true for male labor force participation. Half of the earnings coefficients for blacks and nonblacks were positive, with t-statistics between 1.3 and 1.9. The other half had mixed signs and were far from significance.

Analysis of Racial Differences

Differences between black and nonblack regression coefficients were tested in either four or eight separate cases (pairs of regressions) for the variables under discussion. Each test involved subtracting the nonblack coefficient from the black coefficient, dividing the result by the computed standard error of the difference, and interpreting the result as a conventional t-statistic.

Table 12.3 summarizes the outcome of these racial difference tests. The rows pertain to the ten original relationships in the model, numbered as in Figure 12.1. The fourth column of Table 12.3 lists the expected black-minus-nonblack differences from Table 12.1. The remaining columns describe the determination or whether or not the regression results support the expected pattern.

There is no definitive way of constructing a joint test for multiple differences of regression coefficients estimated in the present manner. If the four (or eight) coefficient estimates were independently distributed for each racial group, a joint t-statistic could be developed by averaging the t-statistics for individual differences and dividing the result by two (or the square root of eight). Still, the regressions performed here for alternative versions of a given relationship were obviously not independent. The chosen procedure therefore was to consider a difference of coefficient significant if its sign conformed to expectations and fulfilled any two of the following criteria:

1.   The difference is significant at the 5 percent level for the benchmark regression (this being the combined version containing a female-

TABLE 12.3

Results of Tests for Significant Differences Between
Black and Nonblack Regression Coefficients

	Variables		Expected Racial Difference	Significance Criteria			Racial Differences Considered Significant
Relationship	Dependent	Independent		Benchmark Regression	Half or More Regression	Mean t-statistic	
(1)	MLF	BCE	Positive	*	*	*	Yes
(2)	FMSP	MLF	Indeterminate				No
(3)	FERT	MLF	Negative	*	*	*	Yes
(4)	FERT	FMSP	Negative				No
(5)	FLF	FMSP	Positive	*	*	*	Yes
(6)	FLF	FERT	Positive	*	*	*	Yes
(7)	FHF	FERT	Positive	*	*	*	Yes
(8)	FHF	MLF	Negative		*		Possible
(9)	FLF	BCE	Positive				No
(10)	FLF	FHF	Positive				No

denominated male labor force variable and/or an unadjusted employment-growth variable);

2. The difference is significant in at least half of the regressions for which it is tested; or

3. The mean of the four or eight t-statistics for coefficient differences in the given case exceeds the critical level for 5 percent significance of a conventional t-statistic.

Based on these criteria, the regression results support the existence of racial differences for five of the ten relationships in question. The coefficient difference for a sixth relationship fulfills only one of the criteria and is considered "possible." The regression results clearly fail to support racial differences for three other cases in which differences were expected. In the remaining case (relationship 2), no difference was either expected or identified.

These findings are stronger than anticipated, given that tests of coefficient differences are usually more stringent than tests for the existence of relationships. Of forty-eight individual tests, twelve establish the significance of coefficient differences at 1 percent and another ten establish significance at 5 percent, with all of these significant differences bearing the expected sign.

BLUE-COLLAR JOB LOSSES AND MALE LABOR FORCE PARTICIPATION

Eight pairs of cases were available for testing racial differences in the regression coefficients that relate male labor force participation to blue-collar employment. All of the differences were significant—three at 1 percent—in the four regressions containing the unadjusted employment-change variable. The mean of t-statistics for all eight cases would be significant at 1 percent in any reasonable joint test.

Eight additional difference tests were conducted for this relationship since many of the same individuals were enumerated in both the dependent and independent variables. (There was about a one-third overlap in both directions for blacks in 1980; that is, black males aged sixteen to thirty-four who held blue-collar jobs constituted about one-third of all black blue-collar employees and one-third of all black male labor force members in that age group.) These tests simply involved using nonblack rather than black employment change to explain black male labor force participation. The resulting racial differences in regression coefficients were comparable in significance to the differences already discussed.

Figure 12.3 depicts the magnitude of racial difference in the impact of blue-collar job changes. The independent variable in this case is the 1980–

FIGURE 12.3

Influence of Blue-Collar Job Availability on Labor Force Participation by Young Males

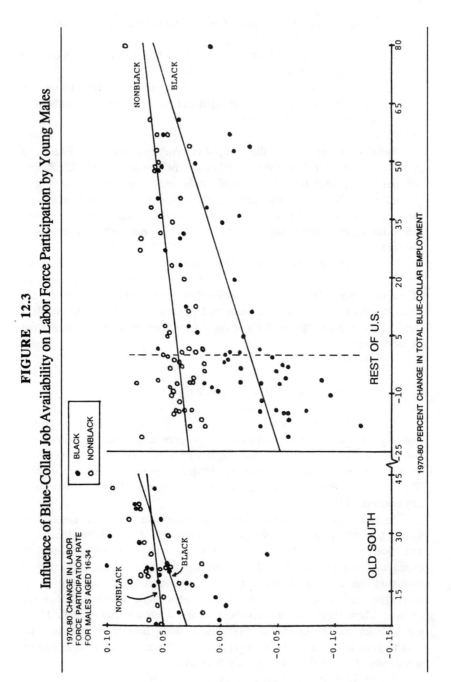

to–1970 ratio of total (not race-specific) blue-collar employment. Regressions were run in this form so that a common quantity could be plotted on the horizontal axis as predictor of black and nonblack labor force participation. The dependent variable for both racial groups is the male-denominated measure, that is, change in conventional male labor force participation rates. This choice of variables does not reflect the most significant black-nonblack differences observed in the study but is convenient in other respects. The graph is divided into two panels, with regression lines and data points plotted separately for Old South metropolitan areas and areas located elsewhere.

Racial variation is minimal in the Old South for both the regression lines and the individual data points. Elsewhere in the United States, however, the racial pattern is striking. Nonblack labor force participation did not decline between 1970 and 1980 in any of these metropolitan areas, whereas the labor force participation rates for black males declined in more than 60 percent of all cases. Figure 12.3 shows an essentially complete separation of black and nonblack data points for the non–Old South metropolitan areas in which blue-collar employment declined between 1970 and 1980. These areas, plotted to the left of the dashed line, constituted half of the non–Old South sample.

The racial difference tests used here consider only the slopes of regression lines, not their overall position. The difference in slope between the black and nonblack regression lines in Figure 12.3 is easily appreciated. The nonblack line shows relatively little sensitivity of male labor force participation to blue-collar employment change, although the relationship is very significant statistically. The black regression line has much greater slope due to the severe deterioration of male labor force involvement in areas with declining blue-collar job opportunities. Table 12.4 summarizes this impact in another fashion.

DIFFERENCES IN FEMALE BEHAVIOR

No racial difference was expected or found for the relationship predicting the share of females married with spouse present. For each of the three other female behavior variables—fertility, female family headship, and female labor force participation—the analysis established significant racial differences.

The findings for these three variables followed a common pattern. Underclass behavior had been expected to influence the dependence of each on two or more other variables but instead affected the regression results significantly for just one independent variable. This outcome implies interactions among the explanatory roles of different variables, which perhaps should have been expected.[5]

TABLE 12.4

Employment and Labor Force Participation
of Black Males Aged 16 to 34

	Number of Metro Areas (Outside the Old South)	
	Blue-collar Jobs Declining	Blue-collar Jobs Increasing
Male Labor Force Increasing	3	16
Male Labor Force Declining	24	11

Fertility.   In the case of fertility, a black-nonblack difference in linkage to male labor force participation was observed as expected, but it took the form of an unexpected negative relationship for blacks rather than a positive relationship for nonblacks. This difference expresses some mix of underclass behavior and upward mobility of nonunderclass blacks, as noted above. It is partly offset by the fact that the linkage of fertility to marriage, which should be weakened by underclass behavior, involves somewhat larger coefficients on average for blacks than nonblacks. The net outcome is a racial pattern that might or might not be considered to reflect underclass behavior but that clearly tends to promote recruitment to the underclass. This pattern is illustrated in the numerical examples presented below.

Female Family Headship.   The results for female heads of families came closest to meeting expectations, with a significant black-nonblack difference in linkage to fertility and a possible difference in linkage to male labor force participation. The observation that childbirth creates more female-headed families among blacks than nonblacks is a straightforward reflection of underclass influence. The linkage of female family headship to male labor force participation has been considered an important element of the underclass syndrome. The lack of more than a "possible" racial difference in this case is due not to a weak relationship for blacks but to the unexpected existence of a nearly equivalent relationship for nonblacks.

Female Labor Force Participation.   For female labor force participation, the lack of significant and racially different linkages to female family headship was counterevidence with regard to underclass influence. Family headship affects females by making employment both more difficult and more necessary; these offsetting motivations seem to apply similarly to both blacks and nonblacks. Likewise, the lack of a significant racial difference in the linkage of female labor force participation to blue-collar employment goes against the hypothesized underclass syndrome, insofar as this syndrome involves special job adjustment problems for blacks. On the other hand, the highly significant racial difference in the relationship of female labor force participation to marriage with spouse present gives very strong evidence of underclass influence. This finding reflects the two-workers-or-none incentive noted earlier. Lastly, the racial difference in relationships of female labor force participation to fertility (arising from the absence of a negative relationship for blacks) is attributed here to income-related restrictions on black female choices rather than any aspect of underclass behavior.

Numerical Example of Responses to Job Losses

Since it is difficult to assess the importance of these racial differences from significance tests and coefficient magnitudes, Figure 12.4 provides a numerical example. The example shows the estimated impacts of a hypothetical 1,000-worker decline in blue-collar employment for each racial group. The impacts include the direct effects of job losses upon male and female labor force participation plus the indirect effects produced by female responses to male labor force behavior. Effects are computed from the regression equations, starting with employment change in the male labor force equation and working through the model from independent to dependent variables. (The denominators are based upon sample means for 1970 and 1980 so that the computations estimate what would have happened in a typical metro area if the job losses occurred during the 1970–80 decade.) The regression equations used here are those containing female-denominated male labor force participation rates and unadjusted employment-growth variables.

The two panels of Figure 12.4 describe the hypothetical job loss effects for blacks and nonblacks as estimated by the combined version of the calibrated model.[6] The individual effects predicted by the model are listed in parentheses on the arrows denoting relationships. The overall effect for each variable—equaling the sum of individual effects on incoming arrows—is listed in parentheses below the variable name.

As shown in Table 12.5, the magnitude of effects is quite striking. The loss of 1,000 blue-collar jobs diverts 253 black males from the labor force, as compared with 114 nonblack males. There are 104 fewer black females and seventy-eight fewer nonblack females with husbands present. Nonblacks respond to the hypothetical job loss by producing 119 fewer children. Regarding black fertility, the negative relationship with male labor force participation outweighs the positive link with marriage so that the number of

FIGURE 12.4
Estimated Behavioral Effects of a Hypothetical Race-Specific Loss of 1,000 Blue-Collar Jobs

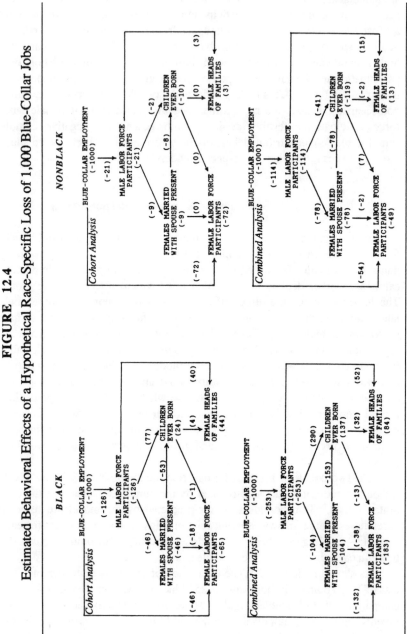

TABLE 12.5

Estimated Effects of a 1,000-Worker
Loss of Blue-collar Employment

	Black	*Nonblack*	*Difference*
Male Labor Force Participants	–253	–114	–139
Females Married, Spouse Present	–104	–78	–26
Children Ever Born	137	–119	256
Female Heads of Families	84	13	71
Female Labor Force Participants	–183	–49	–134
Total Labor Force Participants	–436	–163	–273

black children actually increases by 137, yielding a black-nonblack difference of 256 children ever born. This difference and the influence of male behavior then result in eighty-four additional female-headed families for blacks versus only thirteen for nonblacks.

The job losses directly reduce female labor force participation by 132 persons for blacks and fifty-four persons for nonblacks. Relationships involving marriage and children divert another fifty-one black females from the labor force but offset the nonblack decline by five females. Overall, the hypothetical loss of 1,000 blue-collar jobs results in a loss of 436 blacks from the labor force, or more than two-and-a-half times the corresponding nonblack reduction of 163 labor force participants.

These magnitudes are remarkable in view of the fact that they apply only to persons under thirty-five years old. With allowance for labor force withdrawal by older persons, the example implies that one black person drops out of the labor force for every 1.5 to 2 black workers laid off from blue-collar jobs. The corresponding effect for nonblacks is one labor force departure for every four or five nonblack jobs lost. This summarizes vividly the differential impacts produced by the recent restructuring of the U.S. economy.

Policy Evaluation Needs

The urban underclass is arguably America's most serious domestic problem. All signs indicate that the number of chronically poor and economically isolated urban residents will continue to increase without new interventions. A major reason for the minimal policy response to date has been a fundamental lack of understanding and agreement on causal factors and ameliorative actions.

In this case, the policy distortions and biases created by deficient information are especially severe for several reasons. First, the underclass phenomenon is a complex syndrome of deprivation and behavioral response that involves joblessness, chronic welfare dependency, family headship by never-married females, drug use, participation in the underground economy, and development of an underclass subculture with alternative values. Second, the potential solutions are correspondingly diverse. They involve education, child care, job training, welfare reform, public health, public safety, antidrug efforts, business development, general economic development, and so forth.

A third difficulty for policymakers is that the magnitude and relative intractability of the problem suggest that a simultaneous effort on many fronts will be required to achieve major improvements. Given present knowledge, there is no rational basis for designing and coordinating such an effort. Present information does not allow rigorous comparisons of the most basic alternative solutions. For example, programs to reduce joblessness still lack an information base for assessing the cost-effectiveness of jobs-to-people approaches (for example, business development) versus people-to-jobs approaches (for example, employment training).

For truly informed decision making, we would need the capability to form comparisons among, say, prenatal care programs, changes in the minimum wage, business incubators, sex education classes, drug interdiction, literacy programs, neighborhood redevelopment projects, changes in the criminal justice system, and full-employment economic policies.

Perhaps even more fundamental than the issue of allocating resources among initiatives is the need to motivate resource expenditures per se. The overriding political lesson of the last decade has been the extreme difficulty of gaining public support for measures that are not perceived to benefit the average voter. Serious efforts to assist the underclass will not occur until the middle class understands that chronic urban poverty is a mutual problem.

Specifically, there is a need to show that solutions are positive in cost-benefit terms for society at large. There have been some limited demonstrations of this nature for public health programs (such as research showing that subsidized prenatal care more than pays for itself in lower public health costs after birth). However, this type of analysis cannot be performed for most initiatives without using a formal, quantitative policy evaluation framework that considers interrelationships among economic incentives, labor force behavior, family formation, and so forth.

NEXT STEPS TOWARD A COMPREHENSIVE POLICY EVALUATION FRAMEWORK

The study reported here is an initial step toward development of such a policy evaluation framework. In exploring the economic determinants of underclass behavior, the investigation establishes several basic relationships that have previously eluded quantification. It provides needed statistical confirmation that job losses during 1970–80 contributed to the emergence of underclass behavior.

The findings also demonstrate a number of the family-related linkages involved in this behavior. They attribute substantial but not overwhelming importance to public welfare as a supporting element of the underclass syndrome. This conclusion rests largely upon the observed negative association between marriage and female labor force participation. The other relationships expressing possible welfare influence are either ambiguous or mutually offsetting.

The study establishes a presumption that the underclass syndrome is driven strongly by economic incentives and provides one of the first formal demonstrations that lack of employment opportunity has been instrumental in the formation of an urban underclass. What it does not do, given the inherent limitations of its design, is to:

1. Establish why job losses have been so much more devastating to blacks than nonblacks;
2. Disprove any of the competing explanations for underclass behavior noted at the beginning of this paper; or
3. Demonstrate that lack of employment opportunity has continued to be a leading cause of underclass behavior during the 1980s.

Subsequent research must test the contribution of structural change and job losses directly against the major competing explanations of underclass behavior. These include economic incentives created by alternatives to employment (primarily welfare and the underground economy), race-specific factors, such as residential segregation and job discrimination, and human resource impacts of the drug culture. As demonstrated above, all of these influences and their repercussions can be addressed by aggregate statistical analysis to yield insights and predictive capabilities to guide policy on behalf of the urban poor.

Notes

1. For a more detailed description, see Hammer, 1989.
2. Ibid. See "Table 2. Computed Shortfalls of Black Male Population Relative to Expectations Based on Nonblacks," p. 12.
3. These differences were examined by forming t-tests on the assumption that errors in the estimated black and nonblack regression coefficients were independent (a reasonable assumption since the coefficients came from entirely separate populations). The standard error of each difference between black and nonblack coefficients was computed as the square root of the sum of squared standard errors for the individual

coefficients. The ratio of the coefficient difference to this standard error formed a conventional t-statistic.

4. Hammer, 1989.

5. The interactions in question are substantive rather than statistical. The analysis has given no sign of collinearity problems, which would obviously be minimized by the small number of variables in each equation.

6. Hammer, 1989.

References

Beam, T. *Barriers to Economic Mobility: The Urban Underclass*. Evanston, Ill.: NCI Research, the Institute for Urban Economic Development Studies, 1989.

Hammer, T. R. *Economic Determinants of Underclass Behavior*. NCI Working Paper 89-103. Evanston, Ill.: NCI Research, 1989.

Kasarda, J. D. "Jobs, Migration and Emerging Urban Mismatches." *Urban Change and Poverty*. Eds. M. McGeary and L. Lynn. Washington, D.C.: National Academy Press, 1988.

Van Valey, T. L., W. C. Roof, and J. E. Wilcox. "Trends in Residential Segregation, 1960-1970." *American Journal of Sociology* 82 (1977): 826-844.

Wilson, W. J. *The Truly Disadvantaged: The Inner City, the Underclass and Public Policy*. Chicago: University of Chicago Press, 1987.

Reviewers

Alex Anas, Department of Civil Engineering, Northwestern University, Evanston, Illinois.

Timothy J. Bartik, W. E. Upjohn Institute for Employment Research, Kalamazoo, Michigan.

Jan K. Brueckner, Department of Economics, University of Illinois at Urbana-Champaign, Champaign, Illinois.

Dennis Capozza, University of Michigan, Lansing, Michigan.

Carmel U. Chiswick, Department of Economics, College of Business Administration, University of Illinois at Chicago, Chicago, Illinois.

Daniel Dabney, Economic Development Administration, U.S. Department of Commerce, Washington, D.C.

David H. Geddes, Economic Development Administration, U.S. Department of Commerce, Washington, D.C.

Robert Schnorbus, Federal Reserve Bank of Chicago, Chicago, Illinois.

James L. Shanahan, Center for Urban Studies, University of Akron, Akron, Ohio.

Thomas M. Stanback, Jr., Columbia University, New York, New York.